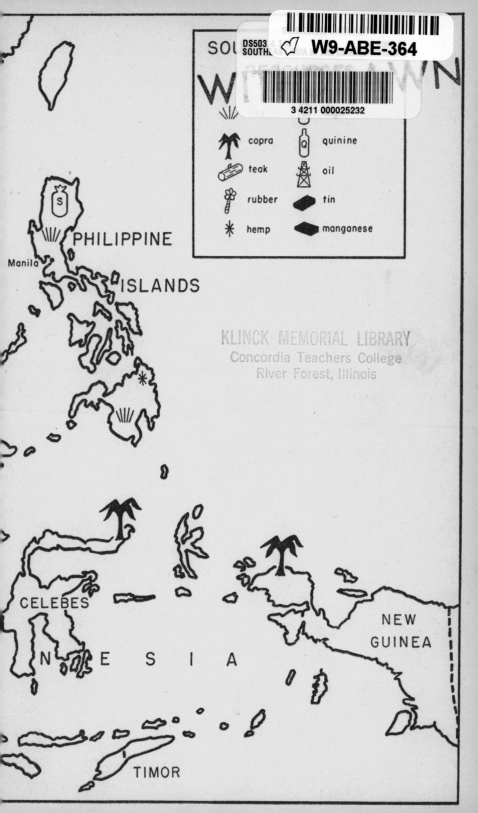

SOU...
RESOURCES
W...WN

	copra		quinine
	teak		oil
	rubber		tin
	hemp		manganese

PHILIPPINE

Manila

ISLANDS

CELEBES

NEW
GUINEA

N...E S I A

TIMOR

Southeast Asia in the Coming World

SOUTHEAST ASIA
in the
COMING WORLD

EDITED BY

Philip W. Thayer

WITH A FOREWORD BY

William O. Douglas

BALTIMORE · THE JOHNS HOPKINS PRESS

Foreword

DURING THE WEEK of August 11, 1952, the School of Advanced International Studies of the Johns Hopkins University, with the generous cooperation of the Rockefeller Foundation, sponsored in Washington, D.C., a conference on "Southeast Asia in the Coming World." Those invited to attend the conference and to take part in its discussions included not only university, government, and business leaders from this country, but also distinguished educators from Southeast Asia: the President of the University of Indonesia, the Rector of the University of Rangoon, the Dean of the Faculty of Political Science of Chulalongkorn University, the Professor of Geography in the University of Malaya, and a Professor of Law from the University of Hanoi. The conference thus brought together an unusually large and varied group of highly qualified authorities on the problems of a vitally important area.

The present volume contains the twenty-two papers which were read in the course of the conference. The order of arrangement is the same followed in the presentation of the papers, in accordance with which the first four days were devoted to a consideration of topics in the fields of politics, economics, culture, and law, while the final day was concerned with a look to the future.

In facilitating the work of the conference and in the preparation of these materials, grateful thanks are due to the loyal energy of the members of the faculty and staff of the School of Advanced International Studies, to the courtesy of the Department of State in making available its air-conditioned auditorium for the meetings, and to the friendly assistance of the officers of the Johns Hopkins Press. A special word of gratitude should go to the Ambassadors of the Southeast Asian countries. The wholehearted support received from their Excellencies James Barrington of Burma, Nong Kimny of Cambodia, Ali Sastroamidjojo of Indonesia, Carlos Romulo of the Philippines, and Pote Sarasin of Thailand, contributed greatly to the success of the conference.

PHILIP W. THAYER, *Dean*
School of Advanced
International Studies

February 15, 1953

Table of Contents

Introduction

SOUTHEAST ASIA is an area little known to Americans. We have had warm sentiments for the people who live there. Yet our understanding of them, their culture, their legal systems, and their customs has not been profound. Southeast Asia has not been well known even to the people who live there. They have been mostly oriented to the metropole of some Western power—the Vietnamese to Paris, the Burmese and Malays to London, the Filipinos to Washington, D.C., and the Indonesians to Amsterdam.

Today Southeast Asia is undergoing a new orientation. The independence movements among nations have established new governments in that region. Those governments are confronted with staggering problems; and all of them are experiencing the dangers of the vortex of politics which the Communists generate. The sturdiness of the independence movements, the proven ability of people without prior experience to govern themselves, the increasing awareness among Asians of the dangers of Soviet imperialism—these add up to solid achievements among the peoples of Southeast Asia since the end of World War II. But the area—rich in people and in resources and a prize for the Soviet empire builders—will long be turbulent and uneasy. It will also need for years to come help and guidance in solving problems as perplexing as those which any Western country has ever known.

We must therefore come to know and understand the region and its people. The ties of language, customs, literature, and blood which we have had with Europe are lacking in the East. It will therefore take great efforts to bridge the gap. The task is one for educators, scientists, businessmen, diplomats, and scholars in all branches of knowledge. The treasure of Asia in material things is great. The treasure she possesses in matters of the spirit and the mind is even more precious. The men whose papers make up this volume reveal some of them in as solid a contribution as can be found in the English language. The importance of the project they tender is evident from the war and wreckage of our policies in Asia during the last half-century and the shadow they cast of events yet to come.

WILLIAM O. DOUGLAS

January 31, 1953

Part 1: POLITICAL SCIENCE

John M. Allison

UNITED STATES POLICY IN

SOUTHEAST ASIA

It is interesting and important to note that the first treaty between the United States and any country in Asia was with a country in Southeast Asia—with Thailand, or Siam as it was then called. It was on March 30, 1833, that a treaty of amity and commerce was signed with Siam which was the beginning of long official American contact with the nations of that part of the world.

It is also important to realize that a study of Southeast Asia involves in fact some consideration of the problems of all of Asia. This has been made increasingly clear since the triumph of Chinese Communism on the mainland. The aggression of the Communist Chinese in Korea—with their aim probably Japan—and the threat by the Chinese Communists of invasion as well as the definite help they are giving to the insurgents in Indo-China, if nothing else, ties Northeast and Southeast Asia together.

I have just returned from Hawaii where I attended the first meeting of the ANZUS Council. Much of the talk which took place around the tables and in the Officers' Club at Kaneohe dealt with Southeast Asia: with the nature of the Chinese Communist threat to that area and what we could do about it. In discussing what we could do about the Chinese Communist threat to Southeast Asia, we naturally had to consider what we were doing already in other areas and how this affected what we could do there. What is the United States doing elsewhere in Asia?

There are those who say that our foreign policy treats Asians as "second-class expendables"—that only Europe gets any attention. I think, however, only a brief review of what we are doing and what we have done will show the shallowness of that charge. For seven years the United States bore the main burden of the occupation of Japan. Not only did we do much to eliminate the vestiges of the old Japanese militarism, but we spent nearly $2 billion to help feed the Japanese and make it possible for them to raise their war-shattered standard of living. The United States took the lead under the energetic and imaginative guidance of John Foster Dulles, with the strong backing of President Truman and Secretary Acheson, in giving the Japanese people a liberal peace treaty enabling them to take their place in the world community as equal partners. There were no onerous treaty restrictions. The treaty made them completely free. We have signed a security treaty with Japan and are keeping United States forces in that country in order to defend the Japanese against attack, as for the present they have no adequate defense force of their own. Is that the treatment given to "second-class expendables"?

When Communist aggressors invaded the Republic of Korea, we, along with other members of the United Nations, took immediate action. Since then United States casualties in Korea up to July 25, 1952, have exceeded 113,000, including over 18,000 dead. We have lost some 2,000 planes. We are spending approximately $5 billion a year for Korea, not including troop pay, food or training costs, and in addition we have given over $700 million of economic aid to the people of Korea. All this was in addition to the contributions and sacrifices of our United Nations partners in Korea. We have refused to agree to an armistice in Korea, although that meant continuing loss of American and other free nations' blood and treasure, on terms which would force Koreans and Chinese to return to Communist slavery and probable death. More than one third of all United States division strength is now in the Far East—more than there is in Europe—more, in fact, than there is in the United States itself.

In the Philippines, as a result of the Bell Mission Report and the Quirino-Foster Agreement, the United States has been carrying on a program of economic aid envisaging the expenditure of $250 million over a five-year period. This is in addition to the large sum—almost one billion dollars—which we have contributed to repair the damages of war in the Philippines. In addition to this economic aid we have military agreements with the Government of the Philippines making clear that the American people have not forgotten what the Philippine people did between 1941 and 1945 and making it clear that, if trouble should come to the Philippines again, they would not stand alone.

In Formosa the United States has a military and economic aid program involving the expenditure of hundreds of millions of dollars. Our Seventh Fleet makes certain that any Communist aggression against Formosa shall not succeed. It will continue to do so.

Let us look for a moment at the other nations of Southeast Asia. Although the Philippines, of course, are a part of Southeast Asia I have treated them separately because of the long and intimate relationship between America and the Philippines and because of our special treaty relationships. In Indo-China we see the other large-scale war in the world today. There the French and Indo-Chinese are carrying the chief burden—it is not often realized that France has spent more in Indo-China than she received through Marshall aid, that for the last seven years one-third of France's professional armed forces have been engaged in Indo-China, and that France is now spending more than a billion dollars a year defending that area. For our part the United States is contributing approximately one-third of the cost of the Indo-China operation. In addition, we maintain there a Military Advisory Mission to assist in equipping the National Armies of the three Associated States and the French Union Army.

In Thailand, Burma, and Indonesia there are smaller programs of economic aid. In the case of Thailand there is also a program of military aid and a Military Advisory Group.

When we look at the Far East from Japan and Korea, down through Formosa, the Philippines, to Indo-China, Thailand, Burma, and Indonesia, American blood or treasure—in Korea both—is being poured out with that of other free nations to keep those countries secure from Communist aggression—actual or potential—and to give them an opportunity to develop as free and independent nations. In that area we keep more than one-third of our ground troops. Would these more than 100,000 American casualties and billions of American dollars have been sacrificed for people whom we considered "second-class expendables"? I think not.

Now what are we doing in Asia? What is our policy? The brief survey I have given above shows what we are doing in part. But how do we feel about the area itself? Why do we deem it important, as we must in view of all that we are spending there? What do we see as the main problems—what are the chief desires of the peoples of those lands and what can we do about it? I should like to say at the outset that American policy in this area is not directed merely at building up bulwarks against Communism so that our own lot will be made more easy. Nor, as I hope to indicate shortly, does it ignore that aspect of the matter.

As I said in the beginning, our first treaty with any part of Asia was with a nation of Southeast Asia—Thailand. Thirty years ago an American scholar, Tyler Dennett, concluded his study of American policy in the Orient by the assertion that most-favored-nation treatment is the tap root of American policy in Asia. To him this meant equal treatment for all and he went on to say that "American interests in Asia are best promoted by the growth of strong, prosperous and enlightened Asiatic States." That is still true. That is still the basic philosophy, I believe, that underlies our policy in Asia. It is in accord with the strong desires of all the peoples of Asia for freedom and independence. If there is one thing all of them agree on, it is their desire for independence and freedom.

In this struggle they have had for freedom and independence, we must not forget what the effect of the war was—the effect of the Japanese occupation of most of the countries of that area. Japan's attempt to create her Co-Prosperity Sphere came to naught, but it left behind seeds which are still sprouting. The Japanese occupation did not succeed, except in cutting off the areas from their normal markets, and, because of the effective submarine and air action in the Pacific, Japan herself was then cut off from economic contact with the conquered areas. The result was not merely to increase poverty, but to reduce production and create economic chaos. At the same time the occupations strengthened the demands of the peoples of those areas for independence. To some degree it helped to develop leaders by giving them opportunity to come to the fore. And certainly it left behind arms for the use of those who wanted independence quickly. After the war, the former colonial powers saw the need for change. While some are still dissatisfied and think the change has not gone far enough, we should not forget that in the short space of seven years since the end of the Pacific war eight Asian nations with a population of over 600 million have attained independence, six of them in Southeast Asia. Wherever possible and proper, in accord with our world-wide commitments, the United States has encouraged this development. However, there have been factors which have held back the development and have made it more difficult—such as the lack of trained leadership, only to be expected in areas where the people had not had an opportunity to run their own governments. The economic chaos created by the war also must be remembered. This has created problems which have been further complicated by active Communist aggression.

At about the same time when Tyler Dennett was pointing

out that United States interests would be best served by the creation of "strong, prosperous and enlightened Asiatic states," Stalin was talking about the Far East, and in his lectures on Leninism he stated that "The road to victory of the revolution in the West lies through the revolutionary alliance with the liberation movement of the colonies and dependent countries against imperialism." More recently, in the *Moscow University Herald* of December 9, 1951, the Communists set forth a seven-point program which forms in fact a blueprint of Communist aggression. It begins with instructions to incite nationalism—something which all people want and are interested in—to promote a "united front," and then goes on through various steps to the point where the Communist Party seizes complete control and ousts all others. Point 6 in their seven-point program is worthy of special mention. It says, "Remember that true national independence can be achieved only in unity with the Soviet Union. There is no third, middle or neutral road." Note that it is the Communists themselves who deny the possibility of neutralism and of co-existence.

What is their ultimate purpose? To make the nations of Asia free? No. Remember, Stalin said that it was the road to victory in the West—that is what they are interested in. They are attempting to use the people of Asia to achieve that victory. It is the Soviets, the Communists, who really believe the people of Asia are "second-class expendables." There have not been 100,000 Soviet casualties on behalf of their North Korean and Chinese Communist friends. No—they let them spend their own blood.

What are the Soviet objectives in Asia? The first, as I have said, is to promote world revolution through revolutionary activity in the East; the second, it is almost self-evident, is to get Japan into the Communist camp or at least to weaken it so that it can be no danger to the Soviets. Stalin has said that Russia, with Japan, would be invincible.

Now when we look at these two aims and look at the aims

of the Chinese Communists, we see that for the time being and for probably the foreseeable future their aims are identical. It doesn't matter a great deal whether we can make up our own minds that Communist China is a true satellite or is a potential Titoist state—whether they are going to be more Chinese than Communist. The fact remains that for the time being and for the foreseeable future the interests of Soviet Russia and the interests of Communist China coincide and as long as that fact continues, they will continue to work together. Obviously the Chinese want to weaken Japan. Japan has been their traditional enemy. Or if not to weaken it, to get Japan better into their camp, to get control of it. And how do they expect to do this? One way, of course, is to get control over Southeast Asia. It is an indirect way. They have tried in Korea. They have not succeeded in Korea in getting in a position to threaten Japan. But in Southeast Asia they are trying again. Not only does this help them threaten Japan by taking over Southeast Asia and preventing the rice and raw materials from that area from going to Japan, but it also coincides with old Chinese imperialist desires to go back and take over Indo-China again and perhaps some of the other countries of Southeast Asia. Both the Soviets and the Chinese Communists realize Japan cannot survive without the rice of Southeast Asia and that with that rice in Communist control, they have the possibility of controlling Japan and making it come to terms. They remember that in 1940, Japan took over one million metric tons of rice from Thailand, Burma, and Indo-China, and that in 1951, in spite of the fact that the war had cut down the production of rice, Japan took over 500,000 metric tons of rice from Southeast Asia.

Now how does the United States meet this threat? We have in general a three-pronged attack—economic, political, and military. We believe that no one of these is sufficient of itself. If we emphasize only the military, we undoubtedly will lose in the long run because that is, of course, fundamentally a negative approach. We must have the positive approach of economic and political progress hand in hand. But we realize that without some military barrier to the extension of Soviet and Communist aggression, there is no opportunity for political and economic measures to have a chance to succeed.

Very briefly, I am going to discuss one or two of the areas and what we are doing there. The key probably to all of Southeast Asia is at present Indo-China. This is the area, where, as I have said, a shooting war is going on. It is along the borders of Indo-China that we find some 200,000 Chinese Communists poised ready for attack. Whether they will or not no one can say. But at least they have the capability. We know that there are probably some 10,000 Chinese Communist volunteers in Indo-China with the forces of Ho Chi Minh, not as active combat troops, but as technicians, as trainers, and assistants in one way or the other. Here then is the real, immediate threat.

There had been considerable misunderstanding about United States policy toward Indo-China. Many people have said we are there only to help the French continue to impose colonialism upon the peoples of that area. That, I state flatly, is not true. The French have shown by their actions in recent years that they are looking with the rest of us toward the freedom and independence of these nations in Southeast Asia. Thirty-three world powers have already recognized the Associated States of Indo-China as independent states. Some of them have exchanged diplomatic representatives. The three Associated States took part as equal members of the conference at San Francisco which signed the Japanese Peace Treaty. They did not sign as part of the French Delegation. They signed as independent nations. Since 1950 the peoples of Indo-China have assumed a constantly greater share of the responsibility of government. In Laos and Cambodia they have elected assemblies which are functioning. In Viet-Nam a beginning is being made toward the creation of an assembly. They have practically all the powers they can exercise at the present time while a war is going on; and there is a war going on and it cannot be forgotten.

Back in 1950 the French also took the great decision to create national armies in the Associated States. It seems to me that once that decision was made, there can be no back-sliding. The only way in which the peoples of that area can be truly independent is, over a period of time, to create national armies, by which they can defend themselves so that they will not have to depend upon the French or the United States or anyone else—so they can stand on their own feet and be truly independent. In that effort to create national armies the United States is helping. We are doing all we possibly can in view of our commitments elsewhere. Since 1950 there have been created in the Associated States fifty-two battalions of troops in their national armies. Out of that number, twenty-one of those battalions have six or less French officers in them. Two of those battalions have no French officers in them. The Chief of Staff of the Viet-Namese Army is a national of that country. Progress is being made. We are moving in the right direction. With France, there is a real hope that the peoples of that area will have true freedom. With Ho Chi Minh and his Communistic friends coming into power, there would be no hope for true freedom. There would be only the certainty of Communist domination.

We have recognized that this struggle in Indo-China—the struggle by the French and by the armies of the Associated States—is part of a world-wide resistance to Communist aggression. There the French, as I have said, are carrying the chief burden. In Korea it is the United States. But it is the same war.

In other parts of Southeast Asia what have we been doing? In the Philippine Islands real progress is being made with United States help. I have mentioned the economic aid program—a five-year program. That is beginning to bear fruit. The Philippine budget is being balanced. Their economy is being stabilized. In addition to that, they have had, a year ago, the first really free election in their history. This was done by the Philippine people themselves and it gave them heart and encouragement in carrying on democratic processes. The Huk movement—the Communist movement in the Philippines— has had its back broken by the energetic and imaginative work of Ramon Magsaysay, the Philippine Secretary of Defense. Here is one place where many advances are being made in the fight against Communism, and it is being done on both fronts. It is not only military suppression. There is plenty of that. It is severe. But there is also rehabilitation at the same time. It is realized that these people—many of them—are in the Huk and Communist camp because of genuine grievances. When such is the case real attempts are made to meet these grievances. However, the leaders of this movement are a few Moscow-trained Communists. There is much yet to do but the number of armed Huks is probably down to less than 5,000 at the present time. In this struggle, America has contributed. It has contributed through economic aid, through a Military Advisory Group, and through other help.

In Burma and in Indonesia we have a somewhat different situation. These two countries have come to full independence only since the war. They are young countries. They are interested in standing on their own feet. They are non-Communist. But they wish to be neutral countries. My own personal opinion is that eventually they can't be neutral, but that is not something I can tell them. It is something they must decide for themselves. We want to help them. We stand ready to help them. We are helping them in programs of economic aid. But we do not want to force our aid upon them. We do not want to give what is not wanted. We want them to know that we recognize their right to decide their own problems. We recognize their right to do as we did ourselves for many years—remain aloof from the world struggle, until we found through bitter experience that we couldn't do it in the world of today. We hope that through our aid and effort they will not have to find that out through bitter experience. They can be assured that we are friends who want to help when they recognize the need for help.

In Thailand, the oldest independent state in Southeast Asia, we have, as I said, a small military program and a small aid program. We are helping them to build up an efficient army to take care of internal problems and helping them to meet their Communist problem.

There are one or two general things I would like to say about the area as a whole. In Southeast Asia there are over ten million Chinese living in these various countries. These ten million Chinese are a potential fifth column—if they have nowhere to look except to Communist China, obviously they will ally themselves with Communist China and will in these countries of Southeast Asia be, as I say, a dangerous potential fifth column. There have been many arguments about the strategic value of Formosa. I am not a military man. It is not for me to say whether Formosa is vital from the strategic point of view or not. I think it is. But aside from that, it seems to me that it is vital from the general political point of view. If there is some area where there is a non-Communist Chinese Government to which these millions of Chinese in Southeast Asia can look, it will be less of a temptation to them to turn to the Communist Government on the mainland. If that Government on Formosa begins to create the type of government which they can respect and honor—one which is doing something for the people—then it will be still easier. That is what we are trying to help that Government on Formosa to do. We think it is making progress toward creating the sort of government which deserves support. We think it is going in the right direction. We shall continue to help it do so.

I should like also to mention briefly the effect of the war in Korea on Southeast Asia. It has two effects. The obvious first effect is that because of our all-out effort in Korea, we are limited in what we can do in Southeast Asia. We cannot do as much always as we would like to do because of our problems in Korea. But also while that is true and is perhaps a negative factor, there is a positive factor. I am convinced, that if we had not met the Communist aggression in Korea in the way we have and if we had not thrown it back, as we have, beyond the point from which it started, there is good evidence that the situation in Southeast Asia today would be far different from what we see—that the people of that area would not have had the past two years to strengthen themselves, to continue to build up stronger governments economically, politically, and socially, so that they are in a better position to handle their own affairs and withstand any form of Communist aggression, overt or covert.

Allow me to mention briefly the ANZUS Pact—this ANZUS Council meeting from which I have just returned. There again there has been some misunderstanding. There has been some thought that this represents a white-man's pact. That is not so. It is a beginning of collective security in the Pacific. We cannot do everything we want to do at once, so we do the things we can. We found out when we began to study this problem that it was not possible, and we still believe that it is not possible at this time to create an over-all Pacific security system or security pact of the same type that we have in the Atlantic. The problems of the various countries are so different. For one thing, very obviously the countries in that area have different attitudes toward China. While that continues, it is difficult, if not impossible, to get them all into one sort of over-all pact. Practically all of the Asian nations, whether they want to be neutral or not, are non-Communist countries. You might think they have this bond which would draw them together, but there still are differences among them. President Quirino of the Philippines has been very active in promoting a Pacific pact, but as yet he has not had great success. I think a beginning might be made in the association of these countries, not for military or aggressive purposes, but for exchanges of ideas and information—exchange of cultural leaders, educators, and so forth. Perhaps that is the way we must start. But we did realize when we looked over the situation that there were things that could be done. We have our security pact with Japan. We have a mutual defense treaty with the Philippines, and we have the tripartite security pact with Australia and New Zealand. This is a beginning. It is only a beginning. Some time in some way which we cannot now foresee the nations of the Pacific area will begin to wish to have some form of collective security. When they do, when they make it known that it is their desire, they will find the United States willing and ready to help. But we do not think it is something we can force upon them.

I have taken you around the area briefly and sketchily to show you some of the things we have been thinking about. In conclusion I would like to say that we still agree with what Tyler Dennett said—that American interests require "strong, prosperous and enlightened Asiatic states." We believe we are helping toward creating just such states. But in this and in some of the things I have said, perhaps I have given the impression that we think we have made more progress than we have. That is not true. We are very conscious of the fact that our problems are not solved, but that we will have to continue to work for a long time toward the solution of these problems. In closing may I quote from a speech I made recently in Seattle:

I am afraid the United States and the other nations of the free world must learn to live for some time to come with crisis. We shall need all the resolution, firmness and patience we can summon if the tremendous sacrifices we have already made are not to be in vain. Of the above qualities, if any one can be more important than the others, I stress patience. We must not become, as we are all tempted to at times, so dismayed at what is going on that we rush into new adventures which might create more problems than they solve. We must not, on the other hand, at any sign of good news, give way to our natural desire to relax and turn our thoughts and efforts to more pleasant things.

As has recently been said: "The central objective has to be somehow to keep the thread of civilization alive—to avert war, if possible, because war is the second greatest threat to civilized survival; but to be prepared for war, if necessary because the greatest threat of all is totalitarian victory."

Paul H. Clyde

HISTORICAL REFLECTIONS ON CONTINUITY
IN UNITED STATES FAR EASTERN POLICY

Half a century ago a brilliant American, a man of fine mind and fascinating personality and, indeed, a man of letters who happened also to be Secretary of State, told the major powers that he considered their replies to his open door notes as "final and definitive." In that phrase John Hay was making, in terms of continuity, a policy far more rigid, inflexible than he knew. I shall return to his phrase—"final and definitive" —later in these remarks. I mention it here merely to forewarn you that Hay's historic words do not apply to the conclusions I shall present to you. My own conclusions are neither final nor definitive. I suspect that the historian as well as the policy-maker does well in this way to remind himself as well as his audience that in history, if not in policy, there is nothing that is "final and definitive." History by its very nature and function is reinterpreted, if not rewritten, by each succeeding generation.

This being so, I must disclaim all intent of presenting to you anything so absolute as the verdict of history on our American thinking and doing toward and in the Far East. The history of the United States in Eastern Asia assumed its first embryonic forms in the late eighteenth century. These forms grew and new ones were added in the nineteenth century, and the process of history in evolution has continued with increasing complexity of fact and interpretation in the twentieth century. This history is a story of growth, always

17

incomplete, always in process, changing its form with the passage of time as new evidence is revealed and as each generation looks back on the story through its own intellectual and emotional spectacles.

I hope therefore that you will receive my observations in the foregoing context. They present no claim to infallibility. New evidence may render them untenable. Meanwhile you may consider them as no more than the reflections of one historian whose judgments may well be in error.

Historical Thinking in Disrepute

In the turbulence of the present, the task of the historian, always difficult, is beset by the added pitfalls created by a national temper plagued by emotional crisis. Neither government nor that elusive person, the man in the street, moves today in a climate of calm historical reflection. There is an overwhelming pressure upon us to accept this or that interpretation, this or that program of evidence. The historian shies away, and properly so, from absolute judgments in terms of right and wrong; but in the analysis of historic national objectives he cannot side-step value judgments on what was wise and desirable and what was unwise and undesirable. Accordingly, I shall have something to say about the wisdom in our history (and there has been a great deal of it), but the main burden of my remarks will be directed to matters where wisdom, if not lacking, is at least more difficult to discern.

Far East Policy: a Young and Minor Interest

As a first reflection on American historical policy in Eastern Asia, I would remind you that American relations with the Far East are as yet exceedingly young. The first American treaty with a Far Eastern nation was negotiated only a little more than a century ago. This quality of youthfulness—perhaps immaturity would be a better term—is not, however, the unique element in the history of America's Far Eastern relations for, as you recall, all of this country's foreign contacts are young in point of years. The unique element in our approach to Asia becomes clear when one recalls that in conducting relations with Europe and Latin America, Americans have been guided in some degree at least by the common intellectual and cultural heritage this country enjoyed along with those regions and their peoples. In Eastern Asia in contrast, Americans have been and still are as a people, if not as a government, strangers to the civilizations of half of mankind. Moreover, until what I shall call an historical yesterday, Asia was not regarded by this country as a region of real significance. Indeed, until fifty years ago the American horizon in Asia saw only a limited commerce and a glowing prospect of converting the heathen to Christianity. These purposes, of course, were not unimportant. The point is that they did not add up to a vital national interest. For all but a few Americans throughout most of our history, the Pacific Ocean has been very wide and the teeming millions of Asia far away.

The Lack of Historical Studies

This physical and this intellectual and cultural gulf between America and the Far East also reflected itself, and very naturally so, in the poverty of our Oriental scholarship. Men of my own generation can recall the time when American university courses on the modern Far East could be counted on the fingers of one hand. Only since the period between the two World Wars may it be said that recognition in limited degree has been given to the essential place of Far Eastern studies in our unique experiment to educate our entire people as responsible citizens in a democracy. The historical failure of Americans as scholars to concern themselves with Asia, and the historical failure of Americans as a people to be students of Asia are sins of omission not unrelated to the catastrophies which have overtaken our relations with the Far Pacific since the early years of this century. When knowledge is lacking, the views men entertain and the policies they advocate are apt to rest on frail substitutes: emotion, sentimentality, or some species of intellectual crystallization. Not even the fiat of a George Washington could preclude in those circumstances

America's emotional attachment to Japan before 1905 or its sentimental regard for China after 1905. American international friendships in Asia have not been notable for their continuity, and this is perhaps not surprising since they have been founded in the heart rather than the mind. The case of our "little brown brothers" in the Philippines would appear to be no exception to this generalization.

Security in the Nineteenth and Twentieth Centuries

In both the nineteenth and the twentieth centuries the security of the United States has been closely related to the independence and the prosperity of peripheral powers in Europe and also, though this is a newer idea to us, in Asia. Britain's position and British policy in Europe were a guarantee of this security. More often than not, Americans failed to sense this fundamental circumstance. On the other side of the world, in Asia in mid-nineteenth century the United States, after trailing other powers into China, pioneered in the opening of Japan, a second peripheral power of potential import to American security, an importance which seems not to have been noted at the time, not indeed until it was seen fifty years later by Theodore Roosevelt. Commodore Perry was of course concerned with the concept of security; but in general, Americans who belonged to the generation of Perry and Townsend Harris, or to the later generation of John W. Foster, did not see Japan in terms of American security. Eastern Asia for the vast majority remained a concept of romanticism enlivened by Japanese kimonos and cherry blossoms.

Apart from this romanticizing on strange and quaint peoples, the opening of Japan and the earlier inception of treaty relations with China rested on a simple premise of commercialism common to American interest in all parts of the globe, and upon the manifest destiny felt by some Americans to carry Christianity to those who were unenlightened. I am suggesting that in the opening of Japan, American action out-

stripped American thought since the action did not comprehend well-considered motives of security save in a very remote
and limited sense. But perhaps this lack of insight in mid-
nineteenth century into the road America was travelling can
be better understood when it is recalled that men of a much
later generation acted with even less regard for, and less insight into, consequences. I refer to the men who made policy
in 1898. They appear to have forgotten what the Fathers of
this country had known very well, that important foundations
of American security lay far outside this continent. Yet from
1890 onward in an era of isolationism this country was su-
premely confident of its security, a security which it attributed
quite mistakenly to superior American wisdom in standing
apart from the sordid affairs of the Old World.

The Philippines

That fateful year, 1898, brought some extraordinary de-
partures in American policy in the Far East. Among other
things, it ended the simple policy of commercialism in Asia
based upon most-favored-nation treatment. Out of a war
fought against Spain for no well-considered or satisfying reasons, fought at a time when measures short of war had by no
means been exhausted, Americans, of all peoples, emerged
with a colony and, of all places, in Asia. It should be chasten-
ing to recall that the naval and military measures which placed
the Philippines in American hands were, as you remember,
the result of a high-level intrigue by a few able men acting in
what they considered to be the highest national interest. Those
military measures, the result of intrigue, were followed by
larger political decisions the importance of which it would
be difficult to exaggerate: for example, the decision to retain
the Philippines. The secret conferences, the official and the
public debates leading to this end were rather violent, but
the arguments advanced often appeared to mean very little.
What seemed to matter was that enough Americans, their
senators, and their most vocal spokesmen had come to like

the flavor of empire. What empire might do to America, its ideals, and its institutions was left to posterity. This ill-considered departure from continuity recalls the earlier decision of 1898 which had fixed the number of troops to be sent to the Philippines before there was any agreement as to what these troops should do.

Looking back over these extraordinary doings, the historian will not jump to the conclusion that the taking of the Philippines was in itself necessarily unwise; but he may well suspect that there was folly in fighting a war that was not inevitable, in creating an empire without due thought to the consequences, and in forsaking tradition and principles before it was clear that these were outworn and no longer useful. Action had again outstripped our thought. But this capacity to forsake principle was soon to be matched, as we shall see, by a tenacious power to cling to principle.

John Hay and the Open Door

As the Philippine issue was moving toward decision in the elections of 1900, John Hay made his request to the powers for observance of an open door and the integrity of China. For the next forty years that compound phrase—the open door and the integrity of China—punctuated American literature and debates on foreign policy with a repetitious force outrivalling historic appeals to another phrase—the Monroe Doctrine. If continuity be a virtue, then American policy as symbolized by the phrase, the open door and the integrity of China, must be counted a supreme triumph. In the long run, however, policies do not justify themselves through some simple process whereby it is simply assumed that they are good; yet this process of justification by assumption was used more often than any other to bolster the open door and the integrity of China throughout most of the history of these doctrines of policy.[1]

[1] The following are the sources on which I have drawn most heavily for the interpretation here presented of the open door and the integrity

The Popular Interpretation of the Open Door

From the beginning the interpretation accepted by American public opinion on what Hay had done, an interpretation carried down to our own day with an almost untarnished continuity in both our official interpretations and our unofficial histories, is illustrated by the following example cited by George Kennan from Mark Sullivan's *Our Times:*

The "open-door" policy in China was an American idea. It was set up in contrast to the "spheres-of-influence" policy practiced by other nations. . . .

The "open-door" is one of the most creditable episodes in American diplomacy, an example of benevolent impulse accompanied by energy and shrewd skill in negotiation. Not one of the statesmen and nations that agreed to Hay's policy wanted to. It was like asking every man who believes in truth to stand up—the liars are obliged to be the first to rise. Hay saw through them perfectly; his insight into human nature was one of his strongest qualities.[2]

Legend versus Fact

Bearing in mind the Sullivan interpretation commonly accepted to this day, one may seek with profit to re-examine

---

of China. The limitations placed upon the Hay policy by reason of existing spheres of influence were first developed by Paul H. Clyde, "The Open Door Policy of John Hay," *The Historical Outlook* (May, 1931), 210–14. An extended treatment of the Hippisley-Rockhill background of the Hay notes was first presented by A. W. Griswold, *The Far Eastern Policy of the United States* (New York, 1938). The most penetrating analysis and the most dynamic presentation of the nature and application of the open door policy is George F. Kennan's *American Diplomacy, 1900–1950* (Chicago, 1951). For concise interpretations of the open door throughout its history see Paul H. Clyde, *The Far East: A History of the Impact of the West on Eastern Asia* (2nd ed., New York, 1952).

[2] *Our Times: The Turn of the Century* (New York, 1926), 509, cited by Kennan, *American Diplomacy*, 21–22. For an official reiteration of the traditional interpretation see *United States Relations With China*, Department of State Publication 3573, Far Eastern Series 30 (Washington, 1949), 1–37.

what really happened. From such re-examination there is now emerging a more realistic historical appraisal of the open door. It appears that the Hay notes of 1899 prepared by Alfred Hippisley of the Chinese Maritime Customs Service, and by W. W. Rockhill, Hay's chief counsel on the Far East, were basically a summary of the hopes of the Chinese Customs Service at that particular time. Moreover, it would seem that in content the notes were directed against current policies of the British Government. Hippisley was in fact using the United States to force the British into a line of action less threatening to the Customs Service. Neither Rockhill nor Hay appears to have been aware of this, nor do they seem to have known how far by this time, the autumn of 1899, the British Government was moving away from an open door and toward a policy of a sphere for Britain.

The Replies "Final and Definitive"

In response to Hay's notes, the replies of the Powers were reluctant, deeply qualified, and in essence amounted to no acceptance at all. Nevertheless, Hay described them as satisfactory assurances, as "final and definitive."

He thereby gave the impression, which the American public was not slow to accept, that the European powers, who had been on the verge of getting away with something improper in China, had been checked and frustrated by the timely intervention of the United States government and that a resounding diplomatic triumph had been achieved.[3]

The Integrity of China

This open door exchange was no more than completed when the Boxer outbreak led Hay to send his integrity of China notes, July 3, 1900, generally interpreted by historians as a pledge to protect China against foreign encroachment upon her territory. In reality, these various American dicta,

[3] Kennan, *American Diplomacy*, 32.

the open door and the integrity notes, had no practical effect on the current scene in China. If anything saved China from partition it was the mutual jealousies and fears of the Powers. Furthermore, all the chief actors in and about Washington, Hippisley, Rockhill, and Hay, soon lost their illusions about the open door. Hay, himself, was seeking a coaling station in Fukien before the end of the very year in which he had preached our devotion to China's territorial and administrative entity; and when the Japanese asked if we would join them in forcing the Russians to observe our principles in Manchuria, Hay said we would not.[4]

In summary, then, how shall we evaluate the activation of Hay's open door and integrity policy?

First. The Hay open door formula was not really Hay's and there is no evidence that this formula was given critical study by the government which was about to propose it. Supposed to be in line with British purposes, it was actually in conflict with a new and emerging British policy inimical to the Chinese Customs Service. The Service sought through Hay to protect its interests.

Second. The policy was not new and American but old and British. It did have a past but the appearance of spheres of influence precluded it from having a future. The United States did not regard the policy as vital, for this country did not support it in any determined way and was not prepared to accept responsibility for results if it were implemented.

Third. The Hay principles contained other elements of danger because they fashioned a policy Americans were not prepared to follow in their own newly acquired possessions, the Philippines and Puerto Rico.

Fourth. The evidence does not suggest that Hay knew or understood these things and it would be academic to belabor

[4] See Clyde, *The Far East,* 293–300; A. L. P. Dennis, *Adventures in American Diplomacy* (New York, 1928), 242; Kennan, *American Diplomacy,* 34–35.

the thesis that he should have known. He reasoned as you or I might have reasoned. The policy has done well by the British, it surely could do well by us, and there could, he felt, be little harm in asking others to adhere. Hay, of course, did know that the replies of the Powers were meaningless, but he was enough of a politician to turn a diplomatic failure into a domestic triumph. And so he turned from the Powers to the American public proclaiming the same high-minded formula and claiming a great diplomatic victory. In all of this there was something of a double meaning, for indeed the assurances from the Powers were soon to prove "final and definitive" but not in the sense Hay conveyed to his public. Unfortunately, that public accepted Hay's words at face value. A great and a tragic myth was already in the making, and Mark Sullivan did not stand alone in perpetuating that myth.[5]

A Matter of Interpretation

The justification is twofold for lingering on the Hay open door even in an essay as brief as this must be. In the first place, the open door and the integrity of China were to claim American official and popular homage in words, if not in deeds, for the next forty years. American policy in the Far East had been captured by a slogan—the open door and the integrity of China. All the complexities of Far Eastern relations, all the undiscovered, unsolved problems of tomorrow could be entrusted safely, so it was felt, to this benevolent phrase. Its magic was hardly less potent than an earlier slogan—the Monroe Doctrine—which was sometimes assumed by the American public to comprehend powers which lay outside its political or its legal nature. In the case of the open door a credulous public was encouraged in this homage by a succession of administrations both Republican and Democratic.

In the second place, the affirmation of the open door and China's integrity by Hay merits emphasis because this incident appears to have shaped a design for American diplomacy

[5] Kennan, *American Diplomacy*, 35–37.

in the Pacific from that day until Pearl Harbor. This design had the merit of simplicity. As crises, great and small, followed each other in succession throughout the uneasy years of China's twentieth-century history, the American Government following Hay's example called time and again upon a great power to respect the open door and the principle of integrity. The powers so addressed replied as they had responded to Hay. No one of course ever denied Hay's principles, but neither was there any disposition to define their meaning in a China where realities did not correspond to Western concepts of the well-ordered nation state. America's repeated appeals to the Powers, despite their evasive replies, were time and again presented to the American public as diplomatic accomplishments of great value. Yet in none of these overtures did the United States assume any responsibility. There was no suggestion that this country would back its principles by force; no suggestion that it would assist any power that attempted to enforce them for us. There seems to have been a conviction that, since the principles themselves were just and good, reassertion if sufficiently prolonged would eventually bring them to pass. Time, as we now know, has not dealt kindly with that conviction.[6]

Twentieth Century Continuity

The Hay episode did in fact set a pattern of continuity—a continuity in verbal effort to implement Hay's principles in China. The historian can applaud the efforts to implant good principles either here or elsewhere; he is conscious of the power exercised by ideals in American history. But in addition, the historian may, indeed he must ask, why there was not a larger effort by the American Government to determine after the first reverses whether these principles were in a practical sense applicable to China after 1900. No superhuman insight was needed to discover that the first principle, the open door, was never relevant save in the most restricted sense

[6] Kennan, *American Diplomacy*, 38–40.

of consumption merchandise, once the sphere of influence had become an established fact. A sphere in practice meant special privilege, the antithesis of an open door. The fact that America refused to recognize the spheres was a matter of indifference to the Powers. As for the second principle of China's territorial integrity and her administrative entity, the fact here was that long before Hay's pronouncement, the so-called unequal treaties of the nineteenth century to which in most respects America was a party, and the later concessions secured by the Powers between 1895 and 1899 had already made such serious inroads upon China's administrative control within her borders as to make a mockery of the principle unless these special privileges were first surrendered. Hay and Theodore Roosevelt soon recognized the practical limitations but there appears to have been no searching for new or for modified principles on which a more practical and less doctrinaire policy might have been based.

Application of United States Principles

Between Hay's enunciation in 1899 and Pearl Harbor in 1941, a span of forty-two years, the basic policy of the United States in the Far East in terms of principles and objectives underwent no substantial change. Respect for the open door and the integrity of China by the American Government and by the powers remained as the American fundamental formula. What may be said on its application throughout these forty-two years? It must be assumed at the outset that nothing less than the complete diplomatic history of those years can give an adequate answer. Here it is possible only to cite some examples of attempted implementation.

Such examples include the Root-Takahira exchange of notes in 1908, the Lansing-Ishii exchange in 1917, the Nine-Power open door agreement of 1921–22, and others scarcely less striking among which might be mentioned the open door in Manchuria in 1906, the Knox neutralization proposal of 1910, and the Twenty-One Demands of 1915. These were among the positive efforts made by the United States from time to time to revitalize a situation which Hay in 1900 had described as "final and definitive." The frequency with which these efforts were brought forth might lead the skeptic to infer that it was the continuing failure rather than the success of the open door that was so "final and definitive."

Negative Aspects of Policy

There is, however, a far more elusive problem for the historian. Perhaps a satisfying answer will always elude him. The problem is posed by the question: Did the Government of the United States at any time after 1899 regard its China principles as an appropriate and practical basis for a foreign policy over and beyond such value as the principles undoubtedly had in appealing to the high-minded and sometimes sentimental instincts of the American people, especially when this people was thinking of China? At first glance one is inclined to dismiss summarily the implications of this question. Surely a policy marked by such continuity as pertained to American declarations on the open door could not have survived even in the American mind alone without the continuing confidence of the men who enunciated and re-enunciated that policy until it had become an integral part of our American language on foreign affairs. Personally, I have not the remotest doubt that some of our statesmen believed in our China principles as realistic instruments of a noble and practical policy. I am not so certain that their beliefs were wise or that they were based on adequate understanding of the unfolding international and domestic picture in the Far East. Indeed, the question of the Government's belief in its own policy cannot be dismissed summarily.

To begin with, Hay's illusions soon vanished. In 1900 he told Edwin H. Conger in Peking: ". . . we have no policy in China except to protect with energy American interests,"[7] and again in 1902 he wrote to Roosevelt:

[7] Clyde, *The Far East*, 299.

We are not in any attitude of hostility towards Russia in Manchuria. On the contrary, we recognize her exceptional position in northern China. What we have been working for two years to accomplish, and what we have at last accomplished, if assurances are to count for anything, is that, no matter what happens eventually in northern China and Manchuria, the United States shall not be placed in any worse position than while the country was under the unquestioned domination of China.[8]

In 1905 it was Roosevelt himself who was saying:

I do not believe in our taking any position anywhere unless we can make good; and as regards Manchuria, if the Japanese choose to follow a course of conduct to which we are adverse, we cannot stop it unless we are prepared to go to war. . . .[9]

The meaning of these views would need no elaboration even if we did not have the added circumstance of Hay, himself, joining the concession hunters in 1900.[10]

In Conclusion

In conclusion, may I repeat that the foregoing reflections on continuity in United States Far Eastern policy have not been presented as the "final and definitive" verdict of history. Rather their intent is to stimulate re-examination of the official and the conventional framework in which the story has so often been presented and accepted.

Viewed in historical perspective and when judged on the level of American national mores, the record of the United States in Asia need not fear comparison in ethics with the record of any other great power. America's role in the Far East in commerce, in diplomacy, and in education need not be a subject for moral apology. Most of the American statesmen who made and applied policy were responding to benevo-

[8] Roosevelt Papers, printed in Tyler Dennett, *Roosevelt and the Russo-Japanese War* (New York, 1925), 135–36.
[9] Quoted by Kennan, *American Diplomacy*, 44.
[10] Clyde, *The Far East*, 300.

lent rather than to ulterior motives. But these considerations while they demand our recognition are not the real point.

The crux of the matter is that today's historian faces the wreckage of a half-century of American policy in the Far East. What explanation will history offer for calamities as colossal as those which have overtaken the United States in Eastern Asia, an area in which we have been prone to tell ourselves that our wisdom and our sense of justice have been unmatched? There are perhaps some who would maintain that no choices were open to us. That thesis is unconvincing and unproved. Unless the Manchurian fiasco of 1931, Pearl Harbor in 1941, and the Communist conquest of China in 1948–49 are to be counted as the fulfillment of American hopes and of policy objectives, we owe it as a government and as a people to dig more deeply and with greater discernment into our own diplomatic and policy background. If our attitudes and policies have contributed to these disastrous results, we should know in what ways they have done so and thus be better armed, diplomatically speaking, for the future.

The evidence is perhaps inconclusive, but it does point to some grave shortcomings in our Far Eastern record.

First. In the historical view of things we have generally looked upon the Far East as a minor interest and have been too ready to assume that what was good for us would also be good for Asia and welcome to Asiatics.

Second. As a people, as a government, we have been slow to become students of Asia. Many of our mistakes have been the mistakes of ignorance rather than of design.

Third. Having entered Asia in mid-nineteenth century for limited purposes, we intrigued ourselves into acquiring an Asiatic empire at the century's close without first giving due thought to the consequences. It would at least be more satisfying to think that we did what we did with our eyes open.

Fourth. In the twentieth century we affirmed for ourselves and for the Powers—and we continued repeatedly to affirm as the years went by—principles vis-à-vis China whose relevancy as practical bases for a foreign policy was and continued to be open to serious question.

Fifth. The American people were encouraged to believe in the efficacy of these principles long after the original proponents of them had acknowledged their disillusionment.

Sixth. As a result, policy achieved continuity, but it may be questioned whether this continuity was a virtue since by reason of it policy was bound to unchanging abstract principles in which there was no room for "a recognition of power realities in the Orient as a factor worthy of our serious respect." [11]

And finally, when policy is tied to abstractions, when it propounds principles on which we are not prepared to make good, then there is some reason to believe that the men who apply policy are faced by frustration. It was in 1931 that a responsible spokesman of the Department of State, in his official capacity, recorded his own remarks to a distinguished foreign visitor:

. . . both the American Government and the American people [he said], having no selfish political objectives in reference to China, were in fact most eager to help China, but were frankly at a loss as to ways and means. . . .[12]

The open door and the integrity of China had indeed come upon days which in the most tragic sense of those words were final and definitive.

One may be permitted the hope that the historian will have a happier story to tell when he records the policy of the United States toward Southeast Asia in the coming world.

[11] Kennan, *American Diplomacy*, 51.

[12] United States, *Foreign Relations*, 1931, III, 968–69. Memorandum by the Chief of the Division of Far Eastern Affairs (Hornbeck) of a Conversation with the Apostolic Delegate to China (Archbishop Celso Costantini). Washington, June 23, 1931.

George McT. Kahin

POSTWAR PROBLEMS IN THE SOUTHEAST ASIA POLICY OF THE UNITED STATES

Since the end of the war, there have been discernible two phases of American policy toward Southeast Asia [1] which have been manifest to some extent in most of the area and have been clearly apparent in Indonesia and Indo-China. The first of these phases ran from the end of the war until about the middle of 1949; the second we are still in. Whereas the dominant factor in the first phase was the fear of a spread of Communism and Soviet power in Europe, the dominant factor in the second has been the fear of the spread of Communism and the power of the Soviet bloc in Asia.

It is difficult to understand the present phase without some knowledge of the first, for the policies we followed during the first period severely limit our choice of policy today. This results not only from the momentum of these past policies and the commitments we have made under them. It also stems from the fact that they have strongly conditioned the attitudes of

[1] Space does not permit coverage of all of the many post-war problems which have confronted the United States in Southeast Asia. Discussion of American relations with Burma and Malaya have been omitted because the problems involved have fortunately been relatively minor. Exclusion of the Philippines results from the fact that it was expected that other papers in the symposium would treat it rather fully. The primary focus of this paper is on those two areas of Southeast Asia where the most critical post-war problems of the United States have arisen—namely Indonesia and Indo-China.

Southeast Asians toward us and toward whatever new policies we may hope to initiate. These previous policies, *in particular as they have been interpreted by Southeast Asians,* impose limitations upon the latitude of policy open to the United States today which it would be highly unrealistic to ignore.

The First Phase (August, 1945—mid–1949)

It has often been noted and it is certainly true that with the end of the war the peoples of Southeast Asia looked to the United States as the champion of the principle of national self-determination. In general, the leaders of the revolutionary nationalist movements which broke out there believed that the United States would back their bids for independence. It was in large measure because of this that the postwar era opened with the United States commanding a prestige and leadership in Southeast Asia which was enormous, dwarfing that of the other Allied powers, Soviet Russia included. However, with respect to Indonesia and Indo-China we failed to assume the position of leadership that was expected of us. To their nationalist leaders we appeared to sit on the sidelines and let them fend for themselves. By doing so we went a long way in dissipating the high regard in which we were initially held.

From the end of the war until mid–1949, formulation of American policy toward Southeast Asia was dominated chiefly by what were seen as the requirements for an effective policy in Europe. Our concern for the fate of continental Europe was so great as to bring our policy-makers to temporize in Southeast Asia with the principles of self-determination to which in theory we remained committed there as well as in Europe. Enlistment of the cooperation of France and the Netherlands with American policy in Europe and, as American-Soviet relations deteriorated, the strengthening of these two countries against possible Soviet pressure were widely regarded by the State Department and the Pentagon as incompatible with overt American support of the independence movements in

Indo-China and Indonesia. The margin of survival of the two metropoles was deemed so slim, so precarious, as to make inadvisable any American interference aimed at ending their control over these colonies. Though the American Government hoped for negotiated settlements in these disputes, legal, psychological, and economic reasons were held to counsel a policy of neutrality on its part.

Loss of an important colony on top of her recent humiliation at the hands of Germany, particularly if coupled with American pressure to yield to the loss, might, it was argued, turn sensitive French nationalism against the United States to the advantage of either Soviet Russia or the Gaullists. With 40 per cent of the French electorate voting Communist, it was felt that such American pressure might tip the scales dangerously. It was also believed that should France yield control of Indo-China to its indigenous leaders, native leaders in other French colonies would be emboldened to revolt.

American pressure on the Netherlands, it was held, would turn the Dutch away from cooperating with American plans for the economic and military rehabilitation of Western Europe, thereby seriously damaging the prospects for success of these projects. In addition, it was argued that maintenance of Dutch control over Indonesia was indispensable to the recovery of the war-ravaged Netherlands economy. It was held that elimination of this control would, at least for the time being, so undermine the Netherlands economy as to facilitate the spread of Communism within the country, while at the same time weakening seriously the over-all economy of Western Europe.

The inclination to temporize with American principles in Southeast Asia for the seeming benefit of American interests in Europe was somewhat moderated during the earlier part of the first phase of American postwar policy by an important minority opinion within the State Department. Though unable to have its policies accepted, the group holding this opinion was sometimes able to temper the Europe-first policies of

the majority. The principal locus of this minority was in the
newly-created Southeast Asia division of the Department. During this early period most of its membership combined a sympathy with the aspirations of advanced colonial peoples for
independence with the conviction that France and the Netherlands would be stronger financially and militarily vis-à-vis
Russia if they gracefully granted these colonies independence. What Britain was to do in Burma, they hoped France
and the Netherlands would do in their Southeast Asian colonies. Though unable to bring American policy to support
the independence movements in Indonesia and Indo-China,
the efforts of this group contributed a great deal toward keeping the United States neutral in the disputes between their
nationalist regimes and the Netherlands and France. For instance, in large part because of its efforts, the Dutch were for
some time unable to get ships released from the Allied Shipping Pool to carry their troops to Indonesia, and both the
Dutch and the French were refused permission to purchase
arms from the vast American stores in New Guinea.

The ability of the United States to maintain a position of
neutrality during the earlier part of the first phase of our postwar policy cannot be fully understood without some reference
to Soviet policy. During this period Russia's Southeast Asian
policy was fully as Europe-centered as that of the United
States, and in general operated at the expense of the independence movements in Indonesia and Indo-China. This Soviet policy made it much easier for the United States to evade
involvement in the issues in Indonesia and Indo-China and
maintain a policy of neutrality.

Though the influence of the men in the Southeast Asia Division during this period was greatly limited in dealing with
the situation in Indo-China and Indonesia by virtue of having
to share policy-making with the stronger French and Netherlands desks in the Department, they suffered no such limitation with respect to Thailand. Here they were able to press
successfully for a policy which held that the Thai declaration

of war on the United States had not represented the will of the Thai people. With the end of the war we resumed relations with Thailand as if she had never declared war on us.

But whereas we could afford to do this, the British could not. For Thailand had not only declared war on Britain, but had annexed four of the Malay States and two of Burma's Shan States. Consequently the British felt justified in making extreme demands upon Thailand for economic and military rights as the condition for re-establishing peaceful relations. Despite the legitimacy of Britain's grievances, the demands which she presented in September, 1945, were undoubtedly excessive. At the insistence of the Southeast Asia Division, the State Department almost immediately requested the British to suspend negotiations with Thailand pending discussions on the subject between the Department and the British Foreign Office. This move brought higher echelon British officials into the picture who agreed to scale down the original demands very considerably. For this the Thais gave us credit. As a result, and because of our refusal to consider a state of war as having existed between us and Thailand, a substantial reservoir of Thai good-will for the United States was established. Subsequent American policy has tended to maintain that reservoir.

During the third and fourth years following the war, America's policy in Indonesia and Indo-China appeared to be even more subordinated to its policy in Europe than previously. This was undoubtedly in part due to the further deterioration of relations between the United States and Russia and a heightened fear of Soviet aggression in Europe. It was probably also a consequence of changes in personnel within the Southeast Asia Division of the State Department whereby its dominant tone during these years became considerably less sympathetic to the aspirations of the Indonesians and Indo-Chinese for independence than had previously been the case.

During this period the United States still avoided coming to grips with the acute problem in Indo-China. To an important extent this was because the situation there did not come under the glare of the United Nations' spotlight, as was the case in Indonesia.

Even before the Indonesian question came before the Security Council, the United States had appeared to take a more partisan stand regarding it. The first indication of this was an *aide-mémoire* sent by the State Department to the Republic of Indonesia on June 28, 1947, at a time when negotiations between it and the Netherlands based upon the Linggadjati Agreement were being superseded by Dutch ultimata. The American note called upon the Republic to "cooperate without delay" with the Netherlands in the formation of an interim federal government for all Indonesia, a demand which the Republic—in the face of a Netherlands ultimatum—had just accepted. In addition, however, the *aide-mémoire* asserted: "The Linggadjati Agreement specifies an interim period from now until January 1, 1949, during which the Netherlands is to retain sovereignty and ultimate authority in Indonesia." Since this concept actually appeared nowhere in the Agreement and because this constituted one of the main demands in the Dutch ultimatum, Indonesian leaders could only conclude that the United States was backing the Dutch against the Republic.

This belief grew following the Netherlands attack against the Republic a few weeks later and became even stronger after the second Dutch campaign launched at the end of 1948. The Republic's leaders were convinced that the Dutch could never have mounted these tremendous military efforts had the United States not sanctioned such action. They were aware how dependent the war-damaged Netherlands economy was upon American financial assistance. The flow of this aid they saw as making possible the release of a roughly equivalent amount of financial substance from the Dutch home economy for military purposes in Indonesia. They were convinced, and they remain convinced today, that this economic dependency of the Netherlands on the United States put the latter in a position to restrain the Dutch from military action against the Republic if it had so desired. In following the debates and the voting in the Security Council they became even more firmly convinced that, despite the statements of its spokesmen, the United States backed the Netherlands against the Republic.

With the spring of 1949 came the nadir in America's position in Indonesia. Disillusionment with the United States grew to deep embitterment. Rightly or wrongly, Indonesians were convinced that in the Security Council the United States held the balance between effective action which that body might have taken to counter Dutch aggression against the Republic, and the equivocal course which that body seemed to them to be following. Were it true that the United States could not effectively work through the UN, it could, they argued, by exerting financial pressure have brought the Netherlands to heel promptly and at the very least have obliged it to carry out the Security Council's resolutions which it had ignored for so many months. With the Roem–van Royen Agreement of May 7, 1949, the United States was seen by Indonesians as backing and pressuring the Republic into signing a political settlement which they believed was for the most part favorable to the Netherlands and an endorsement of the puppet states which it had erected in the Republican territories overrun by Dutch troops during the second half of 1947.

The Second Phase (Mid–1949—to the present)

During the next few months American policy toward Indonesia appeared to undergo a profound change. The United States began to put effective pressure on the Netherlands as well as on the Indonesians to agree to a realistic settlement, demanding that the Dutch make substantial concessions to the Republican point of view. With Dutch forces in Indonesia clearly on the defensive against mounting Republican military successes, the inclination of the Netherlands Government to resist this American pressure was much reduced. On November 2, 1949, agreement was reached at The Hague providing for the relinquishment of Netherlands sovereignty over Indonesia and protection of the Dutch economic stake there.

For an understanding of present-day Indonesian attitudes toward the United States and the potential of American policy in Indonesia, it is important to appreciate the way in which the Indonesian leaders interpret this change in American policy. They were and remain convinced that it did not come about primarily because of an altruistic regard for Indonesia's right to independence. Rather, they believe it was based principally upon America's concern for its own strategic interests within the general context of the Cold War, a concern which they believed was heightened by Communist victories in China. They were not aware of any real change in American policy until after the increasingly successful resistance of Republican armed forces had made it clear that the Dutch could not enforce a political settlement, and until after there had begun a dangerous drift among Indonesians away from the anti-Communist leadership of the captured Republican officials still interned by the Dutch. American policy then changed, Indonesians believe, because of a realization that the Dutch could not control the course of events in Indonesia and that their futile attempts to do so only increased the prospects of Communism there.

Undoubtedly, this Indonesian analysis of the change in American policy contains much that is valid and much which was relevant to the change in American policy toward Southeast Asia as a whole. There had developed an increased American concern over the threat of Communism in Asia, and also the belief had now become fairly general that Western opposition to independence movements among colonial peoples is likely to turn them toward Communism. However, there were also other important factors which helped shape the new American policy. Important among these was the success of the Marshall Plan in strengthening the economic structure of

Western Europe. By mid–1949 the economies of both France and the Netherlands were in much sounder shape than they had been during the preceding few years. It could no longer be plausibly argued that retention of their colonies in Southeast Asia was vital to their economic well-being. The military rehabilitation of Western Europe was now a more critical problem than the economic. It had become clear that the fighting in Indo-China and Indonesia was denuding France and the Netherlands of a major part of their military strength. As a result, both were falling far short of their obligations for the defense of Western Europe. Thus, where a year or two before the economic requirements of Western Europe had provided a major argument for military campaigns by the Dutch and French to regain control over their colonies in Southeast Asia, European military requirements now provided a potent argument for abandonment of these ill-fated attempts. Another factor of importance was the power of an increasingly aroused public opinion in the United States which had begun to realize the extent to which American policy in Europe had compromised American principles in Indonesia and Indo-China, a public opinion which was commencing to receive substantial representation in the American Senate. Also, there is no doubt that the increasing indignation of Burma, India, and Pakistan with Netherlands policy in Indonesia had some effect.

To understand the relationship between the United States and Indonesia subsequent to the transfer of Netherlands sovereignty at the end of 1949, one must keep in mind the keen disillusionment of Indonesians with both the Soviet Union and America during the period since the war. In addition, one must note that though Indonesians have credited the changed American policy with significantly expediting the Dutch withdrawal and transfer of sovereignty, they are strong in their conviction that it was primarily Indonesia's own efforts which won Indonesia's independence.

It is from this conditioning more than anything else that has stemmed a major controlling factor in current Indonesian-

American relations—Indonesia's independent foreign policy. The most recent elucidation of this policy was made in late July, 1952, by President Sukarno. He declared that Indonesia had resolved to occupy "the No Man's Land" lying between the camps headed by the United States and Soviet Russia so that "in concert with others of like mind" Indonesia could serve as "a buffer between the antagonists," reserving to itself "the right to associate with this or that country, irrespective of membership in a bloc, on specific issues." "Thus," he stated, "while not taking sides by tying itself to a bloc, Indonesia does not intend to keep aloof from every incident that may arise out of controversy between the opposed blocs. Therefore our role is not only one of passive neutrality, but of active independence." "We will," he concluded, "judge issues on their merits and then decide to act or not as our conscience dictates."

Though it is undoubtedly true that between the two world camps Indonesia has in practice tended to incline to the side of the United States, her dedication to this idea of an independent foreign policy is sincere and has constituted the dominant factor in Indonesian-American relations during the last two-and-a-half years.

Though some aspects of American policy since mid–1949 have tended to bring Indonesia closer to the United States and to diminish her insistence upon an independent foreign policy, they have been offset by others which have antagonized Indonesians and reinforced their determination to follow an independent policy. Among the most important positive aspects have been: (1) the general American support of the Republic of Indonesia at The Hague conference on the majority of key issues; (2) the Export-Import Bank's $100 million loan to Indonesia; (3) the more appreciated assistance of the Economic Cooperation Administration; and (4) the enlightened labor policies of some of the major American companies doing business in Indonesia.

On the negative side the following have been of most importance: (1) American support of the Netherlands position in the debt settlement provided by The Hague agreement; (2) the Indonesian belief that in the spring of 1950 the United States Ambassador put strong pressure on the Indonesian Government to recognize the Bao Dai regime in Indo-China; and (3) the recent ill-fated agreement with the Mutual Security Agency.

This last matter requires some elucidation. Apparently it resulted from an overestimation by the American Ambassador of the political backing of Foreign Minister Subardjo and Prime Minister Sukiman and from his serious underestimation of the strength of Indonesian dedication to the idea of an independent foreign policy. In early February, 1952, the Ambassador undertook to induce Foreign Minister Subardjo to sign an agreement obliging the Indonesian Government to subscribe to a statement which Indonesians interpreted as implying military alignment with the United States.

When the agreement was made public in Indonesia a month later, it resulted in such an explosion of public indignation and protest as to topple the Sukiman cabinet. The cabinet which has succeeded it is much more insistent upon following an independent foreign policy. The Indonesian reaction to the agreement has been so strong as to remove almost all remaining chance of Indonesia's ratification of the Japanese Peace Treaty signed at San Francisco.

Basic change in American policy toward Indo-China began to be discernible at approximately the same time when our policy toward Indonesia was changing. But whereas in mid–1949 non-Communist elements were still dominant in the leadership of the Indonesian nationalist movement, this was no longer the case in Indo-China. Thus by the time American policy had belatedly become reconciled to the necessity of working with the nationalist movements in Asia, we had forfeited our main chance in Indo-China.

For though the Communists had been a potent element in the Viet-Namese nationalist movement from the outset, they do not appear to have emerged into a position of complete dominance until shortly before the commencement of the second phase of American policy. Prior to this time, within the movement there had been a substantial, though diminishing, non-Communist fulcrum which an American policy in support of self-government could have utilized. It is probable that American use of that fulcrum for such an end would have significantly increased the power of the non-Communist majority within that Nationalist movement. Though there is no assurance that this element would have triumphed, it possessed much wider popular support than the French-sponsored Bao Dai regime which we now back.

Our long period of neutrality on the Indo-China issue, a neutrality which had been somewhat benevolent toward the French, began to be discarded in favor of a more positive backing of France at least as early as June, 1949. This came after the French had finally admitted the impossibility of reaching a political settlement through force alone and had embarked upon their policy of setting up a rival nationalist regime under Bao Dai. This was to compete with Ho Chi Minh's Viet Minh regime and draw nationalist support away from it. If Bao Dai could attract an appreciable amount of nationalist support, American policy might be provided again with the sort of non-Communist nationalist fulcrum which had existed before, but which we had ignored and lost. It now became a major objective of American policy to give this fulcrum substance. American backing of the Bao Dai regime, which had been offered in a reserved and unofficial manner the previous June, became full and official on February 7, 1950, when we extended it regular diplomatic recognition. Soon thereafter we began to grant it substantial economic assistance, and we put strong pressure on the French to transfer real authority to it. Though initially France's response to this pressure was grudging, she is now probably as anxious as we are that the Bao Dai regime replace her as custodian of Viet-Nam. For France's responsibilities in the defense of Western Europe are now interpreted by French and American policy-makers alike as possible of ful-

fillment only if the awesome drain of French wealth and manpower into Indo-China is stopped.

In July, 1952, the United States was reported to have increased to 40 per cent the amount of the total cost of French
military expenditure in Indo-China which it is willing to assume. But this still leaves France with an Indo-China outlay
of around $600 million for the coming year, an amount equal
to about one-third of the total French war budget. It is reported that as a result of the demands of her Indo-China war,
France will only have twelve divisions available for Western
Europe at the end of this year as compared to the fifteen she
promised. It is estimated that the French officers and N.C.O.'s
now in Indo-China represent the cadres of ten divisions.

The envisaged solution to this problem calls for the training and arming of a Viet-Namese army loyal to Bao Dai which
will gradually replace French troops. A substantial beginning
appears to have been made, forty battalions of Viet-Namese
having now been trained and armed. The French have claimed
that this process has now reached a point which makes it no
longer necessary to dispatch French replacements to Indo-
China. The United States now appears to be sending military
equipment there at a rate roughly equal to this training program. Apparently the hope is that in a year or two more the
French will be able to pull their troops out and turn over all,
or at least primary, responsibility to the forces of Bao Dai.
Presumably, it is calculated that these would be strong enough
at least to hold their own against the Viet Minh.

Whether or not this American-backed French plan will
prove successful will be contingent upon a number of unpredictable factors. It is still a matter of conjecture whether the
political reliability of Bao Dai's troops in 1953 is going to be
much greater than many of those of Chiang Kai-shek in 1949.
This will depend primarily on the success of Bao Dai's Viet-
Nam Government in convincing them it is worth supporting.
Whether or not they think so will depend not only on whether
France turns over full authority to Bao Dai's government and

whether the United States continues to shore up its economy. It will also depend upon the ability of Bao Dai and his group to govern in a way which will satisfy these soldiers, command their allegiance, and attract support away from the Viet Minh. Thus far the prospect of this does not seem very bright.

But assuming this plan does work out, there remains an outside factor bearing on the situation—namely China— whose potential is enormous. In the event that Bao Dai's regime begins to win a major amount of support away from Ho Chi Minh, it would seem unlikely for Mao Tse-tung to sit by idly while a friendly regime was displaced by one closely linked to the United States. Despite involvement in Korea, China apparently has sufficient mobilized strength available in her southern areas to tip the scales dangerously in favor of Ho Chi Minh should she undertake to intervene in his behalf. The most the French can count on to off-set such a move would be American and British air and naval support. The American Government has been reported as unwilling to promise the support of ground troops, and it seems improbable that American public opinion would sanction such a move.

This dismal prospect has prompted some people to urge that solution of the problem be attempted through the United Nations. One great impediment to this path of action is, of course, the French Government's fear that this would establish a precedent which might be extended to its troubled territories in North Africa.

Whether for this or other reasons, those charged with framing American policy are apparently still reluctant to bring the Indo-China problem before the United Nations. During the course of the coming year, it should become fairly clear whether or not this has been a wise decision and the Indo-China policy we have chosen the best of the very few now open to us.

Amry Vandenbosch

OUR FRIENDS AND ANTAGONISTS

IN SOUTHEAST ASIA

THE UNITED STATES and the free world have bitter enemies
and loyal friends in Southeast Asia. There are also in the region
large groups which are difficult to classify. One cannot be certain where they stand.

Our chief enemies are, of course, the Communists. Politically, economically, and strategically, Southeast Asia is of great
importance for Russia and Communist China as well as for the
free world. Control of the oil, rubber, tin, rice, and other commodities of the region would give the Communist bloc a very
great advantage and the loss of these strategic materials would
constitute a severe blow to the West. For whatever reason it
may be, the Communist countries have not attempted to bring
this region within their orbit by direct attack. Their strategy
has been to create in the countries of the region as much confusion and strife as possible, with the object of getting control
of these countries by violence from within, or failing that, of
reducing their value for the West. They have gone a long way
in achieving their purposes. Through their minions they have
succeeded in keeping production of the region below prewar
levels and in making it very difficult for the new governments
to establish their authority and to maintain effective administration. By protracted, bitter hostilities within nearly every
one of the countries, they have succeeded in creating an economic and military drain on the free world.

Communists of the region regard the United States as their

47

principal foe. In their literature the word "American" is rarely used alone; it is nearly always "American imperialists" or "American interventionists." Native non-Communists who oppose them are labelled "lackeys" or "running dogs of American imperialism." The hostility of the Communists towards the United States is understandable; they are convinced that if it were not for American aid to the governments they seek to destroy, Communism would have triumphed in Indo-China and probably also in the Philippines. They are implacable enemies of the United States and of all who are friendly toward us. We had recently another example of this. The Communists of Indonesia put on a campaign against the visit of President Quirino to Java in July on the ground that he is the tool of the United States and wishes to draw Indonesia into the American orbit.

The fact that some of the revolutionary groups in this region claim to be movements for national independence has made American policy somewhat difficult. Some Americans and large numbers of Asians question and even condemn the American policy of supporting existing regimes against such movements. A cursory examination, however, will indicate how invalid these views are. Only in Indo-China does the revolutionary group bear any resemblance to a real nationalistic movement. In the early postwar period the movement there was probably more nationalistic than Communist, but the reverse is true now. Viet Minh is now under the domination of Communists. We have the choice of either aiding France and the Associated States or of seeing Indo-China fall under a new and terrible colonialism of indefinite duration. The Associated States have already acquired considerable freedom and are certain to obtain complete independence, if they desire it, within a relatively short time. France has gone so far toward granting these states independence that it can never reverse itself; it can only go forward. We may assume that this is its purpose. Friendship for France and the people of Indo-

China demands that we aid them in their struggle against Communism.

A very important element in the population of Southeast Asia is the Chinese, who constitute about 5 per cent of the total population but whose significance in the economic life of the region far exceeds their proportionate number. Are the Chinese our friends or antagonists? In the past the Chinese have held aloof from the political life of the countries in which they lived. They were content to be let alone, sometimes even being willing to pay for protection from molestation. In so far as they had any political or cultural interests, these were centered upon China. Under the old colonial regimes little or no pressure was put upon them, nor, it must be added, much incentive offered them, to give undivided loyalty to the countries in which they lived and where many of them prospered. They now find themselves in an entirely new situation. On the one hand, pressure is being brought on them to accept unreservedly the nationality of these countries, and, on the other hand, they are being subjected to considerable discriminatory legislation. In Thailand they have been excluded from a number of occupations. There is hostility toward the Japanese in all of the countries. In a remarkable public address (November 10, 1951), President Sukarno sternly addressed a word of warning to the Chinese who had become rich while the Indonesian people remained poor. He criticized their unwillingness to carry their proportionate share of the public burden and charged them with endangering the economic welfare and undermining the authority of the government by large-scale evasion of government regulations. He likewise spoke a word of caution to those elements among the Chinese who were continually preaching Communism and social revolution. He warned them that a social revolution in Indonesia would quickly turn into a racial revolution of which they would be the first victims. President Sukarno's concern about the Chinese in Indonesia is not without reason. The East Coast of

Sumatra, where large numbers of Chinese laborers are concentrated, is a strongly Communistic center. Many of the Chinese papers throughout Southeast Asia have a Communist slant.

Can the United States win the friendship of the Chinese of Southeast Asia? There is very little that it can do directly. Much will depend on developments within the various countries and the treatment they receive from government and people. Undoubtedly the Chinese have been guilty of some sins against the societies in which they live, but they also have performed highly necessary economic functions and have contributed much to the general welfare. Memories of bitter experiences, including discrimination and extortion, do not make it easy for the Chinese to accept the citizenship of the new states with enthusiasm. On the contrary, it has made them look for a strong China to which they can appeal for protection. Whatever the United States can do to help the countries of Southeast Asia to improve their economic lot will ease the pressure on the Chinese and tend to create the conditions which will make an easier amalgamation or absorption possible. This is quite evident, for example, in the matter of education. Chinese private schools are frequently centers of active Communist propaganda, due in part to the fact that the teachers of these schools are very poorly paid. One obvious means of combating this evil is the extension of sufficient public-school facilities to meet the popular demand for education. A universal primary-school system would serve as a powerful unifying influence, but this would require far greater funds than the economy of any of the countries of the region can afford.

The present American policy of helping the countries of Southeast Asia in strengthening their economic and military defenses is probably affecting the Chinese attitude. Overseas, Chinese have the reputation of being shrewd and calculating and it is said that some of them hesitate to commit their loyalties irrevocably to the new independent countries in which they reside or to take a positive stand for or against Communist aggression. They desire a reasonable assurance that they are going to be on the winning side. A positive American policy will encourage them to climb down from the fence on the side of the West.

From the point of view of their foreign policy and their relations with the United States, the six countries of Southeast Asia may be divided into three groups or pairs, namely, Thailand and the Philippines, Malaya and Indo-China, and Burma and Indonesia. Thailand and the Philippines are cooperating wholeheartedly with the United States, and in Premier Pibun and President Quirino this country has two very loyal friends. Thailand and the Republic of the Philippines are thoroughly committed to the defense of the free world; they have fighting units with the United Nations' forces in Korea.

American-Philippine relations have long been enshrouded in an air of unreality. Americans have overglorified their policies and the achievements of their administration, while Filipinos have overestimated their strength and maturity. American policy towards the insular dependency has been a strange mixture of noble purpose, magnificent generosity, contradictions and irritating demands. The recent crisis in the Philippines and the report of the Bell Economic Survey Mission has had a salutary effect in bringing both Americans and Filipinos down to earth.

There is in the Philippines a group which is rather strongly anti-American. Its leaders are the politicians who collaborated with the Japanese during the war. Chief among them is Senator José P. Laurel, who was the "president" of the puppet Republic which declared war on the United States and Britain. Typical of Laurel's attitude was his recent reference to the Honolulu conference on implementing the Australia–New Zealand–United States defense pact as "a modern version of prewar colonialism." Unfortunately, the United States Congress sometimes needlessly and foolishly provides Laurel and people like him with ammunition to use against us and our friends. It did that when it wrote the so-called "parity" or "equal rights" provision into the Philippine Trade Act, which demanded for American nationals the right to exploit the natural resources of the Republic on the same basis as Philippine citizens. The extremely unfortunate thing about this was that compliance with this provision made it necessary to amend the Philippine constitution, which in turn necessitated a submission of the question to popular vote. The referendum on the constitutional amendment put the Philippine Government in a difficult position and gave Laurel and all antagonists of the United States a marvellous opportunity to spread their propaganda. Of this opportunity they made full use.

Friends can sometimes be an embarrassment, and that is the way some Americans have felt about the Philippines and Thailand. It is true that the governments of these two states have not yet reached the acme of democratic perfection; far from it. Nor have the present heads of these states faultless records. In any consideration of postwar developments in the Philippines it should be remembered that the country suffered terrible devastation and that it was confronted with very grave difficulties after the war. Many of the experienced political leaders and public administrators could not be used because of wartime collaboration with the Japanese. For a while the Filipinos floundered badly, but they are again finding themselves. They are earnestly tackling their problems and with American aid they are making progress in mastering them. Of President Quirino it must be said that he has steadily grown up to the measure of his responsibilities. One need never be embarrassed by friends who are moving in the right direction.

That Thailand should be on the side of the free world, in view of its record and that of Marshal Pibun in World War II, may seem a bit ironic. If the Thai Government is making any progress in the direction of democracy, it is imperceptible to foreign eyes. Sometimes it seems to be moving away from it. However, we have no choice but to support the regime. We cannot intervene in the internal affairs of friendly states. To do so would be wrong and foolish. Diplomacy, like politics, is rarely a matter of first choices in the midst of ideal situations. Moreover, so long as a country is not subject to a totalitarian regime, however undemocratic the government may be, it still has a chance to move toward freedom, but once it accepts or falls under the control of Communism its chances for determining its own destiny within the foreseeable future are dim indeed.

With respect to our relations with them, Malaya and Indo-China constitute a second set of countries. American relations with the states in these areas have not been direct, though in the case of Indo-China direct relations have begun and are certain to increase. France and Great Britain are our partners not only in the defense of Southeast Asia against Communist aggression, but also in organizing the defense of Western Europe against attack by Russia. The programs and commitments of these two states in this region must therefore always be related to the effect which they may have on the position and strength of these countries in Europe. In both Malaya and Indonesia the metropolitan countries are engaged in a costly and bitter war against what is after all the common enemy. It has not been until recently that Americans have had an awareness of the extent of the military operations in which France and Britain are engaged, or the burdens which they carry because of them. Not long ago many Americans wanted France to withdraw from Indo-China; now we are afraid that they may, and the United States Government has felt compelled to give steadily greater economic and military aid to France and the Associated States.

With respect to the British in Malaya—and indeed to nearly all of the countries of the region—certain American policies have had peculiar, and, we may assume, unintended results. The encouragement of the production of synthetic rubber in this country and the determined effort to lower the price of tin have created grave economic difficulties in Malaya and also in Indonesia. Since the production of rubber and tin have made Malaya one of the chief dollar earners in the Empire, the fall of the prices of these two commodities has adversely affected the British position all along the line. On the one hand, the United States is trying to help these underdeveloped countries raise their standard of living, which until per capita productivity can be greatly increased, means higher costs of production; while on the other hand, the American policies under discussion have the effect of depressing living standards. I am not arguing for a policy of supporting unsound economies or unfair price policies, for economic conditions cannot in the long run be improved by such means. I merely question the wisdom of pressing such policies in the present critical situation without counterbalancing measures. We are not likely by such policies to gain new friends or strengthen the loyalties of those who are now friendly toward us. In my opinion, Americans have suffered from an underestimation of the difficulties involved in attempting to raise the living standards of underdeveloped countries, and especially of Eastern tropical countries. We assume that what we did, others can do, forgetting our natural advantages and favorable conditions. Experience is tending to make us a wiser, if sadder, people.

Indonesia and Burma make up the last group of countries we have to consider. These two countries are of very great importance. Together they account for over half of the total area of the region and considerably over half of its population. I have bracketed them for the reason that their foreign policies are similar—both received their independence after the war—and each is troubled with grave internal difficulties which the governments are trying to overcome with practically no outside help.

Burmans and Indonesians characterize the foreign policies of their governments as that of neutrality. The present Indonesian Government prefers the term "active independent foreign policy" as more accurately defining the fundamental principle on which its relations with other countries are based. However described or defined, this policy tends to keep these two countries aloof from the United States. It was an alleged

violation of this principle of foreign policy by Foreign Minister Subardjo which last February precipitated a cabinet crisis
and shortly thereafter caused the fall of the entire Indonesian
cabinet. In order to secure Mutual Security Agency assistance, Subardjo had signed an agreement which included
the acceptance of the conditions stipulated in Sec. 511a of the
Act. The Indonesian Parliament was especially offended by
the requirement to contribute to the "defensive strength of the
free world." Most of the members of Parliament felt that by
accepting this condition Indonesia would formally align itself
with the United States and move into the American orbit.

What is the origin of this policy and what its justification?
The inspiration of the policy comes from India. Nehru is the
hero of the young intellectuals who now largely determine the
policy of these two countries, and India is the model for their
foreign policy. Indonesia, however, has at times shown greater
independence than Burma, not always following the leadership of the great neighboring state. Indonesia would probably reject this suggestion but the prewar example of Holland
may also have influenced the adoption of this policy which was
exactly the policy followed by the Dutch from 1815 to 1940. If
the example of the Netherlands has been such an influence,
we have here a strange survival of colonialism.

The leaders of these countries have no difficulty in finding
ample grounds to justify this policy. The chief and most urgent
task of their countries, they argue, is the improvement of economic conditions and the creation of internal unity. Prime
Minister Wilopo recently set forth this view succinctly to the
Indonesian Parliament when he declared on May 9, 1952:
"An atmosphere of unity and solidarity at home is most needed,
if we are to arrive at satisfactory results in our undertakings in
the fields of reconstruction and stabilization. The commitments or consequences resulting from our foreign relations
should not be such as to disturb or even trouble Indonesia's
internal atmosphere." Sometimes the argument is put in this
fashion: "We are weak; the greatest contribution we can make

to peace is to become strong, and in any case, until we are strong we can make little contribution to world peace."

A factor in explaining the attitude behind the neutrality policy is the mistrust of the West and the resentment toward it which is the heritage of centuries of imperialism. It will take more than a few years to overcome these feelings. Sometimes this attitude takes extreme and irritating forms. The acceptance of a small American loan or grant of assistance may expose a government to the charge of having sold the national birthright for a mess of pottage. Most any act of American leadership in world politics is likely to be regarded as a new form of imperialism, or neo-imperialism.

Occasionally it is argued in justification of this foreign policy that it was also the policy of the United States in its early years and for long thereafter. In reply to this argument it need only be pointed out that Burma, India, and Indonesia became full-fledged members of the family of nations not in the world of 1776 but in that of the mid-twentieth century, which is quite a different world from that of nearly two centuries ago. The attempt to follow an isolationist policy in the contemporary world is to invite disaster, as the Dutch and others learned to their sorrow. So long as the dike of collective security holds, and only so long, is it possible for any state or group of states to follow a policy of neutrality.

Americans find it difficult to understand the fear of so many of our South-Asian friends of the return of Western imperialism when the only imperialism which now threatens the world is that of Russia and Communism. If it is imperialism which these people really fear, they ought to join the United States and the free countries in preventing its spread. Need it be pointed out that neutrality and absolute sovereignty were logical concepts in the old juridical system in which imperialism flourished? Not only do Americans find it difficult to understand this spirit of neutralism in the face of a grave common danger, they find it disheartening, to say the least, to have their willingness to help peoples raise their standard of living interpreted as an attempt to refasten colonialism on the world. They feel that they deserve better than that, especially after all of their sacrifices in men and materials in upholding the principle of collective security.

There are some Indonesians who maintain that their country in the formulation of its foreign policy has the full scope of freedom permitted under the traditional rules of international law. To disprove this contention it is only necessary to point to the fact of Indonesia's membership in the United Nations. By the acceptance of this membership Indonesia lost the moral right, and under certain conditions, the legal right, to follow a policy of neutrality in case of aggression or threat to the peace of the world. The Charter makes no provision for a limited or associate membership in the United Nations. Indonesia claims all of the rights and advantages of membership in the United Nations; it must likewise accept all of the obligations which go with it. It is undoubtedly because he recognizes these obligations that Mr. Wilopo, the present Prime Minister of Indonesia, prefers the term "active, independent policy" to "policy of neutrality." But is the freedom of action suggested by this term permissible within the framework of the United Nations? If this gigantic struggle between the free world and Russia and its satellites were merely a sport contest, yes; but if, as most people in the free world believe, the issue is aggression and ruthless imperialism and the suppression of aggression where it has already occurred, the answer is no. The principles and purposes of the United Nations to which all members have subscribed rules out an independent policy, regardless of whether the Security Council has or has not been able to take action in the matter.

Two observations must immediately be made to restrict the scope of this general assertion. First, all members of the United Nations do not necessarily have to agree that whatever action the United States and other states may take against what they believe constitutes a threat to the peace of the world is wise, or will achieve the basic purpose; and secondly, not all of American foreign policy falls strictly within the framework of the United Nations. Now with respect to the first, some freedom of judgment and action is permissible, but surely not neutrality. With regard to the second category of actions, all other governments may have their own independent policy and take such action as they please. Feeling as they do that they are engaged in a desperate struggle to save the world from the complete loss of national and individual freedom, there is the danger that Americans may view any criticism or unwillingness to accept the policies of the United States as the only right ones, as lack of sympathy with their basic objectives. We must be careful not to work ourselves into a self-righteous state of mind. Preposterous as it may seem to us, even some of our friends think to discern an element of imperialism in our foreign policy. We must take cognizance of that fact. Where this view is wrong we must bring these people to a clearer understanding of our objectives; where it has even the slightest element of truth we must modify our policy.

Basically there is no reason why Americans and the people of Southeast Asia should not be the best of friends. What the people of Southeast Asia want above all are national independence and improved living conditions. Colonialism is an elastic term; as now used by the people of the region it generally means a resentment against their low standards of living, which they ascribe almost altogether to their former subordinate political status and to the foreign capital operating in their country. Now these ideas—namely, national self-determination and higher living standards—are of the very heart of the American national creed. The idea that a good life, at least on its material side, is possible for all of the members of society and not merely for a part of it, is an American idea, and we gladly see its operation extended to the whole world. Americans have always rejoiced to see peoples, even when they were not quite ready for it, receive their national independence.

The governments of Burma and Indonesia find themselves

in a dilemma. As I interpret Prime Minister Wilopo's explanation of Indonesia's foreign policy, his government fears that
if it too frankly encourages foreign capital to invest in the country, or if it accepts economic, and especially military aid from
the West, the Communists and extreme left-wingers may create difficulties, even threaten the internal security of the country. The Indonesian Government must therefore proceed cau-
tiously. One can sympathize with these governments in having
to deal with this problem, but they cannot escape the fact that,
unless economic conditions improve perceptibly and soon, the
Communist movement will gain strength and become bolder.
Now the sad truth is that the countries of this region cannot
out of their own resources provide for even the bare minimum
of development needed to prevent living standards from falling even further. It can only be done with help from the outside. The task is so enormous that it can only be met by the
closest cooperation with the technologically advanced countries of the West, and even with that kind of working together
there is no assurance that we can succeed.

If the United States and the countries of Southeast Asia are
to cooperate to their mutual advantage, the former will have
to exercise patience and understanding and the latter will have
to overcome their distrust of the West. The United States
should avoid attaching conditions to assistance which are likely
to offend, especially when there is nothing to be gained by it.
When the demand for our economic and military assistance
is far greater than our economy can supply, there is naturally
a strong urge to place it only where we can be sure that it will
do the most good in strengthening the free world, and to make
certain that it will be so used. But we must be careful lest we
defeat our own ends. To illustrate, let us take the recent political crisis in Indonesia. Powerful groups of Indonesians objected to the condition of the MSA loan to which we have already referred, namely, that Indonesia would undertake to
"make, consistent with its political and economic stability, the
full contribution permitted by its manpower, resources, facili-

ties, and general economic condition, the development and maintenance of its own strength and the defensive strength of the free world." The term "free world" seemed to constitute the chief stumbling block. To many Asians that term has become a flag covering a cargo of great variety and not collective security only. To them it also means purely American national policy, and not merely support of the principles and purposes of the United Nations. The Indonesian Government proposed that the term be interpreted to mean "free, independent, and sovereign" countries of the world. Apparently this interpretation was acceptable to the United States Government, but it came too late to save the Indonesian cabinet. The Indonesian Government is interested primarily in obtaining light arms for its police forces in order to strengthen its internal security. This is certainly in the American interest, for anything which strengthens the Indonesian Government internally will give it greater freedom to move toward the free world in its foreign policy.

The people of Southeast Asia will also have to make a contribution to mutual understanding. They will have to modify some of their views and attitudes. The people of Asia want to enjoy all of the benefits or fruits of industrialization and modern technology, but they are unwilling to pay the price necessary to obtain these advantages. The people of the West did not get them for nothing. Certainly the peoples of the underdeveloped countries should be able to avoid many of the miseries which the West endured in the early days of industrialization. They can learn from the experience of the West, but they cannot escape all of the difficulties and adjustments which go with so profound a change in society. The peoples of the East will have to face the issue of the necessity of bringing their population and production capabilities in balance. They will have to revise their views with respect to foreign capital and foreign aid. And it would be helpful if they would take their national independence as an established fact and not as something which they still precariously hold and of which the powers of the West seek to deprive them. That is not the attitude of a mature people. An English wit once said that youthfulness was the oldest characteristic of the American people. It ought never to be possible to make that kind of a jest about any Asian nation.

Rupert Emerson

OUR RESPONSIBILITIES
IN SOUTHEAST ASIA

We have travelled a long way in the last decade or two. In the mid-thirties it would have occurred to virtually no one that we had responsibilities in Southeast Asia, or, if any were acknowledged, they would have been so vague and general in character as to be almost meaningless. By the middle of 1952, it would occur to virtually no one to deny that we have responsibilities in that part of the world and that they are real and urgent. Whatever other grievances we may have, the Second World War and its aftermath have left us with no ground for complaint that our responsibilities are not ample or that they do not adequately cover the surface of the globe. We are already deeply involved in the affairs of Southeast Asia and there is every reason to assume that we will become more rather than less involved as the days go by.

It is a far easier task to secure agreement that responsibilities exist than to define them in a fashion which will at the same time win general acceptance and be sufficiently coherent, clear, and precise to be meaningful. No particular problem arises if we are prepared to linger in the realm of large abstractions and say that we want the peoples of Southeast Asia, as we want the rest of the world, to be free, democratic, prosperous, peaceful, wedded to our side, and wary of the Communists; but when this has been said, the cause has not been much advanced. These beautiful words are indeed, or should be, the substance and goal of our policy, but it is when the effort is made to translate them into concrete programs applicable to the particular realities of the area that the troubles start. At that point we run inevitably into confusions and contradictions which are inherent both in the more direct relations between the United States and the countries of Southeast Asia and in the world setting in which those relations must operate and by which they cannot help being sharply influenced. Even without the cold war and the threat of Communist imperialism, the problem of working out appropriate and effective relations with Southeast Asia would be difficult enough. With Moscow and Peiping just around the corner, it assumes a complexity which borders on the intolerable and the insoluble.

One highly interesting issue which should be faced squarely at the outset (and which I shall do my best to evade because I frankly do not know the answer to it) concerns the source of our responsibilities. That issue, it seems to me, cuts across the whole of our foreign policy and is in some part the cause of our confusions, but the more I have studied it the less I have been able to emerge with any clear-cut answer which really covers the facts of the case. In terms of the concept of national interest which is currently so fashionable in some quarters, I suppose that the answer is that our responsibility runs direct to the American people and ultimately solely to them. The difficulty with that answer is that the American people seem not to be content with a purely egocentric and hard-boiled policy which looks only to the American interest without regard to the interests of other peoples. Whether it be admirable or deplorable, we appear to have a sense of responsibility for the world at large and expect from our leaders the shaping of policies which will not benefit us alone but will help others as well. Not infrequently we are prepared to make larger sacrifices for a program which is at least portrayed in altruistic terms than we would be prepared to make for one which was directed exclusively to our advancement at the possible cost of others. I am by no means suggesting that the

American people are either unmindful of their own interests or that they are always concerned to do good deeds for the rest of the world, but I am confident that to line up American foreign policy as being always and basically self-regarding is to pretend to a realism which misses a large segment of reality.

We have ourselves achieved a democratic political system and social structure which we profoundly believe can be of benefit to others, and we have come to an unprecedented material prosperity which we are convinced other peoples can at least approximate if they will follow our example. Recognizing our unique material good fortune, and being even a little fearful of it, we are in some minor measure prepared to share our riches with them. Our concern with freedom and democracy throughout the world, our Point IV and Mutual Security programs, our participation in the United Nations and its specialized agencies, and the gifts of many private individuals, churches, and other groups, all bear witness to the fact that our sense of manifest destiny is not confined to the American people alone. As it is possible to construe all actions of all individuals as being equally self-centered and selfishly motivated, so it is possible to lead all American actions and policies back to a central core of narrow national interest. The only trouble is that in neither case is it true to what actually happens.

Particularly in relation to peoples such as those of Southeast Asia, it is deep-rooted in the American tradition that we should seek to give them a helping hand. We have a strong anticolonial and anti-imperialist tradition, and the underdog stirs our sympathy. The struggle of the Southeast Asians for independence and material progress has a natural appeal to us and we would like, within limits of modest costs and involvements, to assist them both in establishing and maintaining their freedom and in developing their human and material resources. This is not to say that we are prepared to go all out for the freedom and prosperity of the people of Southeast Asia, but merely that we have some distant sense of responsibility for their survival and well-being and would be happy to have a share in doing something about it.

In return we would hope, somewhat overardently perhaps, to receive their gratitude and friendship, and we would be pained to see them take any actions contrary to our policies or interfering with our trade and intercourse with them. But, as I have been suggesting, I am confident that beyond any returns which we would expect there is a significant residue of essentially disinterested good will on our part. Whether the Southeast Asians welcome our assumption that we know what they want and how they should go about getting it is a question of a quite different order.

This felt sense of responsibility to aid the Southeast Asians as they come into the modern world on their own feet is one facet of American responsibilities, but there are a number of others which by no means always fit harmoniously together. It is in the interweaving of our different and divergent responsibilities that our troubles begin to multiply.

In contrast to the altruistic picture which has been drawn above, there must also be a recognition of the American national interest somewhat narrowly interpreted in terms of a self-regarding promotion of the well-being and protection of the American people themselves. Despite the current vogue of the idea, I am not able to number myself among those who regard the concept of the national interest as furnishing the answer to all problems in the sphere of foreign relations. When an effort is made to apply it in any concrete case, it all too frequently proves an exceedingly weak reed. Either it embraces all the various and often opposed interests which Americans may have, including their altruisms and idealisms, in which case it includes too much to be of any use, or else it is narrowed down to the advancement of some selection of exclusively American interests regardless of the impact on other peoples, in which case it will be unacceptable to most of us. In this latter version it is the obvious implication that the United States has responsibilities only toward its own people.

On this oversimplified basis—which still has ample complications when it is brought to the point of implementation —the American national interest in Southeast Asia might be boiled down in its crudest form to a few simple propositions. We would not want the area to fall into hostile hands for strategic, economic, and political reasons of direct concern to us, and we would want stability enough maintained within the several Southeast Asian countries so that our peace and trade would not be disturbed by their upheavals. We would want unrestricted access to an abundant supply of the vital raw materials, the rubber and tin, vegetable oils and petroleum, of the area and the denial to our enemies of those materials and such surplus of rice as may exist. The Southeast Asian countries should be open freely to American persons, goods, transport, and communications. Any aid which might be made available to the area would be limited to a strict calculation of what returns the United States would get out of it in one form or another.

It is perhaps arguable that a policy based on this egocentric version of the responsibilities we owe ourselves would meet the needs of an American *Realpolitik,* but it is hard to believe that it would measure up to the standards of what the American people feel they want from a foreign policy. It is at least equally hard to believe that it would draw to us the friendship and sympathetic support, which we so seriously need and desire, of the peoples of Southeast Asia and of the rest of the non-Communist world. And if it does not do these things, there must be the gravest doubt that it can be a true representation of the American national interest in times like these.

To the two versions of American responsibilities which have already been given, there must now be added a third which immeasurably disarranges the picture. Given the present structure of the world and the main lines of America's foreign policy, it is obvious that we cannot deal with Southeast Asia merely in terms of the kind of relationships which we should like to see established between ourselves and the peoples who live there. The major responsibility which we have assumed on a global basis is the leadership of the non-Communist world against Communist imperialism, and it would be idle to seek to ignore that what we do and do not do in Southeast Asia is in substantial measure determined by our estimate of the needs of that gigantic campaign. There can be no question that a considerable part of our present involvement in Southeast Asia derives directly from our determination to contain the Communist drive and to meet its challenge wherever it arises. For us, as for the Communists, there is no part of the earth's surface which can be regarded as standing aside from the conflict.

In a world truly at peace we would still be concerned with Southeast Asia and still be perplexed by the problems with which it confronts us, but our concerns and perplexities would be significantly more remote and less pressing. At least as seen from our present unhappy vantage point it seems as if they might, under such circumstances, have an air of innocence about them which today's pressures exclude. It would be pleasanter for us, as it would for the Southeast Asians, if we were able honestly to say that our policies were dictated by our view of their immediate needs and our own without an eye to the ulterior considerations of the cold war; but that is excluded by the circumstances. No one likes to be considered an instrument to be used and manipulated for some one else's purposes, yet that is inevitably how some of the Southeast Asians must regard a good part of American policy as it affects them, since they are by no means sure that they want to travel the same road which we would have them travel.

At this point the discordant elements in our responsibilities begin to come clearly into view. In the world at large and in Southeast Asia in particular, there is no universal acceptance of our compelling sense of obligation to lead in rallying all forces against the Communist threat of which we are so vividly aware but which others evaluate quite differently. Even at home there are sharp variations of view, resting on different estimates of the probabilities in the situation. Ignoring the small minority in this country who would deny the existence of Communist imperialism or regard it rather as blessing than as menace, there still remain large areas of divergent opinion as to the type and timing of the Communist threat, as to the best means of countering it, and as to the scope and nature of American responsibility in different sets of circumstances. If there is imminent danger of armed Communist aggression, be it from China or from a combination of Chinese and Soviet forces, the problem is of one order; it is of quite a different order if we may run the calculated risk of assuming that the real threat for any present purposes is of an internal seizure of power within one or more Southeast Asian countries with only covert and limited support from established Communist centers. Even assuming the first and worst alternative of an outright Red attack, should the United States feel itself obligated, either in its own interest or in that of others, to meet it by full force wherever it may occur?

Let me introduce one further facet of the array of American responsibilities and then have done with them, although no doubt a number more could be brought forward, including an examination of our commitments under the United Nations Charter. The United States has both allied itself with the Western European powers and given priority to the needs and problems of Europe in its general strategy of world action. In blunter terms, our major allies are also the major colonial powers and three of them—Britain, France, and the Netherlands—still have colonial territories in Southeast Asia at a time when the whole of Asia is more vigorously up in arms against colonialism than ever before in its history. For us to hold an even balance between our responsibilities in Western Europe and our responsibilities in Southeast Asia requires acrobatic skill of the highest order.

We have already found to our dismay that what may appear to us as an even balance is likely to have the look of prejudiced favoritism to one, or perhaps both, of the other parties in any particular case. The most striking example is the reaction to our role in the postwar transition of Indonesia to independence. To many in the Netherlands it appeared that we were misguidedly and foolhardily forcing abandonment of a colonial trust which it was neither necessary nor desirable to abandon with such speed, and by many Indonesians we were charged with salvaging for the Dutch far more than they deserved from a colonialism which should long since have been wiped from the books. Although our increasing involvement in the affairs of Indo-China involves some quite different considerations, it also has cost us heavily in the opinion of neighboring peoples. Our contention that we are not bolstering up the French colonial regime against a popular nationalist movement, but aiding in the defeat of one important thrust of Communist aggression has a hollow ring for the bulk of the Southeast Asians. To them it is markedly more significant that we are supporting the French than that we are opposing a largely Communist regime backed by Moscow and Peiping. In the eyes of the peoples of Southeast Asia there can be no compromise with imperialism, and any support of the colonial powers is inevitably tainted with sin. It does not enhance our moral stature when they see us barring the door to a discussion in the United Nations of the Tunisian grievances against French rule.

I have been suggesting a series of categories of responsibilities which the United States has either assumed or has had thrust upon it. If these responsibilities are mutually harmonious or can be made consistent with each other, then no very serious problem arises in the shaping of American policy. Regrettably there is every reason to believe that there are a number of points at which they clash with each other or at which our effort to implement them brings us into serious and even profound disagreement with the peoples whose aid and friendship we seek.

Under the best of circumstances it would be no easy matter to bring the United States and the Southeast Asian countries into working harmony. Where we are advanced, rich, and powerful, they are underdeveloped, poor, and weak. Despite the potentially complementary aspects of such a relationship, it is also an almost infinitely fertile source of friction. Newly come to independence or striving for it, the Southeast Asians are proud and wary, sensitive to anything which threatens to encroach on their freedom and to any possible slight to their dignity and equal status. By descent and ties of many kinds we are closely bound to Europe; they are in process of securing their emancipation from Europe, and the imperialism to which they are vibrantly attuned is the European imperialism from which they are just emerging. If they want aid and guidance from us—and they know that there is still much that they need and that we have it in our power to give them—they are also acutely suspicious that any acceptance of aid may carry with it an implication of subservience.

The distortions which the cold war in general and the Korean entanglement in particular have forced upon the relationship between the United States and Southeast Asia have served to emphasize and bring into sharper focus some of the least happy elements in the situation, but it should be pointed out immediately that to generalize about the entire area in this context is a dangerous process. It is tempting to take Indonesia—with its firm insistence on a neutralist policy much like that of India—as the model for the whole region, but in fact there are great variations between the official policies of the different countries and further variations in public opinion in its many segments. Among the other countries only Burma, which is at all events too seriously torn by civil strife to play a very serious role, can be taken as on the whole lining up beside Indonesia. Malaya with its own lesser but painful local warfare still has its official mind made up for it by the British, and Indo-China is divided into two warring parts, one of which as ardently courts American aid as the other denounces it. At the other extreme from Indonesia, Thailand and the Philippines have generally been prepared to follow the American lead with no apparent need to search their souls deeply. Indeed, the policy of the Philippines—the one country incidentally in which our responsibilities have significant historic roots —has posed a further dilemma for the United States because of the efforts to secure a Pacific pact which would be the Asian or Pacific counterpart of the North Atlantic Treaty Organization arrangements and put an end to the neutralism which the Indonesians continue to cherish. I myself would be inclined to surmise that even in the countries which officially line up with the American position some considerable segment of public opinion would prefer to join Indonesia in its aloofness and shares the latter's wariness of the coalition which Washington heads. The pro-American attitude of the Philippine and Thai governments is, however, clearly on the record.

Admittedly setting out from what I take to be the Indonesian stand and running precisely the risks of generalization against which I have just issued a warning, it might be useful to seek to identify some of the key points at which our sense of our responsibilities runs afoul of serious opposition in Southeast Asia, particularly in relation to the cold war and the policy of containment.

The most fundamental breaking point is that in the postwar period we have come to three overwhelming convictions, now basic to our foreign policy, none of which finds full acceptance in Southeast Asia. In the first place, we are convinced that there is now so close-knit a world that all parts of it must stand or fall together and no part can hope to remain aloof from the rest. Our sense of the folly and futility of the isolationism and neutralism of our own recent past is so strong that we find it very difficult to tolerate similar errors on the part of others. To the Southeast Asians the world remains a bigger and looser-jointed place than we are prepared to concede, allowing in their view of it for not only one world or two but several. In the second place, we are convinced of the immediate threat to all the non-Communist world of an implacable and constant Red drive for world domination which only our determined and peace-loving vigilance can thwart. Be it from wishful thinking or from reasoned conviction, the Southeast Asians see the danger as neither so one-sided nor so inescapable and doubt that the finger of doom necessarily points in their direction. In the third place, we are convinced of our unassailable rightness, firmly believing that we and our allies represent freedom and virtue and that the Communist camp represents oppression and abysmal evil. For the Southeast Asians there is no equivalent certainty that the world is so neatly divided into white and black.

These doubts and variant interpretations are by no means unique to Southeast Asia; indeed, there are many in Europe and elsewhere who share them in one degree or another. But in Southeast Asia they have a special poignancy and meaning because of certain aspects of the Asian setting. In revolt against European colonialism, they are suspicious of any policy which carries the risk of attaching them to the coattails of the United States and Western Europe. Even where they have gone along with the main lines of the United States–United Nations policy in Korea, they have had a lingering dread of non-Asian troops operating in Asia and of a war which might be spread far beyond the confines of Korea. The American hostility to the new regime in China has seemed to them to carry the implication of undue intervention in Asian affairs and of a threat to the rights of nations to determine their own destiny, and not all aspects of the Japanese Peace Treaty sit well with them. In Indo-China they are inclined to see the old colonialism seeking to hold on by force, backed, if not by American troops, at least by American munitions and supplies. There is an abiding skepticism that the United States is honestly committed to the creation of a free and new order in Asia—a skepticism which grows with every account of racial discrimination in the United States.

At the present time our overriding concern, based on the presuppositions indicated above, is the maintenance of the free world as we see it, and the general tenor of our policies—

as well as the aid which we are prepared to extend to other peoples—must be adapted to the exigencies of our grand strategy. The scheme of priorities of the Southeast Asians is a different one. There can perhaps be agreement on the broad and general goal of maintaining the peace of the world, although there are different views as to how it can most effectively be maintained, but their first concentration is on their own desperately pressing needs. They are unpersuaded that the American line of attack on the problem of peace gives the answer, or even an appropriate answer, fearing that the United States is in fact creating a situation in which war becomes more rather than less likely. The proposal that they link themselves to the coalition led by Washington opens up to them the dread vista of being drawn into a vast conflict which they might otherwise be spared. Declining to recognize our claim of exclusive rightness, even though their general sympathies may lie on our side as against that of Moscow, they feel under no moral compulsion to accept our version of the crusade in which we are engaged, and they have come to no certainty that their material interests are best served by joining forces with us. Fearing war, wasting no undue love on Europe and the white man, concerned to maintain or to achieve a full sovereignty, and seeking a vitally needed breathing spell from turmoil, they prefer the old path of neutrality to the new path of collective security. Or, to put it in terms possibly more akin to their own thinking, they suspect that what we offer them is less a new-style collective security than an old-style alliance which, like other alliances of the past, has involvement in war as its inevitable end. Collaboration within the broader setting of the United Nations has a markedly greater appeal than the narrower bond with the United States and its major adherents.

The contradictions lurking in our several responsibilities and commitments have been emphasized by the impact of the Korean War, which has forced a speeding up of the rearmament program and a general tightening of the lines of the containment policy. In a material sense it has meant, on one side, that our demand for the raw materials of Southeast Asia went up as did the price we were prepared to pay for them, but, on the other side, it has meant that our non-military aid programs were more carefully scrutinized and pruned, that more strings were attached in the way of insistence on adherence to American policies, and that the availability of goods in the American market was lessened as the price for them started to mount in the inflationary spiral. Even the increase of price for Southeast Asian raw materials was not an unmixed blessing, since it caused a sudden disturbance of markets and then was sharply checked by official American action as the conviction spread that our rearmament needs were being exploited by the producers of the raw materials we needed. In addition, the United States took the lead in securing the imposition of an embargo on the sale of many types of goods to the countries behind the iron curtain including China, which had under American pressure been declared an aggressor by the United Nations. This step both cut into the markets of the Southeast Asian countries and forced a re-examination on their part of the extent to which they were prepared to be carried along by the spreading implications of American policy.

If these comments are in any measure sound and represent any substantial body of Southeast Asian opinion, then it is necessary to carry the argument a stage further and wonder if we have not fallen down on one of our major responsibilities. We have not been adequately able to get across to them our sense of the rightness and urgency of our cause, or, to put it more significantly, to persuade them that fundamentally what we are after is what they must be after too. Perhaps a part of the problem is that, falling prey to the materialist interpretation which we claim to repudiate, we put too much faith in the ability of money to talk, and perhaps another part is that we assume our rightness too firmly and too solemnly without being prepared to pay enough attention to the varying viewpoints of others.

In the realm of technical assistance and material aid also,

is it not possible that a part of our shortcomings derives from a tendency to look down from on high and tell other less enlightened souls how things should be done? I can see no reason to doubt that the American people would sincerely like to see the Southeast Asians move ahead in progress and prosperity, but it must be more seriously open to doubt that we have as yet devised the most effective means and approaches to achieve the ends which we want and which, presumably in somewhat different fashion, the peoples of Southeast Asia want for themselves.

No matter how they are approached, our responsibilities are perplexing and confusing, and they are made far more hazardous by our inability to read Communist intentions with any certainty. If it must be the presumption that Red China or China and the Soviet Union together are likely to strike by military force at any moment, then we must act as our own military and political interests dictate, hoping to carry as much of Southeast Asia with us as possible, but acting whether it is with us or not. Even then it is difficult to evade the question as to the extent to which we are justified in seeking to draw or force into the protection of our armed camp peoples who would rather gamble on their ability to stand aside from the conflict, and fear being dragged into it by us more actively than they fear Communist attack. Nor is it looking too far into the future to wonder whether in developing the armed forces of the Southeast Asian countries we are not running the serious risk of setting up a military clique which will come to dominate the civilian scene. The experience of Thailand, Egypt, and many Latin American countries is ample evidence that this is no matter of idle and academic speculation.

If, on the other hand—and this would be my own interpretation—the likelihood of such attack is remote on condition that we make it clear that, as in Korea, if aggression occurs we are prepared to meet it, then we have an opportunity to move more slowly and to build more surely. We can follow the more congenial path of seeking to build the bulwarks against

Communism within the Southeast Asian countries by assisting them to demonstrate that there is no need to turn to violence and dictatorship in order to move ahead in the world. For the negative goal of the defeat of Communism, which at least in certain areas strikes no particularly responsive chord, we can substitute the infinitely more attractive goal of development and advancement.

To act on the supposition of remote danger of Communist attack removes some of the problems, but even at this level many of the contradictions among American responsibilities still remain. There is, for example, the unresolved issue which our new position in the world has thrust upon us: traditionally we have sought, with marked diversions hither and yon, to stand by the doctrine of non-intervention in the affairs of other peoples; but it has become increasingly clear that that doctrine can have only a limited application under present conditions when inaction on the part of a superpower can itself constitute a drastic type of intervention. At several points this problem ties in with the controversies as to the conditions under which American aid should be extended to countries which seek it or which, in one of the most curious phenomena of our times, have it pressed upon them. It is certainly arguable that in the American national interest aid should go only to those whose policies coincide to a reasonable degree with our own and who are prepared to establish the safeguards, including American supervision, which will maximize the effectiveness of our assistance, but too rigorous insistence on these conditions can defeat our own purposes by narrowing the circle of our associates. How far should we depart from our conceptions of free enterprise in the economic sphere and democracy in the political sphere in choosing among those who will share our bounty? Or, to take a specialized application of the principles of free enterprise, can we modify our own system and conceptions to the extent of entering into long-term contracts for raw materials at stable prices in order to eliminate the erratic boom-and-bust cycle which tends regularly to disrupt the Southeast Asian economies?

For our sake and theirs it is essential that there be mutual trust and friendship between the United States and the peoples of Southeast Asia, but these cannot be achieved unless the Southeast Asians are persuaded that their interests are truly served by collaboration with us. That places upon us a primary responsibility to seek to discover their interests and to join in aiding their attainment wherever that is compatible with our general purposes. It requires that we become more sensitively attuned to Asian ways of thought and outlooks than we have been in the past—to recognize, for example, that in Asian eyes it would be a cardinal betrayal of the right order of things for American troops to join in the Indo-China War, except possibly in case of open Chinese intervention. It requires a greater recognition that the Southeast Asian countries, operating in a different geographical setting and deriving from different histories, cultures, and traditions, inevitably have concerns and interests which are alien to ours. I believe, furthermore, that it places upon us a responsibility for a humility which is all too lacking. Perhaps we can learn something from Southeast Asia, perhaps its attitudes and interpretations have a validity as great as our own, or even greater. If we are prepared to accept the key responsibility of conceding to them in word and working practice a real equality of status, of building a true partnership with them, then there is ground for hope that many other responsibilities will fall in line too.

Part 2: ECONOMICS

Claude A. Buss

NEW RELATIONSHIPS: ECONOMICS AND
DIPLOMACY IN SOUTHEAST ASIA

THE PROBLEMS OF diplomacy in Southeast Asia are deeply rooted in economics. Embassy staffs—and foreign offices—have experts in commerce, agriculture, industry and labor. It is not enough to compose reports; it is often necessary to render advice, or assistance, or even to carry out a demonstration project. People—human beings—are the subjects of economic dilemmas: their level of living is the stake in each decision.

According to the UN Statistical Office, the 1949 average family income in the United Kingdom was the equivalent of $773.00; in Southeast Asia it was $55.00. The nineteen richest countries in the world, with 16 per cent of the population, earned 66 per cent of the total income; the fifteen poorest, with more than half of the people of the world, lived on less than 9 per cent of the total income.[1] The implications of these facts have been clearly stated by the distinguished Liaquat Ali Khan:

It is my conviction that the peace of the world today depends upon the peace of Asia. You cannot allow one third of the world to live in misery and hope that the world at large will live in peace.

The boom in raw material prices which followed the outbreak of the Korean War is a memory. The profits which accrued were used *but slightly* for economic development. They were simply dissipated in the inflation induced by the orgy of

[1] Quoted in *Manchester Guardian Weekly,* June 12, 1952, page 4.

consumption. We are becoming aware again that the normal
state of Southeast Asia is distress. The UN World Economic
Survey for 1950–51 showed that during that year the gap between the advanced countries and the underdeveloped countries was widening, not narrowing. The underdeveloped countries as a whole showed a relative decline in industrial and
agricultural production. This had happened at a time when
the underdeveloped countries were supposed to be enjoying
prosperity. The Food and Agriculture Organization has reported that current rice supplies in Southeast Asia are only
half of what they should be. The International Labour Office
has further noted that population is still outstripping food
supply.[2]

If increasing misery is the quickest way to revolution—and
if Asia is Lenin's promised land—then it behooves us to probe
deeply into our economic perplexities, assess our failures and
accomplishments, and regroup our forces for some new, brave
and bold attacks.

Many of the relationships between diplomacy and economics in Southeast Asia are not new relationships; they are
rather old relationships with new overtones. In some instances,
internal economic problems were not regarded as proper subjects of international relations; in others they were solved by
the metropolitan countries, with little regard for the sensitivity
of Asian populations. Now Asians are vitally concerned with
their own concepts of economic justice. They demand a decent
respect for their own dignity and their own rights.

Land and the products of the soil are fundamental in the
Southeast Asia picture. The second recommendation of the
Bell Economic Survey Mission to the Philippines illustrates
procedures which are vitally needed in all countries throughout the area:

Increase agricultural production by applying modern scientific
methods; improve agricultural extension services; establish rural
banks to make loans to small farmers; expedite opening of new

[2] *Manchester Guardian Weekly,* July 3, 1952, page 8.

lands for homesteads, and simplify present procedures to obtain land titles; purchase large estates for resale to small farmers.[3]

The Government of Burma is pushing land nationalization and division. It is encouraging peasant cooperatives for rice marketing,[4] milling and consumer sales. It wants a special agricultural bank to handle cooperative funds and extend credit. In spite of land nationalization, a debt moratorium, rent restriction, and agricultural loans, the poverty of the Burmese peasant over wide areas has not been conquered. Agricultural methods are backward, the soil yield low, fighting and depredation have hindered cultivation. Ten acres of paddy land in Lower Burma will not bring in much over 900 rupees (£70) a year to its tiller, and the money lender is appearing again in the villages.

The new twist to these age-old problems is the demand for seed-selection centers, more tractor stations in Upper Burma, and more assistance in afforestation. It is hoped that the Technical Cooperation Administration aided irrigation projects and a fertilizer factory will be powerful antidotes to the simple Communist slogans of "no rents and no taxes"—when these projects begin to show results.

In Thailand, Premier Pibun's program places in front rank the objectives of increasing land ownership and other benefits for farmers. As a sign of the new times the World Bank is financing irrigation and hydro-electric projects in Central Burma.

A writer in the Philippines Free Press has expressed his sentiments about the land in these graphic words:

It is about time Americans learn a few of the facts of Asiatic life. Those facts spring from a central one: horrible poverty. Not of a

[3] Department of State: *Background: The Philippines Today,* November, 1951, p. 8.

[4] The Government State Agricultural Marketing Board only pays half the export price of rice to the producer. Peasant cooperatives (80 per cent of the rice growers are tenants) want the profits which go ordinarily to government and middle men.

minority but of the masses. The American, with his wonderful standard of living, cannot understand why anyone should embrace communism. The Asiatic—more and more he cannot understand why he shouldn't. What else is there for him? To the Asiatic sunk in the abyss of unrelieved poverty, the "Voice of America" must seem like the voice of the man from the moon. To be a free man, to eat three square meals a day, to live in a house whose roof is not made of nipa or straw, to be well-clothed, to be treated by a doctor when one is sick, to be able to send one's children to a decent school —not to go half-naked and always in danger of starving to death and having to sell one's daughter into prostitution—the Asiatic will ask incredulously: Are such things possible? Propaganda about the American way of life is money wasted—in Asia. Those who listen to it do not need it; they are already pro-American. Those who should listen—cannot understand what the Americans are talking about. But they can understand what the Communists are talking about. The land, the Communists promise, is going to belong to them. That's all they need to hear. That's all they care to know.

A second category of traditional economic problems is that which stems from Southeast Asia's dependence on raw material. The area is well known for the variety and richness of its resources, but some countries depend on a single crop or a limited number of crops. The Philippines depends to an embarrassing degree on its sugar market in the United States, both Indonesia and Malaya measure their well-being largely in the price of rubber and tin. Mass-purchasing has exacerbated diplomatic arguments. Southeast Asian exporters have blamed unpredictable American purchasers for fatal gyrations in the rubber market; American purchasers have accused the tin miners of price-gouging or conspiring to force the price of tin to unreasonable levels. A few cents per pound in rubber might spell the difference between bust and boom in Singapore. A fall in the price of rubber tends to disrupt the local economy, cause unemployment and wage-cuts—all of which play directly into the hands of the Communists. A rubber recession hurts the government more than it hurts the planter, on account of the sliding scale in taxes. The higher the price of rubber the greater proportion the government collects, and the government gloomily anticipates reduction of U.S. $20 million in rubber export duties for the current year as compared to 1951.

The ghost of synthetics has haunted the Malayan planters. The supernormal demands of rearmament programs have postponed the day of reckoning, but the fear is overwhelming that commercial synthetics will someday take the profits away from tin mines, rubber plantations and the jute factories.

The third economic dislocation which has its roots deep in the past is the disappearance of the prewar international trade pattern, with Southeast Asia's vital contribution to the balance of payments. Raw materials earned dollars from the precious American markets. Those dollars paid for European imports or perhaps migrated to Europe in the form of profits or pensions, and eventually returned to the United States from Europe in payment for Europe's excess of imports over its own exports. No adequate substitute has been found for this old arrangement. The loss of colonial markets and investments has multiplied the troubles of the United Kingdom and the Netherlands. These troubles have been only partially allayed by United States assistance programs.

Singapore continues to be a vital dollar-earner for the Commonwealth, but Jakarta keeps its dollars for direct purchase of American products. Indonesia has often been in the exasperating situation where it has wanted American goods but simply could not obtain the necessary priorities or allocations. Steel, already in short supply in the United States, could not ordinarily be obtained for export to Indonesia.

As one country after another tends to restrict its imports, it also tends to increase its exports. Southeast Asian countries are no exceptions. There are the usual restrictions on products from hard-currency countries, and exchange controls which are accompanied by frenzied efforts at export promotion. Southeast Asia's exports have little trouble when the United States is in a buying mood. But when the United States decides it can afford a breather in its stock-piling program, it is likely to hear Southeast Asian protests against the embargoes on shipments to Russia, to China and to their satellites. Much more thinking needs to be done, for example, along the lines of intra-area trade or regional exchanges—French Indo-China coal for the Manila Gas Works or Malayan iron for the Japanese steel mills. But quantitative revival will have to await the end of these international tensions, internal disturbances and the return of at least prewar normalcy.

A special word needs to be inserted with regard to the trade relations between the Philippines and the United States. The trade agreement of 1946 provides for the continuance of free trade between the two countries until 1954. Then come the graduated duties and declining quotas. The trade agreement provides also that until 1974 Americans will be given equal rights with Filipinos in the development of the natural resources of the islands and that the value of Philippine currency in relation to the United States dollar shall not be changed, the convertibility of pesos into dollars shall not be suspended, and restrictions shall not be imposed on the transfer of funds from the Philippines to the United States except by agreement with the President of the United States. Naturally, the Republic of the Philippines desires "re-examination" of some of the privileges which accrue to us; but we both must be prepared with adequate substitutes for the loss of the advantage of its privileged access to the American market.

A fourth economic-diplomatic problem centers about the ever-old, ever-new, ever-arguable position of the Chinese. Until recently the Chinese in Southeast Asia were not involved in international politics. The metropolitan powers gave them protection approximately equivalent to everyone else, and the Government of China did not bother too much about the welfare of its subjects overseas. The Kuomintang discovered the accessibility of its golden eggs overseas, and the Communist China regime would like to preserve the inflow of remittances from abroad.

Local governments in Southeast Asia have become increasingly aware of the economic position of the Chinese and have tried to recoup some of the gains which they felt the Chinese made from their own nationals. This is quite apart from the politically discriminatory laws.

The problem is much more complicated than it seems. One might argue "why not take the local Chinese for an economic ride. They are usurers, money lenders, trade monopolists, rice manipulators and above all potential fifth columnists." But there is the other side of the coin: they are hard workers—they serve an economic function which native populations deliberately refused to serve and the abuses of their power can not mitigate their social utility. Moreover, many of them are not fifth columnists—they have cut their ties with the country of their ancestors and their loyalties are to the countries in which they have chosen to live and die. They can become loyal citizens or they can become rebels. The role of the Chinese among the Huks, the Viet Minh, and the Malayan guerillas is counterbalanced by the contributions made by the Chinese hospitals, schools, banks or chambers of commerce to the side of law and order.

But what do you do to these Chinese if you launch aid programs which have as their end object the displacement of a Chinese company by a new native company or organization. What do you do to the Chinese whom you accuse of being a fifth columnist or a collaborator with the Communists before you are sure of your facts? In Malaya in particular you will swell the ranks of the Communists if you cause lay-off in the mines or drastic cuts among the plantation workers. Who could blame the Chinese if he would turn to Mao Tse-tung in sheer protest against some local economic or political force which threatened to deprive him of his rights, his job, or his self-respect.

The fifth and last of these old economic problems is that of foreign investments. Investments abroad paid handsome dividends. It hurts to lose them. Recall the story of the British negotiations with Burma, or the Netherlands negotiations with Indonesia. The concept of due compensation clashed with the arguments of abstract justice. Old investors lost out and I believe that none of the investors in other countries received the same degree of compensation which Americans got for their losses in the Philippines. But once bitten, twice shy. New capital hesitates to go abroad and perhaps would hesitate even if the enticement for profit at home were not so alluring.

Governments invite new capital, but capital asks guarantees which governments will not or can not give. While capital idles, both borrowers and lenders suffer. Many also feel that full employment in industrialized countries cannot be achieved except in the context of an expanding world economy in which the development of the underdeveloped countries would form a most important part.

I realize that the distinction between the foregoing section and this section is a shadowy one, but it has the merit of convenience. The problems above were old economic problems with new diplomatic relationships: The problems which follow derive from new and recent relationships between diplomacy and economics in Southeast Asia.

The first consideration must be given to the rehabilitation of the ravages of war. The Japanese aggression snuffed out lives, destroyed property, obliterated channels of trade, and put a complete stop to constructive economic activity. Many parts of Southeast Asia still lie buried in the wreckage of the Co-Prosperity Sphere. The Philippines revived quickly; less fortunate countries were through no fault of their own favored with less substantial encouragement. Perhaps no country has revived so astonishingly as Japan itself. A certain cynicism has characterized the Chinese attitude which deplored the fact that they were on the wrong side. "If only we had lost, the Americans would have been responsible for us and not for Japan."

It is no exaggeration to state that many of the woes of French Indo-China, the Philippines, Indonesia, Burma and Malaya are directly attributable to the heritage of chaos and anarchy which was left after the end of the Japanese occupation: it is costly to restore law and order. In Burma, it is estimated that there are still 19,000 rebels confronted by an improving Burmese army 40,000 strong "with officers from Singapore and Sandhurst." Figures for French Indo-China and Malaya are of greater magnitude, and give some idea of the tremendous costs of military operations.

But the problems are not military alone. Magsaysay has attributed his successes against the Huks to his new tactics. He gave the Huks an alternative program. He offered substantial rewards to informers on Huk leaders and agreed to buy Huk firearms. At the same time he inaugurated a policy of resettling the Huks who surrendered on homesteads of their own in Mindanao. Sir Gerald Templer is not unaware of economic bullets, and the Defense Minister of Burma is on record as saying "one of the most effective recruiting agents for the government would be rapid progress towards economic prosperity and equitable social and economic conditions in government-administered Burma." What is true for these countries is true for all of Southeast Asia: economic remedies are also helpful for the politico-military diseases which have existed since the war.

A second economic problem with new diplomatic relationships is the emergence of economic nationalism. Its most spectacular expression has been in measures against the Chinese. It has flourished with political independence and has spawned an area-wide yearning for self-sufficiency. Before the war, the Philippines were content to grow sugar for the American market and to import their rice from Thailand or Burma.

Sugar meant more money. But this is not so today. The bitter experiences of the Japanese occupation accentuated an inherent faith in the goodness of self-sufficiency.

It is a tragedy that economic nationalism should be so sought after in Southeast Asia at a time when its disadvantages and dangers have become so apparent in the West. It may be argued that the West does little more than pay lip service to economic interdependence, but Southeast Asia is chary of even that. Import restrictions and exchange controls were deemed advisable in the Philippines, and Thailand recently closed down "the only free currency market in Asia outside Hong-kong." [5]

Foreigners generally are finding it increasingly difficult to balance their budgets. Head taxes or registration taxes have risen from a nominal one dollar per year to twenty dollars per year per member of the family. Sterling balances have been devalued, dollar values have gone down with them (except on the black markets), and resulting prices have skyrocketed. The Philippines have been notoriously expensive for dollar earners since the war, and it is wise to scan carefully the date on any post report before planning your expense account.

Economic nationalism in trade extends to barter arrangements. Controlled markets, centralized buying and selling, and strict control of all foreign exchange help to account for the difficulties of at least some of our firms in foreign trade.

State planning, the third of these new phenomena, goes hand in hand with economic nationalism. Examples are the National Development Company in the Philippines and the Rural Industrial Development Authority in Malaya. These institutions are against our ideas of free enterprise, but there is no use in violent opposition to them. Southeast Asians say they cannot afford the costly mistakes of competitive capital-ism—and they are eager to do quickly what has taken us many years to accomplish. They feel that there is not the reservoir of private capital nor of technical know-how necessary for de-

[5] Tellman Durdin: Bangkok, April 3, 1952, *New York Times*.

pendence on individual initiative. In their view, they need the combined strength of the entire state to achieve their ambitions and to cope with the economic grants of the West.

Furthermore, there is no apology for state socialism and no admission that state socialism is a step on the road to Communism. In the past, free enterprise has meant profits to a chosen few—foreigners at that. In the future, they intend to see that profits shall be for themselves, and for all their people, not just the chosen few. You may question the competence of their inexperienced leaders to conceive of and to operate economic plans on a state-wide scale, or you may fear that economic good intentions will be buried under personal temptations or political pressures; nevertheless, their devotion to economic nationalism is unshakeable and inescapable in their own estimation. It seems much more sensible on our part to accept their ideas and to convince them that they have more to gain in the live-and-let-live environment of free enterprise than in the intolerant economic atmosphere of Communism.

The state planners are growing increasingly conscious of the role of labor. We know that the exemplary labor practices of some foreign firms have been eye openers to the new employers of labor. It often happened in the past that labor racketeers wormed their way into unions and caused trouble in companies with enlightened labor policies. Too often the direction of unions went to Communists by default. At the present time labor is attaining a more respected status, unions are interesting themselves in wages and working conditions, and a non-Communist leadership is endeavoring to cope with the problems which beset laborers everywhere. You hear the same charges of irresponsibility and unreasonableness, but you cannot ignore the emerging power of the labor interest.

The third comparatively recent diplomatic-economic relationship is that involved in the current emphasis upon the cold war—the struggle to contain Communism—in every aspect of economic activity. I wonder if there is much difference in the Asian reaction to the Communist dogma that "victory

in the East is the road to victory in the West" and to the pre-
tension of the free world that "in order to live in the kind of
world we want, we must have friends in the East." We too
want our own type of victory in the West. Neutralism is anath-
ema in the teachings of Stalin and Mao Tse-tung; if we are
not careful, we shall be adopting the same position, and to our
detriment.

Last fall, thanks to Professor Dobby, I met with his international relations club at the University of Malaya. A Sikh
student asked me why we insisted upon adopting a missionary
attitude in our policies with Asia. He said: "You do not fool
us when you protest that you are interested in us for our own
sake. We know and understand that you must be interested in
us for the sake of your own welfare and security. We would
respect you more if you did not try to pretend." Or, as the
Foreign Minister of Burma put it: "You Americans need not
warn us against the perils of Communism, we are living closer
to it than you are."

The anti-Communism inherent in our military assistance
programs should oblige us to diagnose the nature and extent
of the thing we are opposing. Is it an ideology? Is it the merest
tactic of chaos? Is it an aggressive nationalism both on the part
of Russia and China? Is it a new totalitarianism? Or is it a
combination of all of these? The accuracy of the analysis will
predetermine the efficacy of the prescriptions we use. Guns
and dollars in themselves are not sufficient to procure friendship, but when accompanied by frankness and a reservoir of
good will on our own part they are likely to inspire return
traffic in sympathy and understanding.

The fifth and last of the new relationships between economics and diplomacy results from the downfall of Kuomintang China, the eclipse of Japan, and the rise of the power of
the United States and the Commonwealth countries. This
omits the problems inherent in the embargo on shipments to
enemies, and the efficacy of an extended blockade of the coast
of China. But it recognizes frankly the power and concomi-

tant responsibility of postwar United States and reminds us of
the basic interest of both Canada and Australia in Southeast
Asia.

Japan has been removed temporarily from a position of
influence, but it is neither disinterested in, nor ignorant of,
its opportunities in Southeast Asia. Some Japanese would like
to think that Southeast Asia can provide markets to compensate for the former trade with China. Barter agreements between Supreme Commander Allied Powers and countries of
Southeast Asia kept many Japanese mills running toward the
end of the occupation. Unfortunately, Japan's sterling balances have piled up precariously as a result of her export
drives—Japan's neighbors are more likely to take action in
restricting Japan's exports since the United States has "gone"
from Japan and are likely to be more uneasy about undue
expansion of Japan's capacity to produce. Japan is eager to
re-enter the economic life of Southeast Asia, in shipping, fish-
ing, trade and technical development, but Southeast Asia cannot be too enthusiastic about Japan or anyone else becoming
a workshop for the whole of Asia.

Industrialization, it seems, is a fetish in all underdeveloped
countries. Plans are not lacking for huge and impressive development schemes. Too often it is believed that industrialization will relieve economic ills, without adequate emphasis on
economic costs. What will happen to those who will be thrown
out of work by the competition of new and modern industries?
Where will the capital and the technical know-how come from?
How much of the total product will have to be diverted to
military purposes or to rearmament? Is production to be for
the home market or for export only? It is rather silly for everyone to be wanting to produce for everyone else and to be hesi-
tating to produce anything for home consumption or to buy
anything from a foreign source of supply.

The magnitude of the industrialization problem can be
seen in a report from the Economic Commission for Asia and
the Far East conference at Rangoon which was held from Jan-

uary 29 to February 8, 1952. It was estimated that to raise the national incomes in the Southeast Asia area by 2 per cent, would require 80 per cent of all capital goods available for export to *all* underdeveloped areas.

A look ahead does not give cause for too much alarm or even too much pessimism. Things are never quite so bad as they appear and there is ample evidence that we recognize and are acting to solve our problems. Maybe success has been elusive or indifferent, but we are profiting, I believe, from our experiences in the past.

The countries in Southeast Asia themselves are dedicating their own resources to the enhancement of the welfare of their people. They want the "better things of life" as we are prone to call them, and they are not likely to succumb easily to any policy or ideology which is inimical to their own desires and their own values.

The United Nations offers an ultimate means of economic assistance which shall be free from the stigma of imperialism, but in the meantime national programs are extending a helping hand. The Colombo Plan, launched in high hopes, is off to a good start although there is a great gap between its plans and availabilities. Some Asians and some Europeans are inclined to be a bit apprehensive and even cynical because of the difficulties of raising capital, meeting rising costs, providing technical aid, and assisting receiving countries to utilize the proffered assistance. At the very least it can be said that in the face of growing difficulties it has helped to keep the Asian level of subsistence from falling any lower.

Our own loans and grants have given rise to much optimism and also to much soul-searching. Is the whole of the Far East treated as the stepchild of Western Europe? Is the philosophy of the Mutual Security Agency most applicable to Southeast Asia or should all our operations there be of an Economic Cooperation Administration–Technical Cooperation Administration type? Are we doing as much as we should in coordinating with local schemes, with the Colombo Plan and with the agencies of the UN? Do we take too much initiative or would we be better advised to be a little more difficult to approach? Do we extend aid only to our proven friends or are there fence-sitters who might be won over by any discreet or modest assistance? Have the amounts of our assistance been cut so drastically that others like Burma will "consider the possibilities of aid without strings from the USSR or Communist China"?

We have inaugurated projects of undisputed value in Southeast Asia and our philosophy is changing from a narrow negative one of containing Communism to a positive philosophy of "advance and development." I think we are also disposed to look upon our assistance activities much more as an *opportunity* than a *responsibility*. Southeast Asia needs help from the outside and it will accept such help wherever obtainable. In extending help, we are doing much more than clarifying the new relationships between economics and diplomacy. In the words of our distinguished colleague, the Ambassador from Indonesia: "The successful implementation of our economic policy is interdependent with national security, political stability, and social progress."

Charles J. Shohan

NATIONAL ECONOMIC PLANNING
IN SOUTHEAST ASIA

IT IS APPROPRIATE to this discussion to paraphrase a meaty saying by a great economist along the following lines: "The case for an economic system based on private enterprise, as I see it, is this: there are occasions on which government enterprise and investment can benefit an economy, provided there is a government wise enough to identify those occasions and strong enough to confine itself to them." The economist who made the original statement, by the way, was speaking of the case for free trade and the limited scope for protectionism, but he is long since dead and cannot personally object to the use I have made of his aphorism. I do not believe, however, that he would have objected to the appropriateness of my usage for this present purpose.

To offer such a statement with reference to national planning in Southeast Asia appears to call for discussion under at least three headings. First, why—and it is a fact—is there such insistent interest in state planning of enterprise and investment in Southeast Asia? Second, are there important conclusions to be drawn from the experience of other countries regarding the wisdom of state planning and are there particular considerations relevant to Southeast Asia? Third, are there general or special considerations regarding the strength of governments to plan wisely in Southeast Asia?

Before discussing the first of these questions, I wish to talk briefly of my use of the phrase "state planning." It is not pertinent nowadays to identify just any government action based upon foresight and affecting the economy as state planning. What, unfortunately, is usually implied by the term these days is at least a fairly systematic action by the state resulting in something approaching total control over the whole range of economic activity. Perhaps consumption may not be directly controlled. Indirectly, however, its volume and much of its character would be controlled by, for example, the allocation of opportunities for investment, the allocation or direct provision of capital to enable these investments to be made, the fixing of prices in major fields of domestic trade, direct control of foreign transactions, as well as last—and possibly least—direct governmental or quasi-governmental production or marketing. It is this sort of government activity that I am here referring to as state planning. It means particularly that for practical purposes the state makes—perhaps by directing others—most investment decisions and substantially makes or directs all major production decisions: the government in effect displaces all other entities as investor and entrepreneur.

To turn now to the first question: the fact of state planning in Southeast Asia in this sense, and the vigor with which the conception is promoted in the area. Each of the governments in Southeast Asia has since the war promulgated, or at least prepared, one or more government blueprints for production or investment in many or all sectors of the economy. Each of the governments has one or more active state planning bodies, on a cabinet level or on a technical level, official bodies and also quasi-official bodies, decision-making, as well as advisory. Each of the governments has provision in its budget for the expansion or institution of state investment in many lines. Each of the governments has established new quasi-governmental action bodies—banks or government corporations—to undertake investment, some of them with resources not deriving directly from the government budget. Practically all Southeast Asian countries have instituted new and far-reaching measures restricting economic activity by foreigners or specifically reserving fields of activity for their own nationals. All of the independent countries of the area have taken steps which have resulted in a major separation between their own price levels and world price levels. Almost all the countries have taken steps directly to finance production or to control trade in several of their most important fields of import and export.

Now there are a number of fairly recent, but nonetheless highly important, reasons of a postwar nature for this feverish activity by the governments in the economic field, stemming simply from wartime physical destruction and financial disruption. In common with many states in other parts of the world, governments in Southeast Asia have felt it necessary to take direct action in regard to reconstruction and rehabilitation, to get and give maximum assurance that the highly limited resources available would be more or less equitably parcelled out and more or less efficiently devoted to activities that were clearly of vital importance if the state were to survive. Furthermore, the great imbalance of world exchanges appeared to require that in order to achieve these primary and highly important purposes, the country could not be left fully exposed to shocks and changes originating elsewhere in the world.

But most countries have experienced extreme economic dislocations from recent wars, and many of them have experienced great physical ravages. Nonetheless, I believe it is true that as an area, no region has pursued more intensely the goal, though by no means also achieving the fact, of state planning than has Southeast Asia. For this special circumstance I am inclined to assign two reasons which are in a relative sense peculiar to Southeast Asia. These are: the strength of authoritarian political traditions, and the absence of vigorous native entrepreneurship. To an extent, these may be viewed as opposite sides of the same medal, but I believe they are in part separable.

It can be argued, although I for one am skeptical, that the village organization typical of many parts of Southeast Asia is fundamentally highly democratic. But I do not believe this more parochial local organization is administratively or intellectually transferable to the national scene, and larger-scale political organization has been traditionally more on the analogy of the relatively absolute courts of the more powerful feudal nobles in what for Europe were the earliest modern times. These important and powerful courts were, of course, circumscribed both by a complex series of relations with various classes of people in the domain, as well as by an amorphous and shifting set of broader relations among themselves and with more powerful and distant forces. Parenthetically, although there is probably strictly no such thing as an absolute monarchy, some of the Southeast Asian countries have had in their modern history governments well entitled to be called such.

Another important element in the authoritarian political traditions of Southeast Asia is the fact that the paramount power in all but one of these states was for periods ranging from less than a hundred to several hundred years a foreign and non-Eastern government. (For two of the states it may not be amiss to mention the existence until fairly recently of at least the claim of Chinese suzerainty.) Again, the absolute freedom of the ruling power was circumscribed by the desires and interests of the people of the country, and perhaps more narrowly circumscribed than it is fashionable nowadays to believe. But nonetheless from the point of view of the people, the government of the country was simply a powerful authority capable of making all decisions affecting their individual interests.

A third factor, antecedent to World War II, has been that much of Southeast Asian intellectual borrowing from the Western world, through both education and propaganda, took place during a period when generally socialistic thought was becoming more and more fashionable in the West. Associated with this fashion, of course, has been the powerful attraction of socialism—even before the Russian Revolution—as an expression of political as well as economic discontent which appealed to more politically-minded people in colonial areas. The further exploitation of socialism for purposes of Russian imperialism, expressed as world communism, is of course too well known for comment.

To summarize briefly at this point then, the most powerful political traditions of Southeast Asia are those of native authoritarian rule, colonial governments and, more recently, socialistic views of no particular dogmatic stripe aside from their partially successful channelization by the Kremlin.

The other important element to bear in mind regarding the magnetic attraction of state planning for Southeast Asian peoples is that as a practical matter there is little to compete with it, once decisions are taken formally or implicitly, to minimize reliance upon foreign investors or foreign enterprise. It is a remarkable fact, subject to little qualification, that in this extensive region of the world and for many hundreds of years, major investment, most finance, and most trade has been in the hands of people not native to the area. This is not solely a matter of monopolistic or competitive activities, aggressive or peaceful, by British, French, Spanish, Portuguese, Dutch, and Americans. It has been as much true, and even more true, for many activities directly affecting the average Southeast Asian, of several groups of Indians, of tribes from several areas on the southeast coast of China, of Arabs, and in this generation of the Japanese before World War II.

I do not believe the reasons for this situation are in most respects material to my paper. The fact, however, is of tremendous importance. There is extraordinarily little native tradition of economic investment and enterprise, either state or private, to use contemporary terms, although these categories are not completely separable. The role of the state has been largely either to protect or tolerate the foreign investor or trader, while maintaining its own power and increasing its own wealth. The foreigner was to be restrained, while permitted to carry on his recognizably useful activities. These might be lucrative for the exchequer, but they were not highly valued by the native society. At the point at which a local government was unable to furnish the foreigner adequate protection or, in its absence, to restrain him, it succumbed to foreign paramountcy.

Now I do not mean to imply that this Southeast Asian attitude toward enterprise and investment is to be deprecated. There are virtues, surely, but by no means without accompanying defects, in a society in which investment and trade are very powerful social interests. The values are not so great as to entitle anyone to consider a quite different set of values as inferior. It is, however, a fact that, unwilling and possibly unable to isolate themselves from the cultural influences of India and China and the West, which were accompanied by skillful and ambitious traders, the Southeast Asian peoples are today without a strong native business class.

In these circumstances, given the recapture of political power by native groups, given the decision to take their destinies completely in their own hands, and given the general tradition of state activity—then the doctrine of state planning has no competitor in popularity or, superficially, for practicability.

I want now to recognize two interesting partial exceptions to my generalizations. First, in areas of direct British control, and they are very important, there is somewhat less emphasis on state planning. Second, in Thailand also, the one country in the area with a continuous history of independence, with fundamental political power always in the hands of the Thais, there has been less interest in state planning.

I turn now to my second question: the wisdom of governments in identifying circumstances in which state planning is advantageous for their country. I will not concern myself at all with the question whether on other grounds fully authoritarian governments are desirable, so that thorough-going state action in the economic field follows automatically as a natural function for the government. The undesirability of states of this nature must be argued on other and largely noneconomic grounds. It is here assumed, and I believe on the whole correctly, that a conscious desire for authoritarian governments is not representative of Southeast Asian thought, and that in this respect the Communists and a few intellectuals both of the left and the right constitute an exception.

The problem of the wisdom required for economically efficient planned economies can be discussed in many complicated ways, all of which I believe obscure the fundamental fact that such wisdom simply does not exist anywhere—in the West, as in the East; in government agencies, or universities, or chambers of commerce; in economists or noneconomists. The simple fact is that quite aside from the important question whether it would be undesirable or antisocial so to use it, economics as an intellectual discipline is not sufficiently well developed to insure in any useful sense "correct" state planning for the further future of an entire national economy, nor are there many economists who while conscious of their intellectual limitations are also capable of using their knowledge of the art or science to the utmost, nor are there sufficient or sufficiently reliable data or facts in most countries of the world to permit the fullest exploitation of the abilities of the best economists.

I may here have overstated my point somewhat, but I feel it is important not to understate it even by a hairsbreadth, in view of the current world-wide fashion for exaggerating the economic element in life and overestimating the role of economics in complex social situations. The institution of state planning is by its very nature a political action, developed and carried out through political processes, and only in part on any grounds that may be called economic.

It is generally believed that the clearest possibility of sensibly agreeing on a socially advantageous national economic plan is in time of war. All patriotic citizens are then agreed that the goal is to "win the war." Within fairly broad limits, no account need be taken of the period after the war, and recognizable waste is countenanced, no matter how heavily frowned upon. Even under these circumstances, however, it is by now notorious that judgments are shaky, interest groups powerful, and results uncertain.

Remembering the great inefficiencies and nightmarish aftermath of war economies, it then becomes a matter of interest to note the ease with which many people conclude, "wouldn't it be wonderful if we could only organize ourselves as efficiently to wage the constructive battles of peace as we organize ourselves for destruction in war?" As complex as is the problem of planning for war, planning for some such simply phrased goal as "raising the standard of living" is much more difficult. Perhaps the arts of military strategy and logistics are no more precise than those of economics, but we are willing to place our endangered values, lives, and wealth in the hands of the practitioners of the military arts when these things we hold dear are in danger of being altogether lost. To place them all at the immediate disposal of a small and powerful group for any other reason is unlikely to be a thoroughly conscious and well-considered action, without duress or without influence by the group interested in wielding such power.

On all these counts—social values, life, and wealth—the great powers of over-all state planning would be unlikely to be wisely limited in Southeast Asian countries. For an area with as strong authoritarian traditions as has Southeast Asia, the exercise of great economic power by political bodies is likely to decrease the vitality and chance for survival of non-authoritarian political organization and, as I have remarked above, I do not believe this to be consciously the intention of Southeast Asians.

As for life itself, the very low standard of living, at some times and in particular areas pressing relatively closely upon a subsistence standard, should be a deterrent rather than an incentive to extensive social or economic experimentation. It is often said that where living standards are extremely low there is little to lose by such experiments, but this doctrine I find hard to understand. To manipulate the very lives of people, even with the intention of improving them, requires an almost boundless self-assurance verging on fanaticism, and I do not believe that in this respect the so-called indifference to human life of Asia is characteristic of the countries we are now talking about, although the Chinese Communists are apparently at some pains to exploit this indifference to the fullest. Southeast Asia is relatively to other parts of Asia a happy land and particularly blessed for the most part with sufficient food. But note what economic experiments by an ardently nationalistic government have done to the food supply of that once wonderful storehouse of agricultural products, Argentina.

Now to speak of the effects of state planning upon wealth. Governments must, of course, have foresight with regard to their own direct activities in the economic field. There is nowadays no practical and little intellectual doubt that these activities everywhere must involve extensive direct use of considerable fractions of the country's resources. For my part, I have a strong preference for sharply limiting the state's direct activities in production or marketing; I feel the burden of proof lies rather heavily against the choice to substitute bureaucratic for private enterprise. Be that as it may, I suggest that it is on the whole unwise to attempt to budget for future periods very far in advance or in very great detail. An example in the experience of other countries has been the great practical difficulty of planning with any accuracy and social usefulness for the notion of a so-called "shelf" of public projects to be undertaken in times of depression. This, by the way, is an instance of a relatively simple conception of a special role for planned state investment activity, palpably sensible, but actually extremely difficult of practical application.

In this very connection, governments of most countries today find themselves charged with responsibility for maintaining within some limits both the value of their money and the general level of economic activity in their countries. Attaining these goals may entail considerable government activity to influence the total volume of investment in the country. To the extent possible, such government actions should be less of the nature of improvisation than based on foresight and judgment regarding the future. But planning actions of this type are largely a matter of monetary, banking, and fiscal practice, and cannot be engaged in firmly, let alone inflexibly, for long periods ahead. It is certainly not vital for this purpose that any government with reasonably adequate instruments of monetary policy and even moderately large sectors of normal state expenditure and investment be required to plan action within the entire range of investment activity in the country. But, of course, the activities I have been referring to are completely beside the major point involved in the exciting idea of state planning, since that refers not to the maintenance of general economic activity or to a relatively fixed area for state investment, but rather to economic development. It generally refers, that is to say, to quite new investment which at least from the government point of view is of the nature of innovation.

It is in this field that bureaucratic activity is most suspect as to its wisdom. I think it is generally agreed that unless based on major political decisions and thoroughly backed by the greatest and ultimate political power, bureaucracies tend to be short-sighted and cautious.

The governmental development of investment in new fields can only take place on the basis of what are fundamentally political decisions. I have already noted the extensive responsibilities of Southeast Asian governments to conduct investment in obviously public sectors, and to maintain the total volume of economic activity in part through influencing total investment. Taking account then of the asserted impossibility of relying on private enterprise and particularly upon foreigners for most important fields of investment, it then might appear understandable that the government should undertake a point by point planning of substantially all investment over longish periods of time. But this creeping extension of the heavy hand of bureaucracy and political determination of investment is by no means inevitable if there exists any true realization of the deficiencies of a thorough-going planned economy and any real determination to invoke the forces of private enterprise.

In fact, it is probable that a governmental tendency to be overly logical and schematic with regard to state activity will itself impair the ability of the same governments to get on with the promotion or conduct of investment in what are clearly foreseen to be the most attractive opportunities in the most important fields of economic activity—transportation or power or agriculture. The pressure for total development plans in some sense derives from the laudable notion of coordination of several sectors of the government's activities and functions, and of the budget proposals of separate government departments. This tends to require the filling in of estimates, which then in some sense become plans or even programs for all types of economic activity contributing significantly to the national income. Of course, it is at least virtuous also to supply guesses about activities which are not necessarily important in the national economy. We may have started with four or five important projects or lines of endeavor, all of which on a rough empirical basis, and for good reasons, received firm support as the truly important things to be done—for example, development of the physical facilities of a major port, exploitation for power and water control of a thoroughly surveyed dam site, further extension of a productive canal system, expanded investment in training and utilizing an agricultural extension service, and encouragement to domestic processing of a familiar local raw material. But after compiling a detailed plan, these four or five tend to lose their importance and vitality among the many dozens of proposals and scores of recommendations approved by the planning body. The laudable goal of achieving coordination by placing all proposals in the setting of a total scheme may in turn actually create a major and awesome problem of coordination.

A special reason for devising such a logically elegant plan is to assess priorities, to use a very popular term. Although in the beginning these may be known with accuracy that is as good for practical purposes as can be attained, after the establishment of a plan the problem of assessing priorities may not be diminished, but rather complicated.

Perhaps the true moral is that total appraisal of an economy from a social point of view does indeed make clear the true complexities of the situation and does properly cloud the confidence with which needs were originally appraised. The immediate point, however, is the questionable virtue of so-called coordination and assessment of priorities through a total plan as a means of getting important things done. Ultimately, given the nature of bureaucracy and political planning, there is no real escape from these handicaps so long as the government tends to assume a major role in determining the nature as opposed to the volume of new investment, and tends to conduct it in large part through government organs.

For Southeast Asian countries, there is an additional serious limitation upon the wisdom of state planning to be mentioned. That is the great reliance of all countries in the area upon international trade—on the movement of world economic activity, and of international markets and prices for their imports and exports. It may be an uncomfortable or an unhappy thought, but it is simply a fact that most countries of the world cannot plan with any rigor or for long periods the nature and volume of their investment programs because the nature and volume of their total economic activity depends as much upon circumstances in the rest of the world as it does upon their domestic resources and intentions to employ them. I have read what purport to be economic development plans for countries so situated, which read almost as if they were classroom exercises in the study of closed economies, to which it was necessary only to append in supplementary fashion some reference to international trade and financial movements and possibly a brief reference to possible changes in terms of trade.

This is patent nonsense for countries which export a tremendous proportion of that part of their national product which originates in a truly monetary and price economy, in order, first, to import many of the materials and services vital for this export production and its transportation and, second, to import most of the goods which are nowadays not merely amenities but in fact necessities to maintain something more than a primitive standard of living for those groups in the population which are fully part of the market and price economy.

The overly simple and ready answer to this problem—and it is too freely advanced even with significant qualifications by serious people—is to decrease substantially the dependence of the country upon international trade. This doctrine might be examined in connection with the examination of the wisdom and efficacy of government planning. However, its real vigor and terrible strength derive so much from its blatant expression and exploitation by special groups that I believe it will be conceded not to be wise in its popularly most effective forms. Therefore, I conclude that it is preferable to discuss it in connection with my third topic, namely, the strength of governments to resist the extension of unwise planning.

The strength of Southeast Asian governments, and particularly those of the newly independent countries, is obviously undergoing, and will continue to undergo, severe tests. In the economic field alone there are necessary responsibilities which are complex and arduous for any modern state, and especially so for Southeast Asian governments, without assumption of the major and additional roles of entrepreneur and investor. Among these responsibilities are postwar reconstruction; maintaining sound government finances while insuring relatively full and stable economic activity; conducting the normal functions of government departments (particularly costly during a period of high international tension); coping with problems of international financial payments; and administering such direct controls on trade as are necessary for vital reasons of international polity and for protection of limited international financial reserves. And as is well known, the governments of Southeast Asia do not have great numbers and deep ranks of experienced public administrators.

It is also commonplace to refer to political weakness or instability in the area, almost as if the reference were to some inner weakness of personalities or national character. At least another view is superficially more apparent, and I believe it also describes the deeper truth. It is obvious that for the moment the countries of the area are experiencing an intense phase of the never-ending political process of defining their constitutional forms and struggling to devise orderly processes for their application—and such political moments are often chronologically of long duration. When I speak of constitutional forms I do not refer only to unique political documents, yet in fact the very written constitutions themselves of Southeast Asian countries are extremely new. National electoral processes are not too clearly tested or even defined, and in several countries have not even yet been given any application. The lines of political groupings and the fissures between them are not precisely known.

There is then not even a sure temporary equilibrium of power forces among various elements in the population— groups wishing power, among other reasons, for its own sake or for the expression of sectional or religious or economic interests. Under these conditions the ability of governments to withstand pressure for ill-conceived or even venal economic schemes, is limited. And it must be pointed out that these are not factors unique in Southeast Asia, but merely that the difficulties are greater there and the problems intensified.

Unfortunately, there is one complex of emotions or interests that is common to most people in most Southeast Asian countries. This is faith in their ability to do almost everything for themselves, combined with distrust in the same things being done for them by foreigners. Parenthetically, it must always be borne in mind that distrust of the foreigner is not at all confined to distrust of the Westerner—in many parts of the area, and for many people in each country, distrust of the Japanese or the Indian or the Chinese may be even more familiar and more intense. As a further parenthesis, it must be observed unhappily that perhaps the greatest danger to the area is failure always to recognize that even native Communism is above all clearly a representative of special, powerful, and highly dangerous foreign interests.

Personal and national pride on the one hand, and distrust of the foreigner on the other, are obviously interrelated attitudes with common roots. It may be unkind but it is nevertheless perhaps useful to point out that the pride rests upon a by no means secure self-assurance so far as many activities are concerned. But the newer countries of the area cannot freely concede the necessity of foreign assistance, technical or administrative, or in enterprise or through capital, without appearing to make some concession to the point of view that they are not thoroughly competent to undertake all their own affairs. And such a concession would call into question psychologically the justification for their successful revolutionary struggles and wars against colonial powers. It must be recalled that stripping away much elaborate verbiage and even sophisticated analysis, the issue of colonialism, on the whole now a dead issue, was in part fought and in great part viewed by the bar of world opinion not in terms of the right to self-government, about which there was little or no argument, but in terms of the simple propositions, "they can't run their own affairs" and "we can."

It is probable that the governments of Southeast Asia are likely to be particularly without sufficient strength to withstand self-interested or emotional attempts to get the government to finance or run any scheme that actually or even superficially represents a lessening of reliance upon the foreigner. Although the motives may be somewhat different, I suppose all this can be summed up in a latter-day phrase as a tendency toward an autarchic system. And I think it can be said dogmatically—certainly I do not have time to discuss it here—that such a direction of movement for the countries of Southeast Asia would have harmful effects both upon the standard of living of their peoples and the prestige of their governments.

In closing, I feel I should make certain disclaimers to you. It goes without saying that what I have given you today are my personal views, rather than an official statement. On the other hand, I hope you will also understand that I have no pretensions regarding the originality of my remarks. And this last disclaimer is particularly important, not only in a personal sense. For my views are indeed in no respect peculiarly an American or even a Western view of Southeast Asian economic problems. It is a fact that throughout my remarks, their gist, and in many places even their very content, could be attributed to some of the prominent and responsible statesmen in each of the Southeast Asian countries. The economic problems of Southeast Asia are not only more keenly felt by the peoples of Southeast Asia, but they are more deeply understood by the leaders of the peoples of the area. It would have been far better and certainly far more illuminating to you if such a statement as mine had been made to you by one of these leaders, as indeed would be consistent with the views of some of them.

As I have been saying throughout my remarks, even though some of my theses today are not only held but vigorously propounded by some statesmen in each Southeast Asian country, they are not popular views in that area. It is easier for me to expound them in Washington than it is for a Southeast Asian to argue them in his parliament, or cabinet, or press. Therefore, it is fitting to conclude with an expression of my admiration and respect for those in Southeast Asia who are continuing to demonstrate that supreme attribute of statesmanship—the determination to exert leadership in a democratic society without abasement before popular misconception and dogma.

Frederick T. Koyle

EXPORT-IMPORT PROBLEMS

IN SOUTHEAST ASIA

SOUTHEAST ASIA IS composed geographically of Indonesia, Malaya, Thailand, Indo-China and Burma; it is a rich tropical area, primarily producing agricultural and mineral products for export as well as for domestic consumption. With few industrial plants, the area is vitally dependent on the importation of manufactured goods of all kinds, especially textiles. Rice is a major import of Malaya and Indonesia. Each country was occupied by the Japanese during World War II, and all have suffered, in varying degrees, the necessity of rehabilitating their economies subsequent to liberation. In Indonesia, economic rehabilitation is overshadowed by the slow return of law and order. In Burma and Malaya, civil strife hinders the restoration of stability. Thailand, where bloodless revolution periodically succeeds revolution, lives in fear of the Chinese threat to embattled Indo-China, the barrier to invasion of Southeast Asia.

With this background of internal turmoil, it is reasonable for the international business man to expect many obstacles to overcome in trading with Southeast Asia. The difficulties are not unusual to this area alone. With few exceptions they are common to the free world, and result from the dislocations in international trade which occurred as a result of World War II, and from the deterioration in the value of national currencies. The factors which complicate trade fall into two groups, one governmental and the other commercial. Governments have been compelled to institute foreign currency control in each Southeast Asian country, accompanied by the licensing of both imports and exports. A restriction of production on some major export commodities has been, and continues to be, under official review. For political reasons, government has placed the import or export of some specific commodities in official hands. Commercially, postwar trading has been burdened by the deterioration of prewar trading standards. More important, lack of internal security does not inspire commercial confidence as to the future. I will discuss each of these as they relate to the countries under review.

The Federation of Malaya (including the Colony of Singapore), as the largest earner of dollars, is an important segment of the British sterling area. All of the regulations controlling the pound sterling are rigidly enforced. The monetary unit, the Straits dollar, is effectively tied to the pound. Long an advocate of free trade, a Malayan merchant expresses concisely his opinion of the effect of government regulations on Malayan trade. In his address to the Singapore Chamber of Commerce at the Annual General Meeting on March 28, 1952, the Hon. E. M. F. Fergusson, Chairman, states: "I must say . . . that it is not easy to follow or understand all the measures that are taken. Import and export controls, Exchange Control and all the other controls, are no way to expand trade. They are obstacles to trade and enterprise, no matter how simply the Government may try to make them operate. Controls mean bureaucracy and forms; they require time, study and staff for the business man; and frustration for the honest trader who sees his less honest competitors find the way to defeat the controls. If the end-point of all these controls is convertibility of sterling, then that end-point is good—but let us not reach it so contracted and restricted in our trade that we may well wonder whether there has been a defeat or a victory. It seems to me that there will have to be boldness and enterprise, qualities which many of us think have been lacking in recent years, in the decisions of those who control the sterling area. Certainly we want no extension of the controls which have forced trade to by-pass Malaya, or made it possible for goods to reach us only by paying much more for them to come by an indirect route than would be the case if they came direct. . . ."

The import and export controls to which Mr. Fergusson refers are administered in Malaya by the Registrar of Imports and Exports. A permit must be obtained by importers covering each import from hard currency areas. Specific permission to purchase foreign exchange to cover these imports is not required, as an import permit itself carries the right to the exchange. Imports may be made more freely from sterling and other soft currency areas than from hard currency areas. These areas are considered to be the whole of North America and South America, Belgium, Germany, Cuba, Japan, the Philippines, Portugal, Spain, Sweden, Switzerland, U.S. dependent territories, and the U.S.S.R. United States dollar exchange is normally granted for few purposes other than the financing of essential imports, for ocean freights payable in American dollars, and for royalties and profits of wholly American-owned subsidiary companies of American firms.

Virtually all foreign exchange arising from the export of goods must be turned over to the exchange control in return for Straits dollars at official rates. The country of destination determines the type of exchange which must be surrendered by the exporter. This restriction has given rise to evasions which are typical of the leakage which arises from all types of control. Foreign buyers of Malayan products with hard currencies, such as dollars, can purchase what is called "transferable sterling" which sells at discounts of 5 to 15 per cent from the official rate of U.S. $2.80. This transferable sterling is only eligible for shipments from the sterling area, including Malaya, to specific countries. However, the buyer, after receiving the goods at destination, promptly reships them to a hard currency area, where the going price for the merchandise corresponds to the sterling price at point of origin translated at official rates of exchange, thereby giving the buyer a 5 to

15 per cent advantage in price over direct shipments (less the additional expense of transshipment, of course). As an undertaking must be given the Exchange Authorities in Malaya that the goods will be consumed in the country of first destination, it is obvious that falsification has taken place and it is only the "less honest competitors" who indulge in this operation. Although this back-door operation may be small relative to the total volume, it is sufficient to handicap legitimate direct trade considerably, as the "honest" buyer must pay more for Malayan goods than his devious competitor.

Due to the precarious financial position of Great Britain, fear of sterling devaluation is ever present. When this fear becomes strongest, Malayan merchants favor possession of goods whose value may appreciate, instead of selling them for sterling currency which may depreciate. This preference temporarily causes an unusual Malayan demand for imports in exchange for sterling, and a decrease in current offerings of Malayan exports. Fortunately, a free market for placing forward exchange contracts exists both in New York and London, where the seller of goods to Malaya for payment in sterling may hedge his risk.

In Indonesia, after the transfer of sovereignty from the Netherlands late in 1949, a new currency, known as the rupiah, was established to replace the local guilder and the enormous flood of currency issued by the Japanese during the occupation. Up until the time of the Korean conflict, Indonesia faced a deficit in international payments. This situation was reversed when the rise in commodity prices after June, 1950, brought to Indonesia a favorable balance of trade and a resultant rise in foreign balances, which was a lifesaver to the new and struggling government. Such steps as incentive payments to producers of exports, actual halving of currency notes to check inflation, one exchange rate for imports and another rate for exports, were undertaken in an earnest desire to rehabilitate the Indonesian economy, so badly disrupted by the Japanese occupation and the struggle for independence from the Dutch. Strict import and export controls were established to prevent wastage of precious foreign exchange.

The importer in Indonesia must submit a proforma invoice, which acts in the nature of a bid, to the Central Bureau for Imports covering all commercial imports. The Bureau awards import permits on the basis of price, quality, and terms of delivery. Exchange permits are usually not granted for goods from hard currency areas when they can be obtained from soft currency areas. Importers established in the prewar era are allotted the largest part of permissible imports from hard currency countries, each prewar importer being given a proportionate share of Indonesia's trade based on past import figures. Preference in the allocation of a certain percentage reserved to newcomers in the import trade is given to newly established Indonesian firms. Trade with soft currency areas is open to all.

A complicated system of dollar export certificates was established in February, 1952, in order to give an incentive to the export of Indonesian goods to hard currency areas. This incentive presently amounts to about 4 per cent of the value of the goods. It is responsible for a discount in market prices of Indonesian produce as compared to Singapore prices, and has upset the historical share of commodity exports to hard currency areas, such as rubber, between Indonesia and Malaya. The value of the incentive has been gradually declining and may eventually be abolished. This type of arbitrary evaluation makes it difficult for the international trader to forecast the value of a given export commodity from Indonesia, and is detrimental to Malaya's exports to hard currency areas. When export duties are changed from time to time without warning, the exporter's difficulties are multiplied. For example, a new and additional export duty of 25 per cent ad valorem was placed in February on rubber and copra; 15 per cent on petroleum, tin, palm oil, palm kernels, pepper and coffee. By August, the export duty on rubber had been reduced to 10 per cent.

Each bid for an Indonesian product submitted by a foreign buyer to an exporter is supposed to be referred to a central bureau before it can be accepted. The bureau determines whether the price bid for the product is comparable to the world market price. In the early part of this year, when the rubber market was declining day by day, an Indonesian exporter I know who had accepted bids from London for rubber because he felt sure that the bureau would agree to the prices, found that his assumption was incorrect. He was forced to cancel the commitment which he had made, much to the delight of the buyers, who could buy the same product elsewhere at lower prices by the time the cancellation was effective. Foreign traders may wonder whether the same risk of cancellation may arise when markets go up.

All foreign currency proceeds from the sale of exports must be turned over to the Foreign Exchange Institute in return for rupiahs, at official rates of exchange which vary from commodity to commodity. Even these rates may change overnight. A dispatch from Jakarta on August 3 stated, "Semi-official sources flatly denied rumors that the government had intended to devalue the Rupiah in view of a worsening economic situation. Indonesia devalued the rupiah 200% (i.e. two-thirds) on February 4th, establishing a rate one U.S. dollar to 11 rupiahs 40 cents. However, today's rupiah is valued at only twenty to a dollar on the free market. . . ." Despite the denials, however, fears of devaluation of the Indonesian currency continue to hamper the operations of Indonesian import and export firms. The placing of contracts for far-forward delivery is virtually impossible. Exporters to Indonesia, however, have no problem, as the price which they receive is in foreign currency fixed at time of contract. It is the Indonesian buyer who does not know what his goods will be worth in rupiahs at time of delivery.

In Thailand the restrictions on foreign exchange have not been as onerous as they have in Indonesia or Malaya, and exporters have been permitted to retain a certain percentage of the foreign exchange resulting from exports of Thai products. At present import permits are required only for automobiles, motorcycles, linseed oil and tung oil. Foreign exchange currency proceeds realized from the export of commodities, except the most important, rice, rubber and tin, may be utilized to procure imports of any commodity. Exporters of rubber are required to surrender to the Bank of Siam 20 per cent of foreign currency proceeds, the exporters of tin to surrender 50 per cent, while exporters of rice may retain foreign exchange in excess of the varying percentage specified from time to time for exports of rice. Importers who do not have a supply of exchange from exports have to buy foreign exchange for general imports on the open market, where rates are approximately 100 per cent higher than the official rate. Arbitrary gradual lowering by the authorities of the local rate for the pound sterling, which affected the rates of all free exchange in the spring of 1952, considerably upset the import-export trade in Thailand, and is another illustration of the uncertainties faced by the foreign trader.

In Burma, import permits are required for almost all commodities from any country whatsoever. Exchange permits are required but are not automatically issued with import permits. Her principal export is rice to other Asian countries, and is officially controlled. In Indo-China, all operations in foreign exchange and importations of merchandise are under government control. All imports are subject to an import license, which carries the right to the necessary foreign exchange. Licenses for imports from the dollar area are granted only for essential merchandise not obtainable within the French franc area.

From controls, we turn to production in Southeast Asia, and its effect on trade. The years 1950 and 1951 were profitable ones for Southeast Asia. The Korean conflict insured a world-wide demand, at constantly increasing prices, for the principal export products, among them rubber, tin, copra, petroleum, palm oil and kernels. Rising prices brought rising costs of production and higher wages. Today, Southeast Asia faces the problem of readjustment to lower prices for its exports. The most important, rubber, has dropped from about 80 cents U.S. per pound in late 1950 to about 30 cents today. Copra dropped from $261.50 per ton in March, 1951, to $112.00 today. Rubber production, which exceeded 700,000 tons in Malaya in 1950, is estimated at only 550,000 tons for 1952. More than half the population of Malaya is dependent upon the export of rubber in one way or another. Therefore, this serious decline in price as well as in production poses a most serious economic problem to the Malayan authorities, harassed as they are at the same time by terrorists. A dispatch from Kuala Lumpur on July 28 stated: "Malaya's rapidly worsening financial position is causing widespread concern. . . . Malaya's money troubles have followed rapidly in the wake of falling rubber prices. . . . Against a favorable trade balance of 981,000,000 Straits Dollars ($320 million) for the first six months of last year, there has been a debit balance of 41,000,000 Straits Dollars (about $13,500,000) in the same period this year. . . ."

The taxes from high profits of 1950 and 1951 helped to defray the expense of maintaining an army of well over 100,000 men, to fight 5,000 bandits. These profits are now being severely curtailed. Efforts are being made to reduce wages, swollen by high rubber and tin prices. The rising cost of living has not been checked by the fall in the price of Malaya's exports. Food prices are still high because many farmers, who have been resettled in new areas to isolate them from the bandits, have been restricted in their work for their own safety, and Malayan food production will continue to lag as long as the emergency continues. A Chinese business man from Malaya told me that many of Malaya's economic problems would be solved if the terrorists could be wiped out. Rice, which is the staple of the Malayan diet, now costs about twelve times what it cost in 1939. The price of rubber, on the other hand, has only doubled. The price of tin, which in 1939 averaged 50 cents per pound, is now $1.20.

The dread spectre of competition from synthetic rubber hangs over the rubber producing areas. In the United States a synthetic with rubber-like properties, called "GR-S" is being produced and sold at 23 cents per pound. In Malaya, the average cost of production of top grade natural rubber from an estate is calculated to be about 26 cents per pound, lower grades somewhat less. While GR-S is not a completely adequate substitute for top grade natural rubber, it appears that it is a satisfactory replacement for 50 or 60 per cent of the total American demand, which is principally for lower grade natural rubber.

It is inevitable that countries which are so dependent upon the production and the price of a single commodity such as rubber, should seek some assurance from the consuming countries, principally the United States, that they will use as much of Southeast Asia's production at reasonable prices as they can. An international working party is now meeting in London to discuss a request from the rubber producing areas in Southeast Asia for an international agreement designed to reach this goal. While consuming countries may well appreciate the necessity, even at a sacrifice, of maintaining the economy of this area to strengthen it against aggression, experience shows that it takes many months to reach a workable agreement, if at all. Therefore, it appears that the volume of rubber moving to America will increase but little in the near future, although the long term consumption trend indicates that there should be a market for all kinds of rubber later on, as the world demand expands.

In Indonesia the Government is dependent for its very existence on a large volume of exports. The currency proceeds make possible, to a major extent, the imports of food and manufactured goods on which maintenance of the Indonesian standard of living so much depends. Unless the present government can satisfy the current needs of its huge population, much less increase its standard of living, I understand that the radicals, who are a very substantial minority, will probably attempt to overthrow the present regime. We can understand then why Indonesia is so anxious for an international agreement to assure a market for its chief export. However, international agreements, either to fix prices or to restrict production, are bound to curtail the full flow of trade. The ultimate solution may be a reduction in production costs which will permit free competition between natural and synthetic rubber. It is very hard to persuade an agricultural population, which has been promised through propaganda that eventually it will no longer need to work, that the solution of Indonesia's present difficulties lies only in greater production and longer hours of labor.

There are several examples of governmental participation in the export trade which may be justified by current circumstances but, in the long run, are detrimental to private enterprise. After protracted negotiations, the Indonesian Government sold 54,000 tons of tin directly to the United States Government, covering delivery over a period of three years. This represents a substantial volume of export business, which in pre-World War years was handled by private exporting firms, and for shipments to the United States by importers. Only recently, the United States lifted its ban on the private importation of tin into this country, but such government to government sales have left little for American importers to buy. In Thailand, the Government has taken over entirely a number of enterprises, in other cases requiring 51 per cent Siamese ownership of companies. The export of rice is handled entirely by the Government, as is also the case in Burma.

The present-day buyer of Southeast Asia's products finds a change has occurred in the marketing structure. Considering the political upheaval which has taken place, it is not surprising. Before the war, in Indonesia, practically the entire export trade was in the hands of long established Dutch merchants. The prewar buyer dealt with these organizations in full confidence that not only the letter, but the spirit of his contract with them would be fulfilled. Complaints against shipments, such as short weight, inferior grading, or late delivery were exceptional, and were always compensated for immediately. Today, some of the same firms are still in existence but their activities have been curtailed, and to some extent they have been replaced by new organizations which have become established in the postwar period. We find that the deterioration in methods of operation and in fulfillment of the details of contracts, which has become so prevalent in other countries since the war, is evident. These conditions have introduced a risk in doing business that the merchant can only compensate for by paying less.

To some extent this same deterioration in standards has taken place in Malaya, though there has not been the same violent political change that has occurred in Indonesia. Years ago the import-export trade of Malaya was handled principally by British trading firms, whose reputation for fair dealing and integrity made it possible for the rest of the world to deal with them unhesitatingly. Much of their business has been taken over in the last few years by new trading organizations, lacking the experience and the standards of the older firms. This situation enhances considerably the risk of doing business with Malaya. As an example, the U.S. Government Agency, which in 1951 was the sole importer of crude rubber in the United States, stated that 42 per cent of all rubber imported from all sources into the United States in 1951 was inferior to the grade purchased. Before the war, such a percentage of inferior deliveries would have been improbable. Deterioration in commercial standards operates both as a burden to the buyer and a loss to the seller. In a free economy the natural selection of the good buyer by the seller and of the good seller by the buyer eventually tends to correct this situation. With the restrictions that exist today, however, it is unlikely that true economic forces will operate.

In an effort to prevent unusual quantities of rubber from going behind the iron curtain, Malaya has instituted destinational control of exports. Licenses are issued for shipments to Russia and satellite countries, in terms of only their normal consumption of rubber. Indonesia offers to sell its rubber wherever it finds the best market, but actually, price control and incentives to sell to hard currency areas effectively prevent shipments to other than politically desirable destinations. In Thailand, a government-to-government agreement has been made with the United States, which expires at the end of 1952, assuring the United States about 80 per cent of the total Thai production. At a time when the United States has practically completed its strategic stockpile, and the use of natural rubber in the United States has been replaced to a considerable extent with synthetic rubber, which leaves an unsold surplus in the producing countries, it is questionable how long these forms of destinational control can continue in the face of pressure from rubber producers seeking to find any outlet for their production. Restriction of outlets, no matter how desirable politically, hampers trade, and is an open invitation to smuggling.

Southeast Asia, separated from its principal market by water, is well served by numerous shipping companies of every nationality, although shipping space in a period of high activity, such as during the heavy importation of textiles in the early part of 1951, may be temporarily scarce. In general, shipping has been adequate. However, port congestion at Jakarta, Belawan, Singapore and other ports has frequently retarded the unloading and loading of ships. From time to time, slowdown strikes have also severely delayed shipments. The inter-island steamer service in Indonesia was re-established after the war and is responsible for the renewed flow of goods from the outlying small ports to the main shipping ports of Surabaya, Semarang, Tanjong Priok, and Belawan. Communications have not been restored to their prewar efficiency. Cables to and from the area are still subject to delays in transit, which makes quick consummation of transactions difficult; even though it is possible to telephone to some parts of the area, such as Java, telephone communication with Malaya is not yet available from the United States.

Being primarily producers of agricultural products and minerals, and with a growing population eager to raise its standard of living, Southeast Asia is a great potential market for the manufactured goods of the industrial nations. Light manufactured goods, such as electrical appliances and refrigerators, also have a tremendous potential market, although at present it is restricted by the shortage of electric power. When I arrived at the Raffles Hotel in Singapore this February, I found it lit only with candles during the daily "brownout" in that city. Heavy equipment, i.e. capital goods, is urgently needed throughout this area, first to replace the destruction which occurred during the occupation and the months of civil strife which followed, and secondly, to provide badly needed additional transportation facilities, electrical power, water supply, etc. If commodity prices had maintained their high levels of 1950–51, the demand for machinery on the part of Southeast Asia would have been considerable, in spite of the restrictions on the use of foreign currency except for essential needs. However, commodity prices have receded in some cases to less than half of their previous high. The sterling area shortage of dollars is now so acute that it is doubtful if any considerable sum will be allotted to Malaya by the British for the purchase of dollar area manufactured goods except for those in most urgent need. In Indonesia, the heavy cost of government and the threatened deficit in payments will make it practically impossible to secure acutely needed capital equipment, except that provided through grants in aid or from government loans. The restriction on transfer of capital funds and of dividends, plus the uncertainties surrounding the question of political stability, make private investment on the part of the foreign investors unattractive.

There appears to be no immediate solution to these problems. They are part of a world-wide dislocation caused by the adulteration of money and the constant threat to the security of free nations. Perhaps the preceding recital of handicaps to trade sounds as if little was being accomplished; yet, the 1951 figures show the greatest trading volume ever. For example, in 1939 total Malayan trade was reported as Sts. $1,378,-300,000; in 1951 the corresponding amount was Sts. $10,710,-857,902. Of course, allowance must be made for the depreciation of currency which has taken place meantime. Some commodities, such as tea, sugar and petroleum have not reached their prewar production levels; others, such as tin and rubber, exceed it.

Last March, I asked an exporter in Jakarta to explain to me how, in spite of all these problems, he was able to sell rubber to me in the United States. After he had given me a lengthy explanation of the forms, permits, and steps essential to the operation, I said, "It is a wonder to me that anything is shipped from Indonesia at all." He replied, "Don't worry. Somehow, there will always be a person with the patience and the determination to get the goods away."

From a businessman's point of view, the primary hope for the future of our increasing trade with Southeast Asia lies in the restoration of internal security in all parts of the area. An order once accepted must be certain of fulfillment. There must be no delay in shipping. High standards of commercial practice and grading must be achieved. The buyer and the seller must be confident that proper financing and foreign exchange is available. When this Utopia is achieved, international trade will flourish. It is too much to hope that the controls which now handicap trade with the area will soon be lifted; that all currencies will be made freely convertible. Meanwhile, private enterprise must do the best job possible under the circumstances.

E. H. G. Dobby

FOOD AND THE CHANGING FUNCTION

OF SOUTHEAST ASIA

It is easy to be preoccupied with political developments in Southeast Asia and miss its shifting economic balance and changing function. Change has been characteristic of Southeast Asia for the last hundred years, involving transformations probably more drastic than most in the West over the same period. Early last century this was a region of transit between the Sino-Pacific fringe and the Indo-European fringe of Asia —for a commerce which used Southeast Asia as a corridor to be passed through as quickly as its physical obstructions allowed. Later Southeast Asia became of interest for what was within it; it began to function as a source of commodities and as a consumer of manufactured goods. This function turned Southeast Asia inside out into the pattern which existed to 1940. Politically the territory became compartmentalized into colonies of the Western industrial powers which penetrated from the seaways and shaped Southeast Asia into political units more sharply defined than previously. These units, now Burma, Malaya, Indonesia, Indo-China and the Philippines, were mostly of parts which had little in common politically except the link to a common metropolis overseas; often they had little economic difference except a different metropolitan focus.

Sweeping economic changes accompanied the contact of Western and Southeast Asian ways in the intimate embrace of colonialism.

The metropolitan powers explored for mineral resources, injected capital into the region, and established new lines of communication within and without. Tin, gold and oil were found and some agricultural commodities like rubber, vegetable oils and sugar were developed for industrial purposes. These gave new significance and new values to Southeast Asian localities. Much less known is the story of spectacular transfers of native agriculture by indigenous people: during the past hundred years, over fifty million acres of virgin land were cleared and converted into an agriculture, primarily serving Asian needs. So tremendous an achievement in this area, whose forest cover is of a kind difficult to clear and forbidding even to our modern equipment, was the more remarkable because it was done by simple peasant methods, neither greatly encouraged by the metropolitan powers nor aided by their equipment or their social and economic techniques. Conversions of whole countrysides to rice farming went on in this manner in new sectors of Lower Burma, Lower Siam, and Lower Indo-China.

The industrial and food commodities which came forward in consequence of both these changes involved large quantities: millions of tons of them moved overland, along the rivers and through the islands, made possible by reason of the West's transport revolution, in particular the steamer and the Suez Canal, which enabled bulky low grade materials to travel cheaply over the great distances between Southeast Asia's producers and their customers, whether Asian or Western.

The change to productivity was accompanied by population expansions and regroupings. People shifted to localities which had not attracted people before. The gravitation was toward the zones which, while of high agricultural value, were also in contact with the new trading streams in Southeast Asia. Fertile deltas were reclaimed and gradually filled with farmers. Older inland centers of influence shrank and regions near the ports assumed dominance. Dozens of new towns and cities came into being. Traditional rural aristocracies retained their form, weakening when there arose rich merchant groups with different values and interests and loyalties.

The transformation made Southeast Asia an El Dorado toward which millions of Indians and Chinese moved. Its industrial commodities offered them wages and prospects denied them in the static economies of their homelands. Its new transport systems introduced them to Western engineering. These Asian foreigners were true colonists; they settled in Southeast Asia. Nationals of the metropolitan powers were transient administrative or managerial types—and never more than a handful of them by comparison. The Asian colonists identified themselves with industry, trade, and urbanization.

The map of Southeast Asia was thus changed by new crops, new materials, new people and new ways, and by old peoples moving into new places. The region came to contain an extraordinary mixture of the ancient and the modern, standing side by side and one above the other: a conjunction of new and old was met on every plane, in the use of land, in social life, in economy, and in politics. By comparison with the pattern of 1840, Southeast Asia was scarcely recognizable in 1940 when its products had become of major importance to the West—for its transport and electrical industries and for food canning and printing.

Whatever its function for the West, Southeast Asia had a critical one for Asia. It was the only source for commercial rice.

At least two-thirds of the new land brought into cultivation in Southeast Asia was for padi. In consequence, rice formed by far the greatest volume of any commodity produced. A huge rice trade developed and by 1940 Southeast Asia was producing nearly 20 per cent of Asia's rice and contributing more than two-thirds of all rice in international trade.

The conversion of Southeast Asia into a large-scale rice producer took place at a time when the rice eating populations of India, China and Japan found their own food-growing capacity reaching its limits. At the opening of the twentieth century, most Asian countries were not far from self-supporting in rice. India, China and Japan brought in foreign rice chiefly to offset the vagaries of their own harvests. Southeast Asia functioned for them as a safety valve, an assurance against fluctuating harvests at home. When the Far East began industrializing and urbanizing as the century advanced, their degree of self-sufficiency steadily lessened. The need of India, China and Japan for external rice became chronic rather than occasional. Their industrialization was only possible providing Southeast Asia continued as a rice exporter, and at low prices. Their first steps in industry were based on labor of a cheapness offsetting its other limitations. As "rice granary" to the countries of the East, Southeast Asia therefore had a function more vital for their domestic and economic stability than were the industrial commodities it provided for the Western world which had alternative sources and substitutes.

The peasant who produced Southeast Asia rice aimed for his family and helpers, if any, to be fed directly by the rice grown from his fields. His was the subsistence mode of farming. Workers in the rice fields ate much of what they grew, as opposed to the Western mode of selling the whole crop for cash by which the farmer's food is bought and the laborers paid. Commercial or cash farming gives flexibility and purchasing power, opening a wide range of foods and other necessities to all concerned: the subsistence system limits a farmer's diet to what his ground can produce, narrowing its range though mostly providing ample quantity.

From his crop, the rice farmer paid dues in kind and then sold what was surplus to feeding his family. Rice in trade was made up of the small surpluses derived from these dues in kind and from the excess to farm consumption, the two being related. The farmer could accept low prices for his surplus because his basic needs and those of his helpers had been met before rice left his farm. Thus the rice flowing to international trade did so at prices not geared to the true costs of production. As a surplus, it could be sold by the farmer at a price not based on the monetary value of labor, work and time needed to produce rice. In this sense Southeast Asian rice was being marketed at a price which was not economic. Our conception of Southeast Asia as a source of cheap food arose because the full costs of producing rice were concealed from the market by the subsistence system. Since the price of rice was not an approximation to its economic value, the structure of costings in Southeast Asia was fallacious. The cost of living for Asians in the towns and industries, dominated by their intake of rice, only appeared to be low because their staple food was not priced on the same basis as the foods, wheat or potatoes or meat, upon which Western costs hinge.

At least three-quarters of Southeast Asian rice farms were cultivated in the subsistence mode by 1940. Today the proportion cannot be less than 90 per cent.

The Far Eastern war and its train of events modified rice production in proportion more than in pattern. After only a brief decline, the over-all acreage under padi in the whole monsoon fringe has risen to nearly 10 per cent above prewar; the reported production totals as high as before. In Burma and Indo-China, about a quarter of the padiland is still out of production. The subsistence mode helped to buffer rice from the paralysis of wartime disruption and the over-all acreage and production in Southeast Asia were only slightly down for the first postwar quinquennium compared with the last prewar one. Most novelty shows in the surplus. The amount of rice now moving into international trade from Burma, Siam, and Indo-China is barely half what it was in the late thirties, though there are at least ten million extra people in the deficit areas of Southeast Asia, and probably fifty million extra in other Asian rice-eating countries.

Part of the explanation for the diminished outflow is of course the substantial increase of population within the surplus countries. Each is eating more of its local rice. This is a permanent feature. A rice surplus disappears fast in subsistence farming whose wet technique remains more horticultural than agricultural. Today between the Southeast Asian producer and the international market stand not only the new mouths in his family but also armed men; whether these be bandits, gangs or armies, they require to be fed, stealing or absorbing the surplus from the cultivator. Even if we expect these to be disbanded in time, the members of the groups will be there in one form or another and, not being in general producers of food themselves, they will still need to be fed, albeit on a more conventional basis. The landlord has retreated or been eliminated from the countrysides of Burma, Indo-China and Java; he no longer receives his rent or dues in kind, which induced many farmers to obtain a surplus and added to the flow of rice into commerce. Redistribution of land, legal or otherwise, removes this inducement. Agrarian reform in a subsistence context, while possibly filling bellies, thus lends weight to the argument that the out-turn of rice into trade must continue to decline unless other changes take place.

We must be reminded that the areas previously having rice surpluses were in each country very small in proportion to the planted acreage. None of the rice exporter countries of Southeast Asia had extensive regions of surplus comparable to the Middle West and Australia. Because of the horticultural technique, these sections where the average population per cultivated acre is more than about one, have no surplus, and few localities of Southeast Asia now have nutrition densities that low.

These are constant factors likely to restrict rice surpluses when internal transport becomes easier. They justify thinking that Southeast Asia is within sight of no longer providing the rice exports to the Asian world.

For what rice surplus there is, the increased populations everywhere in Asia stimulate an unprecedented competition among buying countries. India and Japan must obtain some of it, on humanitarian and political grounds, to hold down the drift towards wage disputes and disorder in their urban areas. China would be in the same position if it were not for its curtain. Malaya is as ever bidding for international rice because it specializes in the production of industrial raw materials. Indonesia and Ceylon, now less self-contained in rice, are major bidders also. Political and currency problems lead the governments of all territories concerned to be actively interested in the rice market. In Burma and Thailand, government agencies monopolize the surplus rice of their nationals. The governments of deficit countries negotiate purchases of rice from the governments of the surplus countries. This is entirely a postwar development. It puts some governments in the position of being able to play politics with the foods of millions, though their expressed object is to eliminate private exploitation of the situation. The price at which the government agents handle rice works in two ways. By it the surplus areas set something like a pegged price for their domestic producers. In deficit countries, the government selling price works to keep down the urban price of rice and sets a level toward which gravitates the price expected by domestic producers for their surpluses.

Together with this change of character, there has been a change in value. Rice has risen to incredibly high prices. No other grain has so steadily advanced on the international market since the war. In 1939, Southeast Asian rice traded at about £7 a ton; in 1945, governments were purchasing from Siam and Burma at about £17 a ton and private dealers were paying more; the 1952 crop in Rangoon is being marketed at £50 a ton. For sterling area countries, rice has multiplied its price sevenfold over the past twelve years. In terms of U.S. currency the rise has been fivefold.

The return moving toward the producer in surplus countries has increased proportionally, though he may not be receiving the full benefit of new prices. They have passed fully to the deficit areas and the industrial workers. Southeast Asian milled rice today costs about 60 per cent more than wheat in Chicago. Rangoon rice costs US $30 more than Louisiana rice.

At such prices a rice diet even in the United States would be a luxury.

Thus Southeast Asia has ceased to be cheap as a supplier of Asian food.

We must weigh the implications.

If economic conditions of the kind which apply in our own agriculture operated among Southeast Asia rice producers, prices of this new order would cause rice productions to expand. They do not. The subsistence context prevents high prices operating quickly as an inducement for the same reasons and to much the same extent that it prevents low prices acting as a deterrent. A more immediate effect is that the rice surplus governments now find rice the chief source of their funds and their chief political strength at home and abroad. The Government of Burma, whose country has the simplicity of economic structure characteristic of Southeast Asian states, depends for its income more on direct profit as a rice trader and less on revenue by taxation. The Burmese and Thai governments, now the chief rice traders, have thus acquired an interest in maintaining the high price.

By remaining consistently expensive, this grain has lifted the cost of living for Southeast Asian urban and industrial workers, the more so because the Asian habitually takes a far larger proportion of rice in a meal than an American or a European takes of any one item in his diet. Other local food produce has moved higher in step with rice: local eggs in rural Malaya, for example, are today more expensive than those in the United States. In several Southeast Asian countries, the cost of living has multiplied four times compared with prewar. In Thailand and Indonesia, the one a surplus and the other a deficit rice area, the cost of living has moved to far higher multiples, complicated for them by currency changes. In India and Ceylon, it has more than trebled. Japan appears to have escaped such steep rises, yet its increasing purchases of rice from Burma and Thailand must lead its costs of living upward.

These changes in the value of the Southeast Asian staple food show little sign of reversing the trend we have been tracing. To import food, principally rice, India must spend about three times as much this year as it did for 1950–51 despite a lower return from its raw materials and industries. Costs of labor and processing in Southeast Asia are taking on new proportions. Producers of raw materials find their costs, tied as they must be to the price of rice, have little resemblance to prewar figures. External pressure on them to bring the selling price of rubber, tin, vegetable oils and sugar back to levels approaching the prewar is worsening the internal situation. Southeast Asian labor employed in these industries is being caught in the cross-fire of a form of economic warfare conducted by other governments. The United States buying agency with its power as the greatest single consumer has been lowering its bids for industrial commodities at the same time as Asian governments lift their offering price for rice, backed by the argument that they must raise the economic return of their own people. There is grave danger that this will end in the collapse of most existing commodity producers and of the factories and local industries which we have been encouraging for raising local standards of living. Factories, businesses, utilities, plantations, mines and governments in Southeast Asia find their costs have risen steeply and that the cost of rice-eating labor is the critical component.

Southeast Asia has clearly ceased to be a region of cheap labor. By its influence on rice exports, it affects costs in town and industrial life in other parts of Asia which therefore is ceasing to be the continent of cheap labor and cheap processing.

Nothing could be a greater incentive to mechanization than these new costs. The mechanical method is, however, slow in appearing in rural Southeast Asia. Its chief industrial commodities, rubber, sugar and the vegetable oils, do not readily lend themselves to mechanization. In rice farming, it is almost nonexistent, though experiments are going on at a number of points. The subsistence-horticultural mode and related social factors weigh heavily against the mechanization of rice in addition to matters of capital and to the technicalities of wet cultivation. But at the new prices, rice-farming offers substantial rewards as a commercial proposition and possibly the mechanized approach is not far beyond the present horizon, though not in the present rice-growing regions. While promising mass production, mechanical farming on existing rice-lands offers no solution to the problem of what to do with the labor it must displace; it offers greatest promise in new places.

Its expanding demand and maintained high price cause rice to draw the interest of other parts of the world. It has become commercially attractive now to regions where it has no heritage, no restriction to old methods and no inertia of society or population to impede profitable manners of producing it. Since the war, British Guiana and Australia have been exporting rice well below Southeast Asia prices, though not in great volume. A general increase of rice acreage outside Asia has become apparent. By comparison with 1940, Asia in 1950 had added thirteen million acres to its padilands; the rest of the world in that time added seven million. Over the same interval, Asia's annual padi production increased about two million tons: that of Brazil alone increased by more. In 1940 less than 5 per cent of the world's padiland was outside Asia; today about 8 per cent of a greater world total is outside Asia.

Rice growing is further from being an Asian monopoly.

The failure of Southeast Asia as a whole to respond as other parts of the world have done, underlines that its subsistence system of rice-growing is more a mode of living that an economic means of production. In territories outside Asia, rice growing is a business. The self-contained mode of Southeast Asia acts to restrict the buying interest as well as the buying power of its farmers. Normally they show little wish or pressure to buy anything. It might go a long way to stimulate them to sell more rice if we could rouse their wish to buy. That was part of the function of the middleman in the past: he provoked and encouraged the buying appetite of the peasant as part of the process of bringing him to sell his rice. The salesman function of the much-abused middleman was a fillip to the rice outflow, and by eliminating him one spur to it is removed.

These factors all contribute to the tension being built up in Southeast Asia. The urban and more vocal workers face an increasing shortage in their staple food at a time when a higher standard of living is expected and is still being promised by those who woo them, whether left, right or center. The West cannot ignore the consequent unease and, if existing systems do not permit or encourage the kind of planning to eliminate the deficit, the West will need to take action in sheer self-preservation. Economic breakdown is a contagious disease that can take ten thousand miles in its stride.

Four methods of expanding Asian food supply can be seen: increasing yields on existing farms; increasing the flow of foods from other parts of the world; increasing the range of diet among Asians; and increasing the acreages under padi.

To increase yields sufficiently to be relevant requires us to reach the peasant and teach him; illiteracy, prejudice, and inaccessibility make that difficult and mostly impractical for the West to take part in. The peasant, we must remember, is already convinced—he has been pressed to raise yields at most points to maintain his extra dependents. Effort to this end from within must be continued in the existing padifields if only to keep pace with increasing populations around them, yet it can make little difference to present rice deficit areas or to urban needs.

The flow of foods from elsewhere has started. Rice has been moving into Southeast Asia from the United States, Brazil, Egypt and Australia. Substantial tonnages of wheat and flour are being absorbed by Indonesia, Indo-China, the Philippines and Japan. Because wheat producers respond readily to change in demand, this trend reminds us how pressure from the padifields of Southeast Asia becomes transferred to the wheatfields of the Americas or Australia—and may increase.

Here is a sign that the eating habit of Asians can change, especially among the accessible ones in towns and industries. By it the range of Southeast Asian diets is extending. Slices of bread covered with tomato, chili or fish sauce are now to be seen in the hands of children and artisans in Malaya. Potatoes are regularly used in curries. Corn as a vegetable and as a sweet is more popular. An expansion of off-season maize growing is developing where fields are suitable, though only the Philippines and Eastern Java do so on a large scale at present. Not all padifields permit off-season use in this way.

But it is the remedy of increasing the acreage under padiland which appears to lend itself best to Western technicians. Hitherto the creation of new padilands has been chiefly by peasant methods involving a few acres per person, scarcely achieving more than keeping pace with the population and often confined to the margins of existing rice-lands. It has been tried also by the process of resettlement, shifting people to small holdings in new areas, only to find the locality filling with people at a rate nearly equalling that of the extra acreage created. The population-acreage correlation in smallholder-subsistence contexts works to that end. No surplus of a major order comes from that device alone. A high out-turn per person engaged must be the objective if we are to get food to the urban and industrial markets. The mechanized attack on new territories on the basis of commercial rice farms has yet to be tried though it does offer an expectation of high production, given virgin land, regional planning and a small cadre of skilled farmers.

Are there any places left which suit this approach? Southeast Asia still has them. The deltas of Borneo and thousands of square miles of swamp in East Sumatra are lying practically empty, suiting rice cultivation and calling for regional planning such as international action, whether capitalist or collectivist, makes possible. Except for a few colonies of transferred small holders in Mindanao, South Borneo and South Sumatra, those regions are gaping holes in the pattern of Southeast

Asian production, neglected hitherto because of the limited human groups in the uplands behind them and because rice prices were uneconomic. They offer today the prospect of restoring to Southeast Asia its functions as a pioneer area, as a surplus rice producer, as a try-out for Western technology and as a safety valve. There is ample opportunity for transforming the land-use map of large sectors of Southeast Asia, as the Burmese, Siamese and Indo-Chinese did not long ago under different sociological conditions and with much more limited power to attack their difficult terrains.

We may think, too, of the virgin spaces around the Congo and the Amazon where rice will also grow, though distance from the Asian market debar them from first consideration.

What is the outlook in rural areas of Southeast Asia where a rice-surplus is already being produced?

The restoration of transport and communications in those countries will carry to the rice farmers news of the price his government gets for exporting his rice. That is certain. Whether these two factors will lead to a significantly greater outflow is open to doubt. If they do, the price may drop a little, though the long-term outlook for this grain suggests it cannot drop far. If they do not, the rice farmer will want part of the high price passed down the line to him for what little fraction of his crop he can sell. Governments may find this most desirable. It is the natural means for spreading purchasing power in the rural areas where the new independencies face the same problems as the old colonial administrations; their farming regions have a high production but a small turnover, little internal trade, and therefore little upon which taxes may be based to provide revenue—revenue these governments desperately need. Without it they have no means of fulfilling the promise upon which they floated into power. They might well solve the problem, not merely by passing on the price, but by working to convert the padifarmer into a commercial farmer, accustoming him to the idea of selling all his crop and purchasing all his needs. In that way lies the one hope of giving the Asian farmer fair value for the time and labor put into his crop. His purchasing power will broaden the basis of life for the rice grower, giving him the whole world to draw upon for food—much as the wheat farmer of the Middle West can purchase greater variety of food than the one or two crops his kind of land produces. In that way lies hope of diversifying the food intake of rural Asians and spreading what rice there is among greater numbers who will supplement it with a range of other foods.

Exploring their own mode of production on lines like these, the new independencies may find complete commercialization of rice to be the long-awaited device to induce money flows and trade in their territories, to widen their economy and get them out of the impasse of having productive land, industrious people, and no revenues. No other solution is more than a palliative or a mere tinkering with the outdated and defective machinery of the subsistence system which is less broken down in Southeast Asia than in India, China and Japan.

For the rest of the world, if rice production by reason of its new price levels or by governmental direction, be transformed into a money economy, besides removing the threat inherent in so many people living without an adequate reward for their work, it must create in Southeast Asia an enormous capacity to purchase. In that way Southeast Asia can help to solve also the problem of the industrial world—how to find markets large enough to use up mountains of products without wasting them in a continuous state of war.

Vu Quoc Thong

SOME THOUGHTS ON THE ECONOMIC DEVELOPMENT OF VIET-NAM IN THE ASIAN WORLD OF TOMORROW

THE PROBLEM WHICH the Government of Viet-Nam faces at present is the transformation of the colonial economy of that state into a national economy; and from a subsistence economy into one of well-being.

It is indispensable to underline immediately the fact that this problem is not one of full employment—as in the industrialized countries—nor one of productivity.

First of all, the problem of full employment. In fact, in Viet-Nam there is no question of remedying a temporary disequilibrium between supply and demand, but rather of reducing the exaggerated gap between the supply when faced with a constantly reduced demand. This is easy to understand. In Viet-Nam the supply of products and even of food is insufficient in the face of a constantly increasing population pressure.

Neither is it the problem of productivity which should be solved. Being underdeveloped, Viet-Nam merely attempts—for the moment at least—to produce more for the requirements of the internal market, and not to produce cheaply.

What should be the solution of this problem? It is hardly deniable that industrialization is indispensable in order to transform a colonial economy into a national economy. Therefore, in order to arrive at a real national economy, Viet-Nam will have to industrialize so as to be able to transform the majority of her products herself instead of simply exporting her raw materials. It is also true that industrialization is one of the primary conditions of any evolution toward a higher standard of living. The Viet-Namese population increases regularly by more than 1 per cent per annum. Of course, this birthrate is not too high when compared with that of other states in Southeast Asia, but in order to absorb this surplus of manpower there is no better method than industrialization, because an exclusively agricultural economy offers little chance for the absorption of additional labor. Likewise, the increase of national revenue, and consequently the rise of the living standard of the majority of the population, cannot be rapidly achieved through an agricultural economy.

Therefore, the industrialization of Viet-Nam is the most urgent solution of the economic problem which that state faces at present.

Moreover, it is necessary to know whether Viet-Nam meets the conditions required for such a task. One must recognize that Viet-Nam enjoys a rather favorable situation in this field. First of all, Viet-Nam possesses the necessary manpower; its population is hard-working and able to adapt itself rapidly to the modern techniques. Secondly, Viet-Nam is provided with abundant and varied natural resources. Through its coal fields in the North, Viet-Nam may be classed as one of the countries in Asia which is best provided with this material. These fields are easy to exploit and easily accessible. The coal mines of Quang Yen, Than Me, Dong Dang and Tuyen Quang, for example, constitute a solid base for the industrialization of the country. Before the Second World War, in 1939, the coal production of Viet-Nam amounted to two and one-half million tons. The events of the war have considerably damaged the coal production. However, according to present plans, coal production in the next decade will total 60 million tons, with an increase of the production from 190,000 tons in 1945 to 629,000 tons in 1951, and to approximately 900,000 tons in 1953, should the necessary equipment arrive.

Besides coal, Viet-Nam also has considerable reserves of hydraulic energy thanks to the existence of a favorable hydrographic system. We are certain that, with a rational program of dam construction, the question of electrical power supply to the industrial centers of the country can be easily solved.

Viet-Nam also possesses large reserves of tungsten, tin, lead, zinc and iron. Certain mines were opened in the days before 1939 and results have been very encouraging.

One must not forget also that Viet-Nam is a producer of rubber and rice, the two products which constitute, in a certain way, the agricultural capital of the nation. So far as rubber is concerned, the war events have had, without a doubt, a detrimental effect upon production. Still, production is on the increase. In 1950, 51,763 metric tons were exported as against 41,555 tons in 1949. According to conservative estimates, this production could easily be increased to 100,000 tons per annum.

While listing the factors favorable to the industrialization of Viet-Nam, one must also underline the exceptionally favorable geographic situation of this state. With its coastline extending for 2,350 kilometers from the Gulf of Siam to the Chinese border, and provided with the excellent ports of Saigon, Tourane, and Haiphong, Viet-Nam constitutes an important maritime transit center for Central Southeast Asia. Viet-Nam is also an important turn-table for all major airlines crossing the Asiatic continent west to east. One may safely affirm that Viet-Nam is called upon to become a major transportation hub between Asia and the other continents.

From what precedes, it should be easy to deduce that the industrialization of Viet-Nam—a nation traditionally engaged in agriculture and handicrafts—is not an impossible feat. Nevertheless, it is a task which cannot be achieved overnight. First of all, it requires foreign help because the national financial resources are very weak. The influx of foreign capital, public as well as private, is indispensable in order to equip Viet-Nam with a new economic structure.

Viet-Nam, therefore, will look forward to investments from abroad, whether they come from international organizations, from the Associated States of the French Union, or from other friendly nations such as the United States. These investments will benefit from a legislation which respects and guarantees their legitimate rights. Viet-Nam is not "a trap for foreign capital," and would place but one reasonable condition upon its influx: that its national independence be respected, and that its efforts to improve the well-being of its population would be aided by the investments of foreign capital.

It is quite certain that if in addition to the American aid which we already receive we should receive more equipment goods, it will help us greatly in solving the economic problem which our country faces at present, and which I have briefly pointed out to you. We do not wish to hide from you that the solution of this problem, conjointly with certain social reforms such as, in particular, agrarian reforms, would be a powerful weapon in order to check the progress of Communism in our state, which occupies a key position in this part of the free world.

Part 3: CULTURE

Richard A. Gard

IDEOLOGICAL PROBLEMS IN

SOUTHEAST ASIA

Political, economic, and social forces are engendering the rise of Southeast Asia in the coming world. They are manifest in diplomatic relations, governmental policies and programs, and in public opinion. Such forces are formed not only by military and commercial aims but also by national and ethnic ways of life. Proposals for the future of Southeast Asia, whether made by governments or private industry, must consider traditional cultural bases, requisite cultural implementation, and eventual cultural evaluation. The peoples of this area already have convictions derived from experience, and may be expected to progress as they reflect and act upon their experience. What, then, are some of the exigent ideological issues and problems prevailing in Southeast Asia which may affect its future?

First, how adequate and reliable is our present knowledge of the cultures of Burma, Thailand, Indo-China, the Philippines, Malaya, and Indonesia?[1] Expressions of their social attitudes, written before the advent of Western colonialism and the subsequent rise of national independence, may or may

[1] Consult John Fee Embree and Lillian Ota Dotson (compilers), *Bibliography of the Peoples and Cultures of Mainland Southeast Asia.* (Yale University Southeast Asia Studies) New Haven, Conn.: Chinese Printing Office, Hall of Graduate Studies, Yale University, 1950. xxxiii, 821 pp. Maps. Also Raymond Kennedy (compiler), *Bibliography of Indonesian Peoples and Cultures.* (Edited by Cornelius Osgood and Irving Rouse.) (Yale Anthropological Studies, Vol. 4.) New Haven, Conn.: Yale University Press, 1946. 212 pp. Maps.

not be pertinent to contemporary issues in Southeast Asia as a whole. Has native scholarship sufficiently studied, digested, and utilized these traditional political and religious writings? Is Western scholarship linguistically competent and psychologically ready to interpret them properly? Certain ideological views are now being evolved and stated by Southeast Asians and other Asians and Westerners. Just how formative will these views be in the future development of Southeast Asia in relation to other areas and peoples?

Ideas, when successfully expressed in action, become beliefs and live as customs. Anthropologists, sociologists, and psychologists are now busily engaged in observing and interpreting Southeast Asian mores. To what extent might their reports be vitiated by non-Asian frames of reference and standards of evaluation? Can the ideologies of some 163 million people of this area be comprehended primarily through empiricial study techniques? Who among the Burmese, Thai, Indo-Chinese, Philippine, Malaya, and Indonesian groups can be rightly regarded as authoritative and articulate spokesmen? To Western students, the question of what we know about ideologies in Southeast Asia involves the problem of how we acquire that knowledge and arrive at a common understanding of life ideals, beliefs, and values. Here, it would seem that government, business, and educational interests are all vitally concerned and that the services of the philosopher are needed.

In our so-called objective study of ideological problems, the subjective factor should never be overlooked: by whom are such problems perceived and stated, to whom do they have meaning, and for whom are they solved? How do ideologies differ according to nation, race, religion, social group, and vocation? What is the relationship between traditional Southeast Asian systems of thought and superimposed Western systems of thought? Does an Asian question require an Asian answer? Would an Asian answer satisfy a Western question? In short, with whose ideology in Southeast Asia are we mainly concerned?

Ideology may be variously defined as (1) the study of the relation of ideas to language, (2) the manner or content of thinking which is characteristic of an individual or a group, (3) a subjective interpretation of observed social phenomena, (4) a systematic scheme of ideas about life. A survey of ideological issues and problems in Southeast Asia today would disclose at least four important types: philosophical-religious, political, economic, and legal.

Philosophical-Religious Ideological Problems

Philosophy is the systematic investigation of the facts and principles of reality and of human nature and conduct, comprising man's attitude toward his environment, epistemology or the theory of knowledge, logic, metaphysics, ethics, and aesthetics. Religion may be defined as an organized body of beliefs and practices concerning human relationships with supra-human ideals or powers. But this conception does not well apply to Buddhism, the principal religion of Ceylon, Burma, Thailand, and parts of Indo-China.

With respect to Southeast Asia, therefore, it seems more appropriate to consider religion as the popular manifestation of philosophic ideas and ideals rather than an institution in itself, distinct from philosophy, as generally viewed by the modern Western world. Certainly, Southeast Asian epistemological, metaphysical, and ethical principles have been traditionally expressed in so-called religious writings. Man's attitude toward his natural and social environment is the philosophical-religious beginning of his civilization. Man's aesthetic expression in the arts and ceremony is the philosophical-religious culmination of his culture.

Accordingly, ideologies in Southeast Asia which may be termed philosophical-religious are those sets of interpretations and beliefs, philosophic in nature and religious in application, which are basic to political, economic, and legal ideologies. The integration of various traditional and contemporary thought patterns constitutes the initial problem of philosophical-religious ideologies in Southeast Asia today. During periods of instability, such as the present, thought processes are sometimes preserved and enlivened through adaptation to current issues—and are sometimes lost through that adaptation. Thus the responsibility of the contemporary philosopher for the welfare of the Southeast Asian peoples has never been greater; the corresponding challenge to the man of religion is truly historic. Communist utilization of Buddhist personnel in the Arakan Province of Burma, interference with Buddhist institutions in Ceylon and Thailand, exploitation of religious assets in Indo-China, and attempted penetration of Islamic practices in Indonesia further complicate this philosophical-religious ideological task in Southeast Asia.

Generally speaking, civilizations in Southeast Asia have been founded upon a profound appreciation of Nature and a consequent harmonious relationship between man and Nature. Accordingly, their attendant cultures are not restricted solely to the field of art but also concern the growth of man in his intrinsic relation to Nature. "Progress" to these peoples, therefore, means spiritual development and not material achievement and masterful technique as is often construed by the Western world. The Southeast Asian art of living is man's realization of his interdependence with Nature, so that he may live in peace with his fellow man and with himself.

In Southeast Asia, the close affinity of the human order with the natural order is characteristically expressed in folklore, literature, architecture, political institutions, and everyday life. For example, the topographical position, physical lay-out, and sculptural decoration of the Khmer capital of Angkor Thom, completed by the Buddhist king Jayavarman VII in the late twelfth century A.D., was a microcosmic replica of an idealized macrocosmic edifice.[2] In Burma, Cambodia,

[2] Lawrence Palmer Briggs, *The Ancient Khmer Empire* (Issued as Volume 41, Part 1, of the Transactions of the American Philosophical Society) Philadelphia: American Philosophical Society, 1951. 295 pp. Works Cited, pp. 262–73. 58 figures, 17 maps, 22 plans.

Siam, and Java, former kings and their officialdom had cosmic roles which were prescribed by Brāhmanical and Buddhist beliefs and symbolized by court ritual and coronation ceremonies.[3]

It cannot be denied that natural resources have been developed and utilized for the construction of palaces, the enrichment of imperial treasuries, and the promotion of foreign trade rather than for the economic well-being of Southeast Asian peoples. But a large-scale, planned exploitation of natural resources seems to be primarily a Western practice, based upon a masterful attitude toward Nature and a consequent separation of man from Nature—in philosophical and religious contradistinction to the Southeast Asian traditional attitude and custom. Hence the impact of the Western type or method of commercialism upon the life of Southeast Asia is causing profound changes in its political, social, and cultural thinking.

Once the human order is divorced from the natural order, politics loses its religious expression and religion loses its political efficacy, living standards are evaluated primarily in economic terms, and the cultural arts face the choice of either enhancing or criticizing social ideals. Communism, if established, with its basic doctrine of dialectical materialism, would climax this Westernized bifurcation of man and his natural environment and would thus repudiate the Southeast Asian correlation of the physical and human orders as an integrated way of life. In this part of the world, Nature has been exceptionally kind and beneficent to man; he should not therefore forsake her, and in consequence forsake his own heritage, by

[3] Robert Heine-Geldern, "Conception of State and Kingship in Southeast Asia." *The Far Eastern Quarterly* (New York), Vol. II, No. 1 (November, 1942), pp. 15–30. Horace Geoffrey Quaritch Wales, *Siamese State Ceremonies. Their History and Function*. With Frontispiece, 45 Plates and 5 Figures. London: Bernard Quaritch Ltd., 1931. xiv, 326 pp. List of abbreviations, p. xi. Kenneth Elmer Wells, *Thai Buddhism, Its Rites and Activities*. Bangkok, Thailand: The Bangkok Times Press, Ltd. (Preface, 1939). xii, 284 pp. Bibliography, pp. 269–79.

exploiting Nature in the proposed interests of a Westernized nationalism or of Asian Communism.

The content of epistemology, logic, metaphysics, and aesthetics is present wherever people think and act reflectively. In Southeast Asia this is evidenced by Hindu, Buddhist, Islamic and other beliefs and folk customs. The comparative lack of formalized treatises on such philosophical subjects does not mean that the peoples of this area have not speculated about the nature of reality and human relationships. It is axiomatic in politics that the formulation and success of governmental policies depend upon their feasibility. Feasibility involves plausibility to those persons carrying out the policies. Such plausibility in turn is contingent upon what is known about a situation, how that knowledge has been obtained and whether it is reliable. Reliability of information means consistency with human reason and past knowledge. In short, the experience of a people conditions, implements, and judges political, economic, and social proposals. Such experience involves human relationships which have been standardized by accepted ethical values. All this culminates in the art of living which finds its cultural expression in the arts and its philosophical idealization in religion.

It would be difficult here to summarize the varying conceptions of reality, methods of reasoning, and ethical standards which have been proposed and believed by the followers of Hinduism, Buddhism, Islam, and other religious systems in Southeast Asia for many centuries. Such a survey must be made, however, before we can properly ascertain and measure the impact of Western ideas upon the thought processes of Southeast Asian peoples. The researches and observations of the epistemologist, logician, metaphysicist, ethicist, and aesthetician should be correlated with those of the cultural historian and psychologist.

At the present time, the most important philosophical-religious ideological issues in Southeast Asia can be stated in their relation to the influx of Communist doctrines. The Marxist tenet of materialism, which holds that all human events are exclusively determined by measurable material forces, is in direct contradiction to the reasoned and experiential teachings concerning the nature of reality and of man and their interdependent relationship, as found in Hinduism, Buddhism, Islam, and animism in Southeast Asia. The Marxist tenet of dialectics asserts that these material forces work themselves out in human history by a process in which the conflict of opposites is inherent in Nature and society and is ever resolved into a new and "higher" condition. This metaphysical dialectic cannot be compared with the Buddhist epistemological dialectic, and the presumption of inherent opposites arbitrarily dichotomizes the unity of reality and of life as experienced by the Southeast Asian peoples. The Marxist materialistic interpretation of history contends that the basic conflicts of the dialectical process in human society operate in terms of the changing forces of production (tools, machines) which place men in certain relations with other men (production-relations); these production-relations (the substructure of society) determine the social, political, and intellectual processes of life (the superstructure of society). This evaluation of life in economic terms not only misconstrues the complex development of Southeast Asian cultures, it attacks the dignity of thinking man by denying him the capacity to make decisions upon philosophical, religious, and aesthetic bases. The Marxist tenet of class struggle argues that production-relations result in certain social relations between men which form classes, and that the historical dialectic works itself out in a series of class struggles. Such an argument can create only social tension and dissension and violate the traditional practice in Southeast Asia of conciliation between contesting parties outside the law courts. And finally, the Marxist theory of the State as a class oppressor, an organ of class coercion by the "ruling elite," discards the Southeast Asian heritage of political and social ideals and customs and discourages present endeavors to develop governments truly representative of the people.

As such, the imposition of Communist ideas upon the thought of Southeast Asia endangers the intellectual integrity of its 163 million people. Current Communist criticism and exploitation of religious personnel and property, whether Hindu, Buddhist, Islamic, or Christian, well illustrates the urgency of meeting this problem.

Political Ideological Problems

Political science is the systematic study of politics or the examination and description of the processes whereby political authority is obtained, institutionalized, and exercised. Political thought, which includes both political philosophy and political theory, formulates, expounds, and evaluates various conceptions of, and attitudes toward, political authority as to its origin, development, nature, objective, exercise or administration, and change. Political ideologies in Southeast Asia, therefore, are sets of interpretations and beliefs about political authority.

After several centuries of Western colonial subjugation, the peoples of Southeast Asia, with the exception of the Malays and the Indo-Chinese, are now institutionalizing and exercising autonomous political authority. But their constitutions are chiefly written adaptations of European and American models; their legislative machinery usually functions according to Western practices; and their nationalism, now in the formative state, is notably inspired by Western examples as well as by native reaction to Western rule.[4] Hence, what elements, traditionally based or currently innovated, may be considered indigenous to contemporary Southeast Asian political beliefs and institutions? Are the existing governments of Burma, Thailand, the Philippines, and Indonesia merely mirrors of Western political forms?

[4] *Government and Nationalism in Southeast Asia.* Part I. Introduction by Rupert Emerson. Part II. The Governments of Southeast Asia, by Lennox A. Mills. Part III. Nationalism and Nationalist Movements in Southeast Asia, by Virginia Thompson. (I.P.R. Inquiry Series) New York: International Secretariat, Institute of Pacific Relations, 1942. xiii, 242 pp.

The ideological aspect of this question lies in the nature of cultural borrowing. Governmental institutions are usually developed and maintained to meet specific social needs. Their rationalization or political theory and philosophy must therefore be meaningful to those persons governing and being governed in the relevant social environments. The administration of political authority without due consideration of its cultural basis, cultural implementation, and cultural evaluation would be short-lived, if at all possible. Recently, the independent nations of Southeast Asia have borrowed and adapted Western political institutions, especially democratic elective and legislative processes. Have they likewise borrowed those Western political ideas and ideals which are environmentally attached to these institutions?

If so, are such ideas and ideals truly meaningful to the various Southeast Asian peoples? Will they coalesce with indigenous thought so as to form new political ideologies? As the Westernized governmental structures undergo necessary modification, will their borrowed Western theories undergo corresponding modification?

On the other hand, if political thought cannot be borrowed and adapted as readily as political institutions, then where, when, and how can the Southeast Asian peoples obtain their own political ideologies which are essential for the vitalizing of their new governments? Will they follow the present endeavor of the Burma Union which is fostering Buddhist teachings and mores, traditional before the British rule, in order to found a new national consciousness and a new cultural unity for its people? Or will they follow the example of the Republic of the Philippines which is apparently grafting American political ideals on its body politic?

Thus, the fundamental political ideological problem in Southeast Asia today is a compounded one of selecting, interpreting, and applying those elements of political thought, as may be adopted from native traditions and adapted from foreign systems, in order that present and future governments will be representative of the people. The cultural historian will assure us that Southeast Asian civilizations are already characteristically compounded of borrowings from Hindu, Buddhist, and Islamic ways of life, to which the Western way is now being added, whether it be Christian or industrial, democratic or communistic.

In this respect, three kinds of political ideology are contesting each other for supremacy in Southeast Asia: ways whereby political authority is obtained, institutionalized, and exercised. They are (1) authoritarianism, as derived from traditional theories of divine kingship and practices of aristocratic ruling elites according to Hindu, Buddhist, or Islamic tenets, (2) democracy, as introduced by Western principles of constitutionalism and parliamentarianism, and (3) communism, as proffered by Russian and Chinese agitators. These three political philosophies have developed interrelatedly in the Western world; they now confront each other as independent ideologies in Southeast Asia.

The doctrine of political authoritarianism in Southeast Asia is traditionally founded in autocratic practices and theories of divine kingship. Prior to the advent of Western colonialism, the various peoples of this area had had their own authoritarian ideologies according to Hindu, Buddhist, or Islamic tenets. The prevailing theory that the ruler, whether emperor, king, or chieftain, is the embodiment of political authority was rationalized and effected through a metaphysical correlation of the natural and human orders, the possession of official regalia, and the conduct of religious ceremonies.[5]

Contemporary interpretation and modification of such traditions of political authoritarianism in Southeast Asia involve at least three important problems, summarized as follows.

The dominant Hindu Brāhmanical theory was that the divine creation of kingship embodied a divinely ordained duty to protect the State rather than, as in Western thought, a divine right to rule. This conception was in marked con-

[5] See above, note 3.

trast to the earlier Vedic principle which held that kings were elected unanimously by the people in assembly (*samiti* in Sanskrit) and were so asked to protect the State from all harm. Thus in accordance with his popular appointment, the king was called *rāja* because it was his duty "to please" (*rañj* in Sanskrit) the people by maintaining good government.[6] Hence the first problem: when rulership in Southeast Asia was being Hinduized, why was this Vedic theory supplanted by the later Brāhmanical theory? Could it be revived now as a traditional foundation for modern democratic ideals?

The Buddhist Mahāyāna theory of rulership emphasized the person rather than the office and was so known and applied by aristocratic and educated groups particularly in Siam, Cambodia, and Indonesia (Śailendra dynasty). On the other hand, certain Hīnayāna texts emphasized the office of kingship rather than the person but were comparatively unknown to the common people even though they followed the Theravāda School. The Hīnayāna theory held that kingship was elective or existed by virtue of public appointment, as precedented in the *rāja* office of the Śākya and allied republics (*saṅgha* in Sanskrit) during the Buddha's time (c. 566–c. 486 B.C.) and as monastically practiced within the Buddhist Saṅgha throughout most of Asia.[7] This theory was further supported by the Indian conception of a hypothetical State of Nature from which chaos elective kingship evolved as a necessary remedy. Thus certain early Buddhist texts preserved the Hindu Vedic tradition that

[6] Kashi Prasad Jayaswal, *Hindu Polity. A Constitutional History of India in Hindu Times.* (Parts I and II) Bangalore City: The Bangalore Printing Co., Ltd., 1943, 2d & enlarged edition. xlvii, 430, 6 pp. Bibliography, pp. 399–410. See especially Chapter IV. "The Rise of Hindu Republics and Hindu Terms for Republics," pp. 23–29; Chapter V. "Republics in Pānini," pp. 30–41; Chapter VI. "Republican Origin of Buddhist Samgha and Republics in Buddhist Literature (500–400 B.C.)," pp. 42–51.

[7] See my *Buddhist Influences on the Political Thought and Institutions of India and Japan.* (Phoenix Papers No. 1) (Claremont, California): Society for Oriental Studies at Claremont, 1942. (iii), 50 pp. Bibliographical Notes, pp. 37–48.

sovereignty originates from, and returns to, the people, that kingship is essentially a human institution and not a divine office, and that government is a contractual agreement between the people and the ruler in which the welfare of the country and its people is the sacred trust. Hence the second problem: how could these Vedic and Hīnayāna views be revived in order to liberalize the traditional interpretation and practice of political authoritarianism in Southeast Asia? Can they culturally reinforce current Westernized ideas of democracy?

The third interpretative problem concerns the nature of the Islamic theory of rulership in Southeast Asia. In Malaya and Indonesia especially, what Islamic influences have been exerted on the established Hindu-Buddhist doctrine of political authoritarianism since the fifteenth century? Elsewhere in Asia, the traditional Islamic concept of kingship, in which the ruler is the interpreter of the sacred revealed law and is popularly approved according to the Koran, has undergone modification by sectarian interpretation and instances of self-aggrandizement. In recent times the absence of a substantial middle-class, which would better correlate the positions of the rulers and the ruled in Islamic governmental practice, has often led to the recurrence of political authoritarianism in Western forms. Is this situation likewise problematic in Southeast Asia? In other words, what interdependent relationships exist between the Islamic, Hindu, Buddhist, and Western institutions of authoritarianism in Southeast Asia and how can they be utilized in the best interests of its peoples?

The doctrine of political democracy in Southeast Asia was activated after the end of World War II as a result of Japanese incitation during wartime occupation, native reaction to the possibility of a return to prewar colonial status, and the inability of the British, French, and Dutch governments to enforce prewar relationships. The main elements of the Southeast Asian democracies are Western in inception: written constitutions, parliamentary procedures, political parties and elections; the nature of their present legal systems, however, needs to be analyzed.

It has been traditionally believed by the Western world that political democracy necessarily embodies individualism —that is, individual legal rights, economic liberties, and religious freedom with respect to the exercise of political authority. Today, however, this democratic principle is being affected by current movements in political organization, economic planning, and philosophical thinking. Collective responsibility is tending to supplant individualism as the basis of democracy in the Western world. Is this trend likewise noticeable in Southeast Asia? Is it possible that the Southeast Asian peoples are already traditionally experienced in social cooperative action and therefore do not need to go through a preparatory period of instituting and then modifying the Western principle of individualism in order to formulate their own political ideologies?

If we Western students recommend that the various governments of Southeast Asia correlate their international political relations, integrate their economies, and further their cultural intercourse, must we not also suggest that they temper their individualistic expressions of nationalism with a spirit of collective responsibility and concerted action for all peoples? If so, then those governments may well strengthen the purpose of the United Nations and demonstrate to the rest of Asia and the world how the ideals and aims of humanity can be politically realized. How can this demonstration be best made?

The doctrine of political communism in Southeast Asia has neither precedent in cultural traditions nor sanction in current national aspirations. It must be regarded therefore as an alien ideology, seeking acceptance by theoretical comparison with the doctrine of political democracy and practical alliance with the doctrine of political authoritarianism. Communism, in both Western and Asian forms, brings nothing of positive value to the formulation of new political ideologies in Southeast Asia. Its basic Marxist tenet that the State is an instrument of class oppression and as such will eventually "wither away" upon the attainment of Communist economic objectives is certainly not a constructive contribution to Southeast Asian political thought. Dictatorship by a Communist Party elite for the so-called proletariat would not be a new experience to 163 million people already well acquainted with their own and Western types of despotism. How to avoid Communism in its Marxist, Leninist, Stalinist, and other forms is an urgent problem in the present evolution of political ideologies in Southeast Asia.

Economic Ideological Problems

Economics is the systematic study of the conditions and factors affecting the production, distribution, and consumption of the material means for satisfying human desires. Economic thought concerns the rationalization of such processes and the clarification of such desires. Economic ideologies in Southeast Asia, therefore, are sets of interpretations and beliefs about economic institutions and values.

An analysis and summary statement of the primary economic ideological problems current in Southeast Asia would reflect several divergent points of view. Again we may ask, for whom do these problems exist: the government, private industry, capitalist and investor, labor, consumer, Western-trained economist, or Communist agitator? Each field of economic activity has its own set of problems which involve a selection and pursuit of human wants and material values. We are concerned here with the possibility of the composite formulation of one or more economic philosophies for some 163 million people and the integration of such ways of thought with their political and cultural life.

The consequences of any major economic program definitely shape the direction of a people's economic thinking. For instance, if it is decided that basic industries and public utilities in Southeast Asian countries can only be properly developed and guided by government instead of by private enterprise, will such an activity induce state socialism or enable a subsequent transition to middle class capitalism or incur some kind of communism? The success of such a venture is influenced and, in the final stage, measured by the life-value which people place upon their own material wants and satisfactions. In other words, an economic program, whether government sponsored or privately undertaken, must be accompanied by some sort of idealization, cultural implementation, and ideological understanding by the people concerned. Collective economic security requires collective economic responsibility, but this does not warrant either fascism or communism.

In the final sense, economic policies are devised and executed by men motivated in certain directions. Ideas and ideals provide such motivations and, when formulated, constitute economic ideologies. The crucial question is then, not whether such and such a program will result in a predictable favorable action, but whether a policy truly emanates from the people and is wilfully supported by them. Democracy is an economic concept as well as a political tenet.

Thus the basic question must be asked of the Burmese, Thai, Indo-Chinese, Philippine, Malay, and Indonesian peoples: is the economic factor all important? does material satisfaction determine the relationship of life-ideals? can human wants be evaluated primarily according to economic standards? Furthermore, what standards of living are applicable to them? Money economy and industrial technology may be new to most areas of Southeast Asia; will they ensure happiness as well as livelihood for its 163 million inhabitants? These and accompanying Westernized economic measures are now affecting the ordinary man for the first time in this part of the world. How will he understand, employ, and judge them? This task is his own and not that of Western economists, however informed and well-intentioned they may be.

The situation may be reduced to the fundamental query: how does the ordinary man in this racially and culturally complex area feel about the consequences of national and inter-regional planning, collective economic security and responsibility, industrial technology, and similar impending modern programs? Upon his response will depend the formulation of economic ideologies suitable to Southeast Asia and the resolution of its economic problems in the coming world.

Legal Ideological Problems

Jurisprudence is the science of law as a social control enforced by authoritative means. Legal ideological problems in Southeast Asia, therefore, concern the nature and sources of law, its administration and enforcement, and its relation to society both national and international.

Today we are in dire need of comprehensive studies of the jurisprudential systems of Southeast Asia. Descriptive accounts have been written concerning public administration and legislative processes in this area,[8] *dhammathat* or so-called Buddhist law in Burma,[9] *adat* or so-called customary law in Indonesia.[10] But such accounts do not suffice in themselves, nor do they provide an adequate survey of the subject in content and geographical area. Consequently, how are we to determine the influence of traditional Southeast Asian legal concepts and institutions upon present national and international developments in this region?

[8] For instance, the series on *Public Administration* being issued by the Royal Institute of International Affairs, London: *Ceylon,* by Sir Charles Collins (1951), *Siam,* by W. D. Reeve (1951), *Burma,* by F. S. V. Donnison, *Hong Kong,* by Sir Charles Collins, *Malaya* by S. W. Jones.

[9] Orby Howell Mootham, *Burmese Buddhist Law.* London, Bombay, New York, etc.: Indian Branch, H. Milford, Oxford University Press, 1939. xxi, 148 pp. Sisir Chandra Lahiri, *Principles of Modern Burmese Buddhist Law.* Calcutta: Eastern Law House, 1939, 4th edition. xii, 430 pp. References, p. x.

[10] B. Ter Haar, *Adat Law in Indonesia.* Translated from the Dutch. Edited with an Introduction by E. Adamson (and) A. Arthur Schiller. (Issued in cooperation with the Southeast Asia Institute with the aid of a grant from the Coolidge Foundation) New York: International Secretariat, Institute of Pacific Relations, 1948. xiv, 255 pp.

Possibly we should first search the native literatures and mores for those elements which will provide a traditional basis for the current Westernized constitutions, civil and criminal court procedures, and international commercial law. But which study approach are we to utilize: the analytical, historical, philosophical, sociological, or the comparative? And which system of law is to serve as the Western frame of reference: the British case-precedent in Burma, Malaya, and Hongkong; the French code in Indo-China; the American case-precedent in the Philippines; or the Dutch code in Indonesia? Must we compartmentalize these areas according to their superimposed Western legal systems? And what of the earlier impact of Moslem law, especially on Indonesia? Historically considered, do we not find that any native body of law in Southeast Asia is already compounded of foreign elements: Burmese law of Buddhist ethics, Hindu regulations, and Burmese folkways; Siamese law of Indian, Chinese, Thai, and other influences; and so forth?

In spite of these difficulties, it seems quite possible to select native legal concepts and practices which would support and implement the introduced Western systems now prevalent. For example, the principle of constitutionalism may be found inherent in the jurisprudence of Burma, Thailand, and Indo-China because of Buddhist Hīnayāna texts which expound theories of elective kingship and government by social contract.[11] Similarly, India, Ceylon, and Burma especially have recognized the validity of conventional law (*samaya* in Sanskrit) in connection with Buddhist monastic regulations (*vinaya* in Sanskrit).[12] Customary law seems to have been in force throughout Southeast Asia for many centuries and is perhaps best studied in its Indonesian form (*adat* in Arabic). Before the advent of Western international law, official relations be-

[11] *Buddhist Influences on the Political Thought and Institutions of India and Japan*, "Theory of Elective Kingship," pp. 15–19.

[12] *Ibid.*, "Conventional Law (samaya)," pp. 11–15.

tween the Southeast Asian kingdoms and empires were usually
guided, if not always enforced, by Indian principles of diplomacy.[13]

The spirit of conciliation in legal disputes, inculcated by
Buddhist and Islamic attitudes of social tolerance, has come
to characterize the flexible nature of Southeast Asian jurisprudence. Its guiding principle is based upon the mutual respect and consideration of both disputants; only that solution
which results in no feeling of resentment by either party is
held to be reasonable and lasting; settlement out of court is
customarily preferred.

The cultural basis of legal ideologies lies in the fact that
concepts of public law connote political ideals, notions of
natural law embody philosophical and religious doctrines,
statements of common law express popular beliefs and mores.
The formulation of legal systems meaningful to the peoples
of Southeast Asia therefore depends upon the proper selection and correlation of traditional legal ideas with current
Western concepts. Thus will philosophies of law in Southeast
Asia implement the political, economic, social, and cultural
programs of its governments. And when law emanates from the
life of the people, it will be observed by them.

Conclusion

These and other philosophical-religious, political, economic, and legal ideological problems current in Southeast
Asia may be viewed in two fundamental respects. The first
view is short-term: what is the ideological position of South-

[13] Benoy Kumar Sarkar, *The Political Institutions and Theories of
the Hindus. A Study in Comparative Politics.* Leipzig: Verlag von Markert
und Petters, 1922. xxiv, 242 pp. Authorities cited, pp. xiii–xxiv. See Chapter IX. "The Theory of Sovereignty in Hindu Political Philosophy." Section 3. The Theory of International Relations: a) The Doctrine of
Mandala (Sphere of Influence) and b) The Doctrine of *Sarva-bhauma*
(World-Sovereign), pp. 214–26. Also S. V. Viswanatha, *International Law
in Ancient India.* Bombay: Longmans, Green & Co., 1925. x, 214 pp.
References, pp. 201–204.

east Asia in the present world struggle over issues created by Communist aggression? The second view is long-range: what will be the ideological role of Southeast Asia in the coming world? These two views may well be interrelated. As a philosopher, may I suggest the following measures to the peoples of Southeast Asia for their consideration and action?

First, the preservation, through proper adaptation, of their priceless cultural heritage. This heritage includes a feeling of kinship with Nature, a realization of the interdependence of all life, skill in craftsmanship and folk expression, and philosophical-religious modes of thought.

Second, the continued integration of the various physical, political, economic, social, cultural and other orders for the sake of the art of living, which is so much desired and needed by the world today.

Third, the prevention of a resurgence of authoritarianism or an emergence of communism, and the development of democracy based upon indigenous Buddhist, Hindu, and Islamic principles and practices.

Fourth, a careful study of the process and consequences of cultural borrowing, especially of those political ideals, economic values, and social customs which are now being proffered by other Asians and Westerners.

Fifth, the recognition that life-values rather than economic motives or military expediency should guide the practice of obtaining collective security through collective responsibility.

Sixth, the emanation of both customary and statutory law from the life of the people, in which social relationships are governed by the traditional principle of conciliation, so much needed in a conflicting world.

For the peoples of Southeast Asia, their way of life tomorrow will largely depend upon their intelligent choice of ways of thought today. Ideological problems in this area concern all of us as human beings and members of the United Nations. Through mutual understanding and friendly cooperation, these problems will be resolved.

Kenneth P. Landon

CURRENT PROBLEMS IN CULTURAL

BORROWING IN SOUTHEAST ASIA

CULTURAL BORROWINGS by Southeast Asia in the past have come from many parts of the world and have been made without plan by either the lender or borrower. Such borrowings have been incidental to commerce, warfare, adventure, travel, colonialism, and religious missions.

The cultural traffic of Europe and Asia has for almost two millenniums passed through Southeast Asia at various rates of speed. The processes of Hinduization went through at leisurely pace for almost twelve centuries before its newness had worn off and as much had been borrowed as could be used. In general, most of the borrowing was done by the ruling class, while the general population continued on its usual way virtually unaffected. It too acquired, however, new gods to add to the pantheon of spirits, and new content for traditional methods of amusement.

Islam likewise led a comparatively leisurely pilgrimage of five or six centuries from Malacca to Moro-land in the Philippines. It too became the special property of the ruling class. Islam added numberless new spirits to be appeased and endless *slametans* to be eaten in the name of Allah.

During these centuries of borrowing from Hindu and Muslim sources, the Chinese had recast the lives of the Viet-Namese people in a Chinese mould and had filtered through the rest of Southeast Asia carrying many valuable things with them which were desired by the indefatigable borrowers of Southeast Asia. I think too little has been made of cultural borrowing from the Chinese. They have probably made more of an impact than has generally been believed. As yet no sound study has been made of this subject; consequently we really do not know how much or how little has been borrowed from the Chinese.

Our attention today, however, is to be focused on current problems in cultural borrowing in Southeast Asia and this probably means, for us at least, the problems involved in borrowing from the West.

Cultural borrowing occurs whenever the people are brought into contact by some means with the culture of other peoples and accept for themselves some aspect of that experience. It may happen when a hill tribesman sees for the first time a manufactured cigarette and desires it in place of the homemade variety of cheroot to which he has been accustomed. To get such a cigarette he may have to work for money for the first time in his life. To continue to get them, after having acquired a taste for them, he may have to change the locus of his dwelling and abandon village authority. This may lead to all sorts of remarkable and bizarre experiences with fountain pens, Ford cars, airplanes, and the radio. And over the radio he may hear the Voice of Moscow, or the Voice of Peiping, or the Voice of America, or the Voice of Bangkok. And he may get ideas which will prevent him from being again the simple hill dweller that he had been. Or he may by an act of judgment on these new things decide that the life of the simple hill dweller is the best for him and so return to the life of the hill dweller, but no longer simple.

Borrowers imply lenders. Some lenders are involuntary in the matter of cultural borrowing but many are voluntary, although the things they lend may not be the things they think they are lending. The teacher of English may think she is lending a new and interesting language and actually be lending a determination to dispose of unmarried missionary ladies and a resolve to use the new knowledge to prove how much better the old language is. The religious missionary may think he is saving souls and lending a more sophisticated outlook on life and may actually be lending the idea that long white trousers are more stylish than short brown ones. The business man selling petroleum and motor cars may think he is in the transportation business, but his chief achievement may be in expediting the movement of illicit opium and the development of the opium habit in new communities. And then there are the government lenders—perhaps through military and economic aid programs, perhaps by providing advisers on such diverse matters as international relations, art, police, architecture, education, and law. Such lendings imply an active self-interest in the lender and the effects to be hoped for by the lender may not be at all the results anticipated by the borrower. And the end result may be far different from anything either lender or borrower had contemplated.

Although my subject implies consideration of only one side of the borrowing, that is the borrower, it seems to me that one could hardly do justice to the subject without at least noting some of the problems of the lender. To show what I mean I will refer for a moment to the problems of the missionary lender.

All missionaries of whom I have knowledge have gone forth according to some scriptural injunction to make known their gospel and to save souls. The souls that were supposedly saved were identified by such evidences as a confession of faith, attendance at church, acceptance of communion, and the giving of some substantive support to the enterprise. A survey of missions was made some years ago which disclosed that the size of any average congregation of converts in most mission fields was directly related to the number of employees hired by the missionaries in their homes, schools, and hospitals. This was very disillusioning. Missionary courage was further dampened when it became evident that while missionaries had gone out to lend religion they had made their major measurable contributions by introducing printing, inventing typewriters, establishing hospitals and leper homes, inaugurating new methods of public health, persuading educational officials to undertake the education of girls as well as boys, and leading civil officials to experiment with prison reform. One of the greatest missionary educators of Thailand, Miss Edna S. Cole, is famed, among other reasons, because she introduced the style of blouse for girls that is now universal among women throughout the nation. The problem for the lending missionary is thus whether to trim his lending to fit his purposes or to recognize what his achievements actually have been and to trim his purposes to suit his accomplishments. And if he did the latter, would there be any more missionary work and would this medium of lending cease?

Among other lenders there are the colonial powers, which during the nineteenth and twentieth centuries controlled the political and economic destinies of most Southeast Asian nations. I view colonialism as a pressure-cooker technique for the acceleration of the processes of acculturation. The Western powers affected every aspect of life of the nations they controlled. In the process there evolved desires, ideas, and abilities among a small percentage of educated persons upon whom the colonial powers depended for successful administration. The more successful the Western powers were as colonial administrators, however, the more certain and the more rapid were they in making it impossible for themselves to continue in this relationship. The very people they educated and trained to help them became the leaders of the nationalist movements which made their continued presence less necessary and virtually impossible. The major problem facing the colonial powers since World War II has been the nature of their post-independence relations with former colonies. No two colonial powers have had identical policies or objectives in mind. And no two colonies have achieved their independence in the same way or at the same pace. And no two colonial powers have developed identical relations in the post independence period with former colonies. It would seem then that all colonial powers in Southeast Asia are or have been trying to solve this problem in various ways, and each is faced with unique factors requiring special and original consideration. The point I am making is that a paper might be devoted to the problems of the lender of culture as well as to the problems of the borrower.

And what are the problems of the borrower? I suppose it would not be incorrect to say that some of the problems are individual, some are of village or commune level, some are of a national sort with chiefly internal reference, and some are of an international variety which have both national and international significance.

I will begin with the last first, as this is an international conference. Governmental borrowing or sponsoring of alien practices, techniques, and things may bring a government to a point of national crisis. This was evident in the experience of the government of Marshal Phibun Songgram shortly before World War II when a concerted effort was begun in 1939 and continued without interruption until 1944 to induce the people of Thailand to adapt themselves to new cultural practices in matters of dress, in manners, in literature, and indeed in every aspect of life. The purpose was to accelerate the Westernization of the nation, although it was not so described. The net result was that although many complied there were many who resented being hustled into hats, shoes, dresses of Western style, suits of European cut. And in regard to the more far-reaching reforms involving education and religion, emotions were aroused and people began to seek ways to avoid being processed. The climax came over the issue of abandoning the traditional capital of the Chakri dynasty and establishing a new one inland at Petchabun. The government fell.

Recently I received a copy of the *Report on Indonesia* from the Information Office of the Republic of Indonesia for February 28, 1952. On the front page I read, "The Sukiman Cabinet Resigns," and under this the explanatory statement was made that the immediate cause was Foreign Minister Subardjo's signature on the Mutual Security Agreement with the United

States. Further explanation was given that the Foreign Minister had been severely criticized for accepting American aid from the Mutual Security Agency without consulting his colleagues in the Cabinet. On page two a further note was added that "Dr. Subardjo had in effect violated the spirit of Indonesia's independent foreign policy by signing an agreement for MSA aid that might draw the Republic even slightly 'into the American orbit.' The difficulty was the rider which the United States inserted in MSA legislation last year. It requires nations receiving MSA assistance to agree that they will contribute 'to the defensive strength of the free world.' Such a clause was bound to trouble Indonesian political leaders who hope above all to remain friendly with both Western and Eastern nations, and to rebuild their country without antagonizing any group of powers." My quotations are exclusively from Indonesian official sources and my point is that there are times in this world, under existing conditions, when cultural borrowing at an official level may cause serious difficulties for a government. Cultural borrowing nowadays is not merely an individual matter without national or international significance. Cultural borrowing at governmental level may pose the problem of a nation's foreign policy and cause it either to dodge the issue or to feel that it has an opportunity to take a position on a world issue.

I trust that no one will feel that there is any ethic in this paper, that there is any implication of "should." My purpose is not to say what any nation should or should not do, but merely to point out the problem that may face any nation when cultural borrowing is engaged in at governmental level, of which a great deal is being done today in all parts of the world, not just Southeast Asia.

Cultural borrowing which is done in an organized and systematic manner may raise the problem of trade relations with other countries as these relations are affected by the world situation. I mean by this that the direction and character of a nation's trade may be profoundly affected by its cultural borrowings. For instance, those countries borrowing culturally from the Soviet Union may be expected to channel their export trade among those nations which admit allegiance to the Communist cause. Or those accepting aid under the Colombo Plan or under the Mutual Security Act may be expected to deal in most matters with the free nations of the world and to give certification regarding certain kinds of trade.

As Southeast Asia is a raw-materials producer of such things as rice, tin, rubber, teak, quinine, rotenone, petroleum and copra, a problem may arise as to the disposition of those products in such a way as to enable the producing country to import the manufactured goods it requires. Again, I am merely pointing out the fact that a problem exists of a national economic nature. What are its possible ramifications?

For instance, there is the possible effect on the nation's currency reserves and accordingly on the strength of the currency in the world market. This is a vital consideration and may spell the rise and fall of governments and may mean all the difference between good living and hardship for the people in the nation.

Or again, there is the problem of the effect of such borrowing on the export-import firms, perhaps developing some new ones and eliminating others. In this connection it may become necessary, in the view of the government, to participate governmentally in international trade, perhaps by establishing governmental monopolies, government controlled companies, and control of currency exchange. This may lead to new opportunities for bureaucratic graft. And again in this connection the nation may find that its traditional markets for certain of its products have been eliminated and that it is necessary to create new ones. With only slight effort one could easily think of numbers of other problems of an economic national sort which might be brought on by systematic governmental borrowing of things and of technological advice.

Cultural borrowing poses problems within the nation which may be on a nation-wide scale. For instance a nation may be faced with the problem of how to make use of certain heavy trucks and heavy construction equipment which are required for new internal trade developments and for new construction of hydroelectric plants and irrigation systems. The existing road system may be adequate within limits for the traditional kind of internal highway traffic. But if these new things are to be obtained, not only more roads are required but roads of a nature able to bear heavy traffic. A deliberate decision must be made by that nation which will have to consider the expenditure of additional millions of dollars and of the effect on millions of people who because of the new hydroelectric plants and the new irrigation systems may be brought for the first time into contact with electrical equipment and with the possibility of planting two crops per year. These are serious problems and hard decisions must be made.

On a national scale, there is also the problem of public health. Not only health is involved but the essential life of the people. A changed psyche is involved when people learn that by spraying DDT they no longer suffer from that evil spirit, malaria, no longer have enlarged spleen, no longer are sick during the rice harvesting season, no longer form an under-populated area but begin to become overpopulated. Good public health is not an unmitigated blessing as it poses count-less new problems: problems of birth control, education, em-ployment, litigation, amusement, price control, and taxes.

Cultural borrowing in the field of agriculture may estab-lish new planting practices, seed selection, new harvesting methods, two instead of one crop per year, and diversification of crops. We have seen how the rise of the Department of Ag-riculture led to the decline of the ancient and honorable Ploughing Ceremony and other associated ceremonial and religious customs which had been depended on to secure good crops. By introducing a new and Western technique the old familiar magic is passing out of life. This poses social and religious problems as well as agricultural, because the foundation pattern of the agricultural community is being altered.

Just how deeply cultural borrowing affects the individual as well as the nation may be shown by the development of a sense of time and space in connection with the coming of the railroads. Until that event the telling of the time of day was done in rough calculation in connection with the sun in its orbit. A peasant family saw the railroad come and decided to ride on it to the next town to see relatives. In their customary thinking the next town was a long way off. They arrived bag and basket at the little station and learned to their dismay that the train had gone and the next one would arrive the next day at 8 A.M. They returned the next day and found they had missed the train again. Taking no chances they camped on the tracks that night and kept watch for the arrival of the train the next day. When they had successfully caught it they noted as best they could what 8 A.M. was in connection with the sun. They were then ready victims for the first salesman of Swiss watches. So sharp has the sense of "being on time" developed that the American Chargé in Bangkok, who was giving a dinner party for the Regent and Cabinet members, was caught completely unprepared when his important guests all arrived fifteen minutes early. When the railroad came through, something more than a transportation system happened. Educators in Southeast Asia have remarked that there is a new sense of hustle and push about the students. Perhaps timetables and competition are getting in their insidious work, for better or for worse. Southeast Asia too now has its deadlines!

Cultural borrowing of the sort that I have indicated may lead to new employment possibilities, to the use of money as an essential of life for the first time. This may lead young men and women to leave the traditional village pattern and to cut loose for an adventure with the Food and Agriculture Organization, or with the World Health Organization, or with the creators of new trades and businesses. This raises the problem of village authority, of family unity, in fact of the structure of the family itself as young people may take advantage of their new freedoms to indulge in unsocial practices which do not lead to the normal establishment of family life. This is in itself a serious problem.

Part of this last problem is the additional one of what to do with foreign trainees who have lived abroad for years, have adjusted themselves to the West, and return home to no job which uses their new knowledge and abilities. I have heard it said that the sending of such trainees is not altogether good and should be reconsidered. But in my observation and experience, the most successful agents in the process of acculturation are not the missionaries, are not the business and tradesmen from the West, are not the Western technicians skilled in erecting dams or building railroads, are not the colonial powers with all their pressures and temperatures of administrative control, are not the experts loaned by Western governments to the governments of Southeast Asia. The most successful agents are the trainees who have been sent abroad for a period of years, perhaps by their parents, perhaps by their government, perhaps by a business firm, perhaps by the missionaries, perhaps by the administrators of aid programs, who become thoroughly steeped in the new practices, the new points of view, the new critical and dispassionate and objective outlook on their own nation, and then return to their cities, almost never to their old villages, to practice what they have learned. Whether they have learned much or little, at least that amount becomes indigenous and will bear fruit, good and evil. The tragedy for them sometimes is that there is no outlet for their learning and they turn to the running of restaurants or the making of local movies, or become country gentlemen. Here is a problem—the trainee who has borrowed enthusiastically and wholeheartedly from the culture of the West.

Implicit in these problems is the problem of personal irresponsibility in which the traditional patterns of restraint have been broken down. It is no accident that a Southeast

Asian nation has recently reorganized its ecclesiastical and cultural affairs activities into a full-fledged ministry and has sent delegates to a Moral Re-Armament Conference to pick up new ideas as to how to cope with the moral breakdown that is an inevitable concomitant of broken culture patterns. They face the problem of how to give a sense of assurance, of belonging in a world of shifting values and of changing ideals and practices.

Perhaps one of the most vital problems which cannot be dodged is that of re-rationalizing the traditional religion to bring it up to date, to adapt it to man's current needs so that it will answer his desire-drives for a sense of security, for food, for prestige, for amusement, for power. To give him a feeling of being at home in this modern world, man's religion must be, in his eyes, free from anachronism, able and powerful to make him feel at home in his environment, worthy of his full faith and devotion. It is well known that although the formal religions of Southeast Asia are Islam and Buddhism and Christianity, traditional spiritism still holds great appeal for many. Most people are apologetic about spiritism, the concept that all of nature is indwelt by the same sort of spirit or soul that is supposed to be in man. This is called superstition. The ubiquitous presence of spirit shrines bears mute witness to the secret importance of spiritism to countless millions of people. I would not be at all surprised some day to read a book of profound philosophic wisdom written by a Southeast Asian who had studied philosophy at Harvard in which he demonstrates with the most approved philosophic techniques, perhaps using the terminology of Whitehead, the philosophic soundness of the world view of spiritism and of the pure ethic involved in ancestor worship as it results in evolving substantial family solidarity. It could be done, I imagine. At any rate, such re-rationalization is being done constantly in the religions which are generally regarded as more sophisticated and suitable to complex modern thinking. One need but read *Out of Exile* by Soetan Sjahrir to know that

Southeast Asia can and does produce a fine philosophic mind.

And there is the problem of how to handle the new literary forms which are arising. What happens when a poetic people become prosaic? This is a problem which I believe has not been recognized by any Southeast Asian. There are only two languages in the world, so I have been told, which contain a complete literature: English and French. It is not surprising that many forms of literature are found wanting in Southeast Asia. Nor, in view of the extensive Hinduization of the area, is it surprising that out of the Ramayana and the Mahabharata have come, by Hindu inspiration and Southeast Asian genius, a tremendous poetic literature which is complex, sophisticated and highly stylized. But prose is now the order of the day. Politics, technology, and commerce are not poetic. First-class prose composition has yet to be produced in Southeast Asia. A fundamental change of character in the writers is required. And such change is in process. Is not this a problem of prime importance and worthy of the most careful study?

And what happens when a people who have been uncritical chroniclers of their own events become historians and develop the objective, analytical methods of the modern historians of the West? As yet this has not happened in Southeast Asia, but it will happen. What will it mean? It will mean that the peoples of Southeast Asia will for the first time evaluate themselves as though they were outsiders to their own experience. When this begins to happen, and perhaps it has begun, we will probably witness some drastic events of a social and political nature.

Let me illustrate this. In the Buddhist areas the peasant people who make up most of the population have been content with a simple life. The average man has been content with a small plot of ground, one wife, several children, a couple of bullocks and a cart, a pair of dice, and a fighting cock. His religion has not encouraged ambition of a personal nature, as he has been convinced that life is sorrow, and when in fact he looks about himself and finds how poor his life is he is not surprised. His monks have always told him so. He has no inclination to revolt to secure a better life, he has no inclination to organize in labor movements to require better pay and to secure more things. He knows that life consists essentially of two truths: "Do good and receive good; do evil and receive evil"; and "We are born, we get old, we sicken, we die." So he leads a life of making merit and doing good, and he lets nature take its course. It is no accident that there has never been a popular revolution in Hinduized or Buddhist Southeast Asia required by masses of discontented people. In the first place they are not discontented. What revolution there has been has been brought about by the Westernized minority. In general, the peasant is a happy man because he has the essentials of life although not its luxuries. What improvements in life he has received in the way of sewage disposal, electricity, and transportation have been made available by his superiors, the ruling class, who make up about 7 per cent of the population.

But what will happen when critical historians and political scientists replace the traditional chroniclers and the children of the peasants read these books? What will happen when they become aware of the full implications of human rights and opportunities and discover such diverse things as the Republican and Democratic conventions, the dogma of Communism, the organized action of Labor, or the "glasses and false teeth for everyone" of Socialism?

It is possible that as they learn about these things critically, with evaluation, they will wish to do likewise. On the other hand, it is possible that they will study what happens in countries which have these practices and will go back to live simply with the bullock cart, the fighting cock, and with leisure for good conversation with village friends.

As you see, I am merely raising questions and providing no answers. Several years ago I sat in the office of an Adviser to the Foreign Office at Bangkok talking with an old friend about Thailand's course in the modern world and the possible effect upon the peasant population. He knew the country people and loved them well, as did I. He said with mixed feelings: "We have launched a series of programs which for the first time in our modern history will profoundly alter the essential way of life of every villager. We believe that it is for their good and for the good of the nation. Yet we know that we are watching the inexorable passing of a happy way of life. We do not know whether the people will ever again be so happy as they have been in their simple village life. Whether for good or evil, however, these changes are inevitable as we are caught in a course of history and for our people and nation to survive we believe we must be pliable and adapt ourselves to the new ways."

Paul M. A. Linebarger

COMMUNISM AS A COMPETING CIVILIZATION IN SOUTHEAST ASIA

THERE ARE FOUR major points which I wish to make. Each is submitted tentatively and each is offered for confirmation or denial independently of the others. It will nevertheless be seen that together the four add up to a family of political hypotheses which, if accepted, might qualify some of our academic approaches, as well as some of our governmental procedures, in the manipulation of political, social, or cultural data from Southeast Asia.

These are the four points:

1. The struggle for and against Communism in Southeast Asia is not a war between political entities, as such, but is the recrudescence of a long-dormant phenomenon—the competition of two civilizations on terms of approximate military equality.

2. World War II and the postwar struggles of the period 1945–52 have involved *two* separate sets of cultural phenomena. The first set comprised a more or less traditional application of the familiar and recognized processes known as "war" in Western European civilization and in other civilizations which have accepted Western European trappings, as this kind of "war" has been fought between sovereign states for the last several centuries. The other phenomenon was the reappearance of the kind of intercivilizational war familiar to Europe in antiquity and in the Middle Ages, but not seen in the Western world since the defeat of the Turks at Vienna.

This old war has been hidden by the apparent problems of the conventional kinds of war whose procedures it accepts as a mask.

3. Specifically, intercivilizational war differs from inter-sovereign war in two important respects. First, intercivilizational war is always—to the uttermost physical limits of the capacity of the participants—ecumenical in character. Any war anywhere becomes a part of a general world civil war. Secondly, all war becomes chronic, rather than periodic. The old intersovereign wars of the recent past have been opened with declarations of war and have been concluded with treaties of peace. Chronic war is neither declared nor terminated. It ends in victory or annihilation. In most cases the participants such as the Huks in the Philippines, the Viet Minh in Indo-China, or the Communist authorities of China proper are incapable of concluding any kind of a peace with their respective antagonists in Taipeh, Saigon, or Manila.

4. My fourth point is perhaps the most contentious. If the three preceding assumptions are accepted, there is no end to the present cold war, and there should be no end to it, not until the Soviet system is destroyed and much of our own system with it—not until the two discordant and competing industrial civilizations of today have cancelled each other out and have yielded their place, after World War III, or after World War IV, or after World War V, to a new and different industrial civilization which can command the assent of all mankind and can solve the problem of reconciling personal liberty with political stability in a way that neither we nor the Communists have yet contrived.

I do not wish to set forth these four points without also presenting at least the elements of a defense of this point of view to which I have been driven as much by personal experience, as by the formal processes of an individual attempt at political thinking.

For working purposes, it will be evident that I am using civilization in a fairly specific sense. I am happy to admit that my own criteria for the concept of "civilization" derives in the first instance from the political philosophy of Sun Yat-sen and in the second instance from the writings of Arnold Toynbee. I accept Sun Yat-sen's identification of a civilization as a reasonably coherent cultural unity, fairly formal in structure, and possessing a recognizable degree of ideological coherency, and of accepted political expression. To Toynbee I would consider that all of us are in debt for his careful preparation of a roster of civilizations and for his integration of a great deal of historical speculation and social theory into a coherent rationale of history. It is easy in any particular to disagree with Professor Toynbee, but it is difficult not to enjoy and to employ the immense scaffolding which his scholarship and imagination have built.[1] I have been further influenced in my attempt to understand what is happening in Southeast Asia and in the rest of the world by the writings of Jan Huizinga, whose *Homo Ludens* appeared in German in 1939, in Spanish a few years later, and in English in 1950.[2]

Huizinga answered—to my own personal intellectual satisfaction—a point which I had noted in both a lay and a professional capacity for many years. It is a very simple point, very deceptive, and indeed very troublesome to anyone who has lived in several different cultures. Every social activity conducted by men has a strictly utilitarian role which is usually visible to a visitor from another culture. Over and above this there is a game-playing role, usually invisible to the operator himself, which has been given by the culture, and which complicates the utilitarian performance of whatever is being done. Everything from the worship of God to the making of

[1] For instance, I myself think that his distinction between Sinic and Far Eastern civilizations is a mistaken one, and that he should have made his division vertically in space instead of horizontally in time, and should have had a Sinic civilization running from the beginnings of China through and including the regime of Chiang Kai-shek, and a Yamato civilization running from the early stone age beginning of Japanese culture down to the present moment.

[2] New York (Roy Publishers).

love or the waging of war all the way over to the writing of
books, the assembling of automobiles or the holding of conferences, is shot through by a greater or less proportion of
nonutilitarian ceremony, included simply because people have
processed that operation so many times before. The proportion of play in an operation such as the writing of State Department policy papers, the preparation of a Master's thesis,
or the winning of a decoration from one of the armed services may not be visible to the participant himself, but I suspect that if a first-class anthropologist had been trained by
Dr. Dubois while she was at Alor, and were returning the
compliment of her visit by making an anthropological study
of Dr. Dubois' presiding over our tribal rituals here at this
conference, he might have some very cogent observations to
make about the particular American techniques for playing
at the game of pretended collective thinking and of the exchange of opinions and information.

I would not wish to be understood as going to the extreme
of the English poet, John Gay, who wrote his own epitaph
two-hundred years ago,

> *Life is a jest, and all things show it;*
> *I thought so once, and now I know it . . .*

and had the couplet engraved on his tombstone. To say that
the play factor in any cultural activity is important is very
different indeed, is it not, from saying that all cultural activities are games and nothing but games?

This brings me, belatedly perhaps, to the common foundation of the four hypotheses which I have submitted. The nonutilitarian function of the social organizations and political
instrumentalities which we and the Communists respectively
command have become so important as to displace the particular utilitarian purposes. The sovereign state, once set up to
protect individuals, now constitutes the greatest danger to
individuals anywhere in the world. An intranational and international structure of law designed to maintain peace is so

overdeveloped that it helps to perpetuate a system of national armaments more important than the civilian economies they are designed to protect. The old democracies which we like to call the Free World claim to offer men liberty, while at the same time increasing their regimentation of property, individual movement, and individual activity, while the Communists offer peace and social security at the price of a revolution more bloody and more terrifying than anything mankind has ever seen. Tamerlane at his bloodiest never killed as many individuals in a single day as did one bomb dropped from an aircraft on Hiroshima seven years ago. We are so busy playing the games of international politics, of strategic security, and of economic procedures, that the means have displaced the ends almost altogether.

In terms of abstract theory, there is not enough difference between the utopian theory of Communism and the utopian theory of free enterprise for two reasonable men to fight each other during a single afternoon of debate, much less to plan mass homicide on an unprecedented scale. But the game is being played. We are both the players and the stakes.

How has the world-wide game been going? Perhaps you will agree with me if I suggest that the Communist practice has been working better than ours, even though the Communist theory is from our point of view wrong. Communists have been winning territory during the last seven years, while anti-Communists have been losing it. They still have a novel, disciplined, and inspiring purpose. That purpose may be polluted with the crimes of the Stalinist oligarchy and debased by the cruelties of Communist conquest, but it is still inspiring.

I found in Korea and in Malaya during the last two years, when I talked to captured Communists, that men who defected from Communism had a very real sense of being spiritually forlorn. What I would like to dub the *teleocratic* factor in culture is a massive strength to the Communists, and a conspicuous weakness to us.

By *teleocracy* [3] I would like to subsume the real or pretended subordination of public policy and military strategy to a stated and understandable purpose. The Communists offer three simple elements of participation to the common man in Asia, particularly in Southeast Asia, which the United States and the United Kingdom do not offer. These are, as I should guess their order of importance: first, *understandability,* or the provision of an explanation which (whether to us historically and economically correct or not) gives the ordinary man an explanation of his own personal role in the history of the present age; second, *action,* or the supply of participation in a social or political role sufficient to bind him to the Communist movement; third, supplementing the first, *purpose,* or the opportunity to make a sacrifice for the sake of the human race, to give up his own property or his own life in the service of a cause greater than that of any one class, nation or race.

The issue is so important and so frequently misunderstood that it is worth restating once more in fresh terms. *Communism is important because ordinary Asians can give to it,* not because of what it may give them someday. It has the fanatic and religious appeal of a new system and its most formidable weapons are those which lie outside most of our own everyday thinking about politics and economics. Rights and wealth are not the issue. The destiny of humanity is.

Of course the Communists have an everyday civilization of their own—a very grim and unpleasant one. But their strength lies in what they take from people (help, loyalty, love, effort) and not in what they give people (food, clothing, bicycles). Hence the Communists can pretend to co-exist in our own politico-economic world without serious interference to their main business. They even have the impertinence to em-

---

[3] The neologism is obviously derived from the Greek terms τέλος, "end," and κρᾶτος, "power," as these have been so often adapted in Western philosophy.

ploy the sovereign state which they have long sworn to obliterate. The Communists use the old trappings of the sovereign state contemptuously. Communist ambassadors usually obey the letter of diplomatic protocol while despising the governments to which they are accredited.

Communist civilization has the advantage of being able to believe in its own values while exploding the values of that older civilization—our civilization—which Communism is attempting to supersede. There is a Gresham's law in politics and war, no less than in monetary policy. Bad values drive out good. We can laugh at the spectacle of Don Quixote throwing the pathetic trappings of chivalry against the modern warfare of the Renaissance, but we usually cannot see the pathos of a General Stilwell, a General MacArthur, or a General Marshall believing in the sovereign state while the essence of sovereignty (real national independence) dissolves before his very eyes.

I myself have seen the mocking superiority in the eyes of Chou En-lai while the American busybodies, anachronistic survivors of a dying age, talked their naive doubletalk in front of a man who thought he had a better grasp of reality than did they.

The process is a two-way process. Dr. George Pettee is preparing a treatise on systemic revolution which will say this, I hope, much better than can I. Let me point out that once intercivilizational war coexists with intersovereign war, there is a two-way exchange. The cultural patterns of intersovereign war are borrowed by the newer phase. The Viet-Nam government, in fighting France, uses for some purposes the ideas and cultural standards which the Prussians and the Imperial French used in 1871; for other purposes it does not.

To take another example, for some purposes North Korea and Red China are behaving as states in the old formal international legal sense in their present war against the United States in Korea; for other purposes they are behaving as the militant public arms of an international revolutionary movement. The reversal of this process can be seen in the attempts by Germany and by Japan in the last war to steal from Russia the pretense of creating new totalitarian civilizations. The Germans pretended that they were as much of a new civilization as was Russian Communism, and the twenty-odd states of the Axis allegedly set up their own new world, when in fact a greater proportion of the cultural elements in their war efforts were traditional factors of nationalism, carried to an extreme, rather than genuinely revolutionary manifestations of the postsovereign community.

Let me conclude by applying this specifically to Southeast Asia. Most of the struggles in Southeast Asia are struggles which cannot be ended by treaties of peace. There can be no treaty between the Huks and Manila, between Viet-Nam and Viet Minh, between the MRLA and the Office of the British Commissioner General for Southeast Asia. The wars in Southeast Asia are chronic. They are ecumenical, and I see no probability that they will end.

Speaking individually, I do not see how World War III can be avoided sooner or later. But, still speaking individually, I would not wish to take away from Providence the condign privilege of setting loose disasters among mankind. Many inevitable things—or things which seemed inevitable in their time—have failed to come about. Perhaps World War III will also fail to materialize. Meanwhile, I would like to recommend that if we look beyond the present structure of sovereign states to some new and different system of postsovereign government, we may find that many parts of our present efforts are directed indeed to the long future. The regional instrumentalities developed under the United Nations, such as the Economic Commission for Asia and the Far East, the structures of cooperation being worked out by the various STEM missions of the Economic Cooperation Administration and the Mutual Security Agency, the public and private cooperation presented by some of the major engineering contracts undertaken in Burma and Formosa, and even the programs of straight military cooperation, represent modifications of older and more rigorous standards of "sovereign" action.

May I express the belief that the long-range hope of mankind lies in an escape from the oppressiveness of the sovereign state through the gradual emergence of co-sovereign and post-sovereign instrumentalities which, like the Supreme Headquarters Allied Powers–Europe, will imperceptibly modify and mitigate the evils and irresponsibilities of untrammeled sovereignty, and that concurrently there will be a development, as indeed there is, for the pluralization of authority within each national community? In this respect, we and the Communists may be performing good deeds for a bad purpose. The bad purpose, of course, is the fighting of World War III. The good deeds consist of learning ways whereby families or groups of nations can learn to function within the cultural patterns of larger postsovereign communities.

The leaders of Southeast Asia have too recently escaped the oppressive jurisdiction of one postsovereign community, the GEACPS, or Greater East Asia Co-Prosperity Sphere of militarist Japan, to be very enthusiastic about creating a postsovereign community of their own at the present time. The three-way division of the area into national independent states, Communist satellites, and colonial territories makes any Southeast Asian federation extremely improbable for the immediate future. Momentarily, the old-fashioned kind of nationalism and assertive independence preached in Southeast Asia may appear to be a rather quaint and remote kind of reaction. The cosmopolitan cultural drives of Islam and Buddhism and the rich social inheritances of the Southeast Asian peoples are such that one can hope that the new states of Southeast Asia will sooner or later escape from the ideological trap of nineteenth-century European sovereignty into which they have now fallen, and that they will have their own highly distinctive contribution to make to the political civilization of mankind in this and the next century.

Kenneth E. Wells

THE CULTURAL IMPLEMENTATION OF

GOVERNMENTAL PROGRAMS

IN SOUTHEAST ASIA

For the purpose of this discussion, culture is defined broadly as the technical, literary and artistic attainments as well as the beliefs and traditions of a nation or social group. If culture thus defined confuses us, the bewilderment increases as we consider it in connection with the numerous and scattered peoples that make up the congeries of nations in Southeast Asia. Their names indicate their racial complexities: "The Union of Burma," "The Federation of Malaya," "The Republic of Indonesia," and "The Associated States of Indo-China"—which are associated with France but do not have direct diplomatic relations with each other. Only Thailand seems to have racial unity and yet we recall that it has a racial minority of some three-million Chinese. In fact the Chinese comprise the one Asian race found in significant numbers in all of the five states just mentioned, and their language and culture must be reckoned with by each of the national governments as well as by the governments of France, Britain, Australia and the United States that carry on cultural activities in that area.

Many of the governmental cultural programs in Southeast Asia are an outgrowth of World War II which stimulated Asian nationalism and Communism. But the spread of technology, of ideas, is a continuous and inevitable process and is only partially conditioned by politics. The Indonesians now speak of world culture to which East and West contribute. The cultural and social programs of the United Nations are conducted by an association of governments and are evidence of the reality of a modicum of universally accepted cultural values. That is to say, all nations, East and West, admit the desirability of technical training in engineering and medicine and agree that science and medicine do not bear the label of any one nation.

By defining culture, in part, as the technical and artistic attainments of a group we note that whatever contributes to the health of a people, to their literacy, communications, working and living conditions, and their political competence has increased the sum total of their culture. Such improvements at least alter traditional culture, e.g., spirit doctors and fertility rites depart when the latest medicines and agricultural methods are brought in. Therefore the technical assistance programs of the United Nations and of the various governments are indirectly if not directly cultural programs as well. Our subject, "Cultural Programs," is thus a large one. Here we can do little more than enumerate the kinds of programs contributing to culture now being undertaken by governments in Southeast Asia and indicate the manner in which they are being implemented. The extent and effectiveness of such programs are beyond our range.

Eight agencies of the United Nations are carrying on activities that are in some sense cultural. The first to come to mind is the UN Educational, Scientific and Cultural Organization (UNESCO) whose budget for 1951 was $8,200,000.00. Some of its stated cultural objectives are the encouragement of education in art, drama and music for youth and for people with leisure time; the encouragement of philosophy as a contribution to education and to international understanding; assistance in the maintenance of museums and monuments possessed of universal interest; the publication of bulletins dealing with museums, libraries, copyrights and translations;

the encouragement of exhibitions of contemporary art that travel from country to country; and the establishment of a clearing house for information on translation, library collections and museums. Apart from these cultural objectives, UNESCO has other educational and scientific objectives as well.

By February, 1951, UNESCO had organized National Commissions in forty-nine nations to help initiate and implement its cultural programs. In Thailand, for example, the UNESCO National Commission has on it a representative from the Thai Ministry of Culture. This Commission sent a Thai delegate to the UNESCO-sponsored International Arts Conference in Venice. In 1950 a UNESCO commission surveyed the educational needs of Thailand, issued a report, and then with the cooperation of the Thai Government started a pilot educational project at Cha-Choeng-Sao, sixty miles from Bangkok. At least five educational experts from different nations are on the staff, and the ten-year program of primary and science education inaugurated there is being studied with interest by school teachers throughout Thailand.

To cite further examples from Thailand, the UN Food and Agricultural Organization (FAO) has established regional headquarters in Bangkok and many of its conferences, surveys, reports and activities arouse in all the countries of Southeast Asia an awareness of their common needs and problems. FAO has held training courses in Bangkok that have drawn students from adjacent countries and it plans to continue this service. The cultural contribution of FAO to Thailand includes the granting of thirty-four fellowships this year, twelve to the United States, and the maintenance of educational specialists in the pilot-training center.

A third agency, the UN World Health Organization (WHO), has a budget this year of over $1,750,000.00 for work in Thailand, Burma and Indonesia. It carries on educational and training services as well as field work attacking malaria and other diseases directly. A fourth agency, the UN International Childrens Emergency Fund (UNICEF), has budgeted over $500,000.00 for Thailand alone this year, to be used for maternal and child welfare work and for public health. The UN Economic Commission for Asia and the Far East (ECAFE) maintains technical assistance and advisory experts in Thailand and elsewhere, and the International Labour Organization (ILO) carries on some educational work by providing specialists who teach vocational guidance. Finally there are the International Civil Aviation (ICAO) and the UN Technical Assistance Administration that promote training and research programs in Southeast Asia.

It should be borne in mind that these United Nations agencies do not work in a vacuum but through the invitation of the various national governments and with the cooperation of officials who benefit by participation and demonstration. The governments contribute funds as well as personnel to the projects and are thereby committed to the programs and deserve part of the credit for the social and cultural improvements which result.

The British-sponsored Colombo Plan should be mentioned if only to note that its Consultative Committee reports that the Australian Government has offered three hundred fellowships and scholarships to the countries of South and Southeast Asia up to last September. The Australian Government is making an effective bid for private university students from Southeast Asia, and it is extending the influence of Australian schools by giving text books and educational films to the governments of neighboring countries.

The United States conducts five programs which have cultural influence on Southeast Asia. These are the Mutual Security Program, the Point Four Program, the Smith-Mundt and Fulbright Programs, and the activities of the U.S. Information Service or International Information Administration.

Dr. Clarence R. Decker, writing on "U.S. Economic Aid to Southeast Asia" and of the Mutual Security Agency program in particular, stated that by June, 1952, the United

States Government had allocated $102,900,000.00 for economic aid to Indo-China, Burma, Indonesia and Thailand. About 10 per cent of this was for advisory and informational services. Much of the material granted—such as surgical and laboratory instruments and radio and communications equipment—has stimulated technical training in countries receiving aid. In Indo-China the MSA program enabled 105,000 people to become literate; in Indonesia it recently sent thirty-one doctors, officials and others to the United States for training; in Burma it furnished some equipment to help rehabilitate Rangoon University, and in Thailand it maintains a number of technical experts whose functions are educational. The Mutual Security Agency was able to consider applications for over three hundred scholarships from students in Southeast Asia this year.

The Smith-Mundt funds, in addition to scholarship grants, enable foreign leaders in government, education and social welfare to visit the United States for three or four months in order to observe methods and techniques of interest to them. The Fulbright Program provides travel funds for an exchange of students and of professors between the United States and countries such as Burma and Thailand that come under the agreement. The American lecturers are often men of prominence and experience who are willing to spend a sabbatical year in foreign universities and cultural circles. Thailand, for example, receives under the Fulbright Program from eight to twelve American teachers per year, several lecturers, and one or more research scholars, and it sends upwards of sixty Thai students and observers to the United States.

There are many information services conducted by local and Western governments in Southeast Asia, and many aspects of these services are primarily if not solely cultural. The French colonial government introduced French culture in Indo-China before World War II through schools, publications, the radio, and through scholarships which took young men to France. At the same time the French made intensive and commendable efforts to preserve ancient Cambodian and Annamese culture by restoring monuments and temples, and collecting and translating manuscripts and epigraphs. Since World War II French cultural activities in Indo-China have necessarily declined, but the French Information Service carries on an active program by radio and press and continues to stress French and Oriental art. The Cambodian Government is continuing archaeological studies and restoration of great monuments in the Angkor Wat area.

In prewar Malaya, British culture made an impact through government, trade, education and the press. School curricula were patterned on British models with students preparing for the Cambridge matriculation exams. As a result, the intellectual and monetary interests of the people became oriented to England as well as to China, and English is now widely used by all races in Malaya. At present there is no British Information Service as such in Malaya, but there is a department of Information Services sponsored by the Government of the Federation of Malaya. The British maintain Information Services in neighboring Burma, Thailand, Indo-China and Indonesia, however. Their programs in each of these countries include offers of scholarships, the issuance of news bulletins, news photographs and books dealing with the United Kingdom, the loan of films and projectors, and the maintenance of libraries and exhibits. They also cooperate with associations known as British Councils which sponsor classes in English language instruction. Possibly the most effective single informational medium is the British Broadcasting Company with its programs of news, music, and addresses, relayed from Ceylon and Singapore.

The extent to which various countries carry on cultural and information programs is illustrated by the situation in Burma. Burman listeners get news and information from the powerful All-India Radio, the British Broadcasting Company, Radio Ceylon, Radio Burma, Radio Saigon, Radio Thailand, the Voice of America, Radio Peiping and Radio Moscow.

There are British and United States Information Services in both Rangoon and Mandalay. In addition, Burma has its own Government Information Office that operates mobile film units, issues press releases and serves as the official mouthpiece of the Government. The Peking Government sent a Chinese Cultural Mission to Burma which brought along an exhibit of Chinese arts and crafts. In turn, a Burmese Cultural Mission visited China in April, 1952.

The U.S.S.R. has started a cultural program by organizing a Burma-Soviet Cultural Society, supplying Russian films and books, and offering an exchange of persons. An Indonesian Good-Will Mission toured Burma in March, 1952, publicizing Indonesian culture through talks and pamphlets, and giving leadership grants to Burmese journalists to visit Java. An All-Burman Indian Cultural Conference met at the University of Rangoon in December, 1951, at which seminars were held on Indian culture, history and philosophy. Burmese Buddhist Missions have toured the Buddhist shrines of India and have been warmly received by the Indian Government. An All-Burma Pakistan League has been formed and through it offers have been made of scholarships for study in Pakistan. In April, 1952, steps were taken to form a Burma-Japan Cultural Association and to interest the Burmese Government in sending students to Japan.

Southeast Asia is thus a crossroad of information, or in some cases of misinformation. The United States Information Service emphasizes American culture because detractors have said that the United States is new, materialistic, and cultureless. This statement has been accepted by many Asians who acknowledge United States technical achievements but are unwilling to believe that the United States can possess everything—including culture in a spiritual, artistic and literary sense. Lacking such culture, the United States in their eyes lacks prestige and fails in leadership. The United States Information Service endeavors to offset this impression by such means as the operation of libraries and reading rooms and the consignment of loan collections of books to schools and organizations, exhibits of photographs and the use of hundreds of cinema films, programs broadcast over local radios which include American music, and a press service that provides news items, pictures and articles to local publications—all stressing American activities and way of living. By-products of such cultural information are requests for instruction in the English language—which are met by language classes—and requests for travel and scholarship grants to the United States. Some indication of the extent of the U.S. Information Service in Southeast Asia can be gained from the observation that American films are shown to about 300,000 Indonesians monthly, and that the magazine "American Miscellany" has the largest circulation of any publication in Indonesia.

The information and cultural programs of Western governments have prompted Eastern governments to engage in similar activities. However much the peoples of Southeast Asia may admire Western technology and English literature, they have an understandable desire to retain their own cultural identity of distinctiveness. National consciousness and racial pride are bound up in this attitude. For some of the complex Eastern states the problems of defining and promoting national culture are extraordinarily difficult. The three states of Indo-China, for example, although contiguous, are quite dissimilar ethnically and linguistically. The principal languages are Viet-Namese, Cambodian, Laos, and Chinese; in addition there are many tribal tongues. The Viet-Namese use a relatively new romanized script which is unintelligible to the Laos and the Cambodians. The Cambodians and the Laos support Buddhism while the Viet-Namese divide their allegiance among many faiths including Cao Dai-ism, Confucianism, Taoism, Buddhism and Christianity. In general, literacy is low, and in Viet-Nam large portions of the population are inaccessible to the government, except possibly by radio, because the people live in Communist-controlled areas. Nevertheless, Cambodia and Laos have newly-formed Government Information Services, while Viet-Nam has a full-fledged service which operates about one thousand reading centers, four radio stations and a press service. At present their information programs are so conditioned by the military situation that political rather than cultural considerations come first.

In the Republic of Indonesia the cultural picture is likewise complex. The population of seventy-seven million is scattered over about two thousand islands, and while it is predominantly Muslim in faith it contains large minorities of Hindus, Buddhists and Christians, and many diverse ethnic groups. Much of Javanese art is Indian and Buddhist, having developed during the Srivijaya and Majapathi Empires, roughly A.D. 700 to 1478. The official Indonesian language contains numerous Indian, Arabic and Dutch words. In November, 1951, the Indonesian Government set up a Cultural Advisory Council in the Ministry of Education to recommend a cultural policy. Dr. R. Supomo, writing on "Our Cultural Policy," said, "Our cultural heritage is in essence characterized by the belief in God. The traditional Indonesian philosophy of life is based on the unity between God and man, unity between Man and other creatures, and unity between the material world and the spiritual world." He went on to say that the Eastern world generally had the same philosophical goal as the Indonesians, namely to achieve harmony between individuals, groups, man and nature. In contrast, he viewed the culture of the West as materialistic and individualistic.

Judging by statements made by the Indonesian Government in its information booklets, the cultural policy of Indonesia will not be narrowly sectarian but will embody religious and humanitarian principles. The Government's first cultural task is to promote education: the present literacy rate, while increasing, is probably not much above 10 per cent and only about 40 per cent of the children are in school.

The cultural heritage of Burma is somewhat less varied and complex than those of Indo-China and Indonesia. The

Burmans, who occupy the central and lower part of the country, are Buddhists of the Southern or Theravada type. Burmese Government leaders support Buddhism in the hope that its code of ethics will counteract corruption in office, lawlessness and rebellions. They consider the present Buddhist revival in Burma to be a revival of culture and patriotism as well. The Government's interest in a national cultural movement is shown by the formation of a Ministry of Religion, a Ministry of Mass Education and Culture, and a Ministry of Information. In 1950 the Burmese Government organized and subsidized a Buddha Sasana Council or assembly of leading Buddhists to advise the Government on religious matters and to assist in carrying out religious programs. Some of the religious measures adopted are: (1) The restoration of ancient pagodas, (2) promotion of Buddhist studies in temples, schools, and universities through subsidies and new text books, and (3) the organization of a Sixth Buddhist Council to begin in May, 1954 (Buddhist Era 2500). The plans for this Council include the preparation of a special site covering one hundred acres for the delegates and the erection of a pagoda to enshrine relics to two of Buddha's disciples. The Council will endeavor to produce complete texts in English and Burmese of the Buddhist Scriptures (Tripitaka).

In Thailand the Government recently organized a Ministry of Culture. This Ministry embraces the Department of Religious Affairs, the Department of Fine Arts, and the National Institute of Culture. The Thai Government supports Buddhism as the state religion and grants an annual temple subsidy of over $500,000. Buddhism is taught in the public schools and set forth in Government radio programs, with the emphasis on good conduct and good citizenship. The Department of Public Relations—which handles publicity and information—illustrates Thai art by examples of Buddhist sculpture and architecture. Recent Government plans for education, irrigation and highway construction have been put on a five-year basis to culminate in 1957—which corresponds with Thailand's date of Buddhist Era 2500. There has been renewed discussion of a proposal to establish a Buddhist religious capital at Saraburi, north of Bangkok, likewise to be completed in 1957.

The Thai Government's cultural program is not, however, limited to religion. Recently it reorganized the five bureaus in the National Institute of Culture, namely, the Bureaus of Mental Culture, Traditional Culture, Fine Arts, Literary Culture, and Feminine Culture. Under the Bureau of Traditional Culture are committees on Customs, Good Manners, Welfare and Legal Affairs. The Department of Fine Arts supports an orchestra that gives public concerts of both Thai and Western music, and it maintains a theater that specializes in classical drama and trains student actors and dancers. The building of a large opera house in Bangkok is under consideration. The Department of Fine Arts and Government Arts and Crafts Schools have done much to preserve, promote and popularize Thai dramatic and plastic art. The Thai Government's consciousness of cultural trends elsewhere, and of Thailand's accomplishments in education, architecture and sculpture has prompted it to offer sixteen scholarships to students of neighboring countries in Southeast Asia to study in Bangkok. The granting of scholarships by various nations to foreign students is increasing yearly and augurs well for future international understanding. In 1952, sixty nations offered the almost incredible number of 38,000 such scholarships.

In conclusion, we may observe that culture can be caught as well as taught, misused as well as resisted. Conceivably there will grow up in each country in Southeast Asia an increased awareness of the cultures of other peoples, a greater consciousness of and loyalty to cultural elements—perhaps religious—in its own society, and an unconscious acceptance of many world or universal customs, techniques and values.

Part 4: LAW

Maung Htin Aung

CUSTOMARY LAW IN BURMA

THERE WERE PEOPLE living in the fertile valley of the Irrawaddy some three-thousand years ago, but we have very little
information regarding them. It is known, however, that they
used a special type of stone tool, they were acquainted with
the rudiments of agriculture, and they had certain affinities
with the stone-age people of those regions which are now
known to us as Assam and Java. But some eighteen-hundred
years ago, the Tibeto-Burman tribes appeared on the scene.
They came from the eastern slopes of the mountains of Tibet,
and their route into Burma was down the rivers Irrawaddy
and Salween. Of those new people, the most important were
the Pyus and the Burmese. The Pyus were probably the spear-
head of the migration, and in any case, they arrived before
the Burmese. Unlike similar migrations of early people, the
Tibeto-Burman tribes did not come in search of fresh sources
of supply of food. Instead they were seeking to preserve their
freedom. Their original homeland was not unfertile, and they
had evolved a culture of their own; but now their nearest
neighbors, the Chinese, becoming organized and powerful,
were harassing them, and they were fleeing southward to unknown lands to preserve their freedom and independence. It
was a perilous journey. They came in groups, and it took them
one or two centuries before they could settle in the valley of
the Irrawaddy. They brought with them to their new home
their own democratic tribal organization—and their fierce love
of freedom. They brought also their own customary law.

Since those remote times, the Burmese customary law has

developed naturally, side by side with the growth and development of Burmese society. The Burmese have no great national
code of laws gathered and authorized by a powerful king, no
great charter forced from an unwilling king, no great statute
passed by a national assembly fighting against tyranny, but
nonetheless the Burmese customary law shows a conception
of justice and a love of personal liberty in which every Burmese must take pride.

To the Burmese, before the partial introduction of the
English legal system, law meant civil law. To them, civil law
was purely customary, and besides custom, there could be no
other source of law. The idea of legislation by a parliament
or a congress, or by executive order of the king was unfamiliar
to the Burmese. In English common law, the king could do no
wrong, and thus he was above the law. But with the Burmese,
the king himself was not exempt from the operation of the
civil law, and the king was often the defendant in civil suits,
usually for wrongful seizure of land. Admittedly the king was
above his subjects, and he had the right to levy taxes in service
or in kind, but he was also under a duty to give protection to
the people. To protect the people and to preserve the peace,
the king must prevent wrong-doing and punish wrong-doers,
and it was for the king to proclaim which acts were wrongs
from the point of view of public peace. Thus, at the beginning
of each reign, the king proclaimed his list of crimes, and the
punishments he would mete out to those who were found
guilty of those crimes.

The list of crimes varied with each king, but the usual
crimes were offenses against the state, murder, robbery, theft,
rape, and serious defamation. The usual penalties were whipping, confinement in irons, maiming, banishment, and death,
with or without forfeiture to the king's treasury of the offender's possessions. In the eighteenth century, adultery was
added to the list of crimes, with the punishment of whipping
for both the woman and her paramour, and proclamation of
their guilt by beat of drums and gongs. In the nineteenth

century, the punishment for abduction of women was enhanced from one of confinement in irons to that of death. Thus what the English lawyer would understand by the term "criminal law" was considered to be the personal concern of the king. Therefore, when the ruling king died, and a new king ascended the throne, all persons undergoing punishment for crimes committed under the previous king, automatically were freed. Criminal jurisdiction therefore was considered to be merely an administrative function of the crown, and it concerned the executive, and not the judicial, officers of the state. Modern European writers have ever emphasized the despotism of Burmese kings, but the Royal Edicts proclaimed at the beginning of each reign clearly showed that the Burmese king was not a blood-thirsty individual devoid of all mercy. In the Edicts, we find the king delegating the function of meting out criminal justice to three of his Chief Ministers, admonishing at the same time that they should temper justice with mercy. The king in the Edicts ordered that even in capital crimes, the punishment should be one of banishment, and the sentence of death was to be reserved for vicious criminals. Even when the sentence of death had been passed, the execution was to be postponed for at least ten days so as to enable the king to consider the case and alter the punishment to one of banishment if the facts justified such alteration.

But as in England, the king was considered to be the fountain of justice, for his was the supreme court of the land. The kingdom was divided into provinces, each under a viceroy. Each province was further divided into cities, each city under a governor. Each city or city area was subdivided into towns and each town or town area into villages, with a headman for each town and each village. The courts of the headmen of towns or villages dealt with suits of small value, and there was a right of appeal from those courts to the courts of the governors of cities. The courts of the governors exercised both original and appellate jurisdiction, and appeals from these courts lay to the court of the viceroy, which also exercised both original and appellate jurisdiction. These officers were executive officers under the crown, but when they sat as judges in their respective courts, they were judges in the full sense of the term, for they were free of all executive control. Finally there was the Supreme Court. This final court of appeal consisted of the king as the president, the crown prince as the vice-president, the four chief ministers, and their four deputies. The king, however, attended only on rare occasions, and thus the crown prince usually presided over the court. The law that these courts administered and interpreted was the customary law of the Burmese people. One special feature of the courts was their attempt to settle the case before actually trying it. Lawyers, who were attached to the courts as officers, although their fees were payable by the litigants, also endeavored to conciliate the contending parties. Often the parties decided to refer their suit to an arbitrator. There was no right of appeal from the decision of an arbitrator, on the ground that the arbitrator was chosen by the contending parties themselves. When a suit had been heard and decided, the successful party offered a dish of pickled tea to the other party, and if the latter accepted, the parties were deemed to have been reconciled, and there could be no appeal from the decision of the court. The refusal of the unsuccessful party to accept the offered dish of pickled tea served as his notice of appeal.

Burmese history, like the history of many countries, records rebellions, invasions, and violent struggles for power, but the development of Burmese customary law has been singularly free from catastrophes and sudden changes. There has never been a revolution in the Burmese customary law. However, the law in the course of its long history experienced three great impacts with the outside world. The first was the impact of Hindu jurisprudence, second was the impact of Buddhism, and the third was the impact of English law as the result of the British conquest of the country towards the end of the nineteenth century.

Some of my colleagues of this conference have already

spoken on the impact of Hindu thought and culture on the countries of Southeast Asia. The Hindu expansion overseas was well underway by the second and third centuries after Christ, and Hindu ideas and Hindu philosophies were beginning to remold the native patterns of belief and culture in Southeast Asia. In Burma, however, only the coastal region fell under Hindu influence. The Pyus by the fifth century had founded their kingdom of Prome, then situated only a few miles away from the sea, at the mouth of the Irrawaddy. The Mons, who belonged to the Mon-Khmer tribes that had settled in the regions now known as Thailand and Indo-China, had entered Lower Burma from the east, and their kingdom of Thaton, also then on the sea, seemed to have become powerful by the fifth century, about the same time as Prome. These two cities, Prome and Thaton, probably first became important as ports of call for Hindu merchant ships sailing between India and Malaya and Java, but even in those two kingdoms, Hindu influence was not strong. Thus Burma is the one country in Southeast Asia which was not Hinduized. By the eighth century after Christ, the Irrawaddy Delta was quickly forming, and Prome became farther away from the sea; the kingdom seemed to have declined rapidly, and the Pyus began to merge with the Burmese, who had now founded their kingdom at Pagan in Upper Burma. In the eleventh century, the Burmese made their kingdom strong enough to conquer and destroy the kingdom of Thaton. The Burmese were now supreme in the land.

But the conquest of Thaton opened the outer world beyond the seas to the Burmese. From the conquered Mons the Burmese became acquainted with Hindu literature and with Buddhist scriptures. Burmese society and Burmese law now experienced the double impact of Hinduism and Buddhism, but, of course, by that time, Hindu power in Southeast Asia was a spent force. Both Burmese society and Burmese law survived those two impacts.

Hindu jurisprudence and Hindu legal literature had

molded the native customary laws in the other regions of
Southeast Asia, and the great Hindu Code of Manu, the hermit,
the sage, the lawgiver, had gained enormous prestige and authority in Southeast Asia. The Burmese scholars and lawyers
of the eleventh century studied the Code of Manu, but found
little in it to interest them. The rigid caste system, which
served as the basis of Hindu law as embodied in the Code of
Manu, made no appeal to the Burmese with their classless
society. The Burmese never had an aristocracy or a middle
class. The king was above others, but others were all equal.
There was no hereditary nobility, and the Burmese have always been so individualistic that family names or surnames
have never existed with the Burmese. The officers of the king
could be said to have formed a nobility, but if that was so, it
was a nobility into which every Burmese could enter by talent
and personality alone. The king, the chieftain, and the headman were originally elected. Thus the idea of dividing society
into classes distinguished only by birth seemed strange to the
Burmese.

Nonetheless, the prestige of the Code of Manu was so high
in Southeast Asia that the Burmese decided to make Manu
their mythical law-giver. In Hindu mythology, Manu was a
hermit, divinely inspired. In Burmese legend, Manu became
a simple cowherd who was later elected king because of his
mastery of customary law. The Burmese Manu also became
a hermit later, but he became a hermit out of remorse because he once gave a wrong decision. This wrong judgment
of the great Manu is well known in Burmese folklore as the
case of the small cucumber. There was a cucumber plant
growing in a man's garden, but as it was a creeper, it grew
across the dividing hedge and bore fruit in the neighbor's
garden. Now the man and the neighbor quarreled as to who
was entitled to the small cucumber fruit, and they took their
case before the great Manu, who decided in favor of the neighbor. But he soon reversed his decision, and feeling remorseful
over his previous judgment, became a hermit. This clearly

illustrates that with the Burmese, Manu had become only an ordinary human being with the human trait of making mistakes, so very different from the divine hermit of Hindu lore.

By the thirteenth century, the customary law of the Burmese came to be collected and written down by jurists and scholars. Throughout the intervening centuries until the British conquest of the country, such collections of the law, and also collections of judicial precedents were made from time to time by scholars and jurists. But those collections were not codes, and were not fully binding on the judges. In all these collections, Manu was mentioned as the law-giver, and this lip-service paid to the prestige of the Hindu Code of Manu has misled modern scholars, especially European scholars of Burmese history and Burmese law, into thinking that the Burmese law was merely the Hindu Code of Manu modified and transplanted almost overnight in Burma of the eleventh century.

But in the eleventh century, the Burmese did become Buddhists almost overnight. The Burmese took to Buddhism with great enthusiasm, because the way of life preached by the Buddha seemed to be identical with their own democratic way of life. The Buddhistic revolt against the rigid caste system of the Hindu society could be appreciated by the Burmese, who called the Hindu half-playfully and half-seriously, "kula" or "caste people," and the Buddhistic emphasis on the equality of all men appealed to the Burmese with their classless society and their own emphasis on individual freedom. The jurists and the scholars waxed enthusiastic over Buddhism, and they gave a Buddhistic coloring and a Buddhistic background to their collections of Burmese customary law. This misled the early British administrators and judges in Burma into thinking that Burmese customary law was Buddhistic in origin, and gave to it the misleading official name of "Burmese Buddhist Law."

The impact of the English legal system introduced into

the country after the annexation of 1886 shook Burmese customary law to its very foundations, just as Burmese society itself rocked with the shock of the impact. But Burmese society soon regained its balance, and so did Burmese customary law. The British, by statute, superseded the Burmese customary law of contract and tort with their own English common law, but recognized the Burmese customary law regarding marriage and divorce, adoption, inheritance, and religious usage, and these branches of the customary law remain valid today. Thus, whereas in India the legislature now struggles against strong public opposition to pass new statutes introducing changes in the Hindu law of marriage and inheritance so as to adjust Hindu law to new developments in Hindu society, the Burmese, after their hard-won independence, have not found it necessary to modify by statute or to codify their customary law. With regard to the English law of contract and tort that was introduced into the country after the British annexation, the Burmese did not find the new law strange and mysterious, for the fundamental principles of Burmese law of contract and tort had certain similarities with the fundamental principles of English common law. Thus the principles of specific performance, of damages, of a period of limitation, and a remoteness of damage were known to the Burmese law also. Even the English legal plea of "Act of God" for exemption from liability has its Burmese counterpart in the plea of "ill fortune." The following rules of law relating to ferries will illustrate this aspect of Burmese law:

If a man, for the sake of hire, becomes a ferryman, let him follow these rules. He shall carefully consider and take only the correct fare. If he is careless, or jocular, or immodest, and as a result, property of a passenger is spilled or damaged, let him make good the loss to the owner. But if he crosses with proper care and proper behaviour, and property be lost or damaged, let him blame ill fortune, and he shall not be liable. Women with child, monks, and sick persons shall be ferried across, even if they have no money to pay as fare.

Although the kingdoms of Prome and Thaton probably based their wealth on trade and commerce, and the kingdom of Pagan based its power and wealth on commerce, the Burmese have been simple agriculturists throughout their history, and therefore Burmese customary law of contract and torts dealt with the business of agriculture, such as water-rights, land-rights, hire of cattle, carts, and implements, and with the relations between employers and laborers. As has been stated before, the Burmese law of contract and tort is no longer valid, and although the Burmese still remain agriculturalists, their business of agriculture is no longer simple as in the days before the British annexation. Nonetheless, some of the rules of law in contract and torts are still of interest. For example, let us consider the law relating to payment of wages to laborers. The Burmese law did not give emphasis to that part of the wages which was to be in the form of money. But it specifically laid down that (1) in the case of an agricultural laborer, he was to receive, in addition to wages in money, a suit of clothes at the end of each "season"—i.e., the "growing season" and the "reaping season," and (2) in the case of a non-agricultural laborer, he was to receive, throughout the period of his employment and in addition to wages in money, "regular meals of rice and curry." For the agricultural laborer, who had his own store of paddy, clothing was of great consequence, and to the nonagricultural laborer food was of great consequence. Thus the Burmese law ensured that the fluctuation either in the general level of wages or in the value of money should not adversely effect either the laborer or his employer. Moreover, as both the laborer and the employer wore the same homespun clothes and ate the same food, the arrangement was fair to both parties. With regard to professional services rendered also, the Burmese law attempted to be fair to both parties, as could be seen from the following rules of law regarding physicians and lawyers:

If a physician has been called for fee to attend to a sick person, but the sick person recovers or dies before the physician reaches his bedside, the physician shall be entitled to his fee if he has reached at least the doorway of the sick person's house. In the same way, if a suit is withdrawn or settled, or the judge does not find it necessary to call upon the pleader to argue, the pleader shall be entitled to his fee if he has spoken even a few words, or if he has just pulled up the sleeve of his gown in a gesture of speech. If a client wishes to call in another physician, he shall pay the full fees to the first physician, and shall also offer him a cup of water in token of friendship. If a client wishes to engage another pleader, he shall pay the full fee to the first pleader.

The following rules regarding void sales and purchases will further illustrate the essential similarity of Burmese law and the English law of contract:

There are four cases when a sale or a purchase is void: (i) if the price fixed is below its value; by value it is meant market value at the time of the sale, and even a ruby worth a kingdom before may be sold for one-eighth of a basket of rice, if that is the prevailing market value of rubies; (ii) if the buyer is aware that the ownership of the property is being disputed; (iii) if the whereabouts of the property are not known; and (iv) if the owner of the property is in confinement or under duress.

Just as in the English law, under the Burmese law a person was responsible for any injury which was the foreseeable consequence of his acts. Thus, it was a rule of law that if a person induced another person to accompany him to a place full of perils, and the latter suffered injury, the former was to pay damages to the full amount of the injury; however, if the second person was aware of the dangerous nature of the place, the damages payable were only half the amount of compensation for the injury. Under the same principle, if a host entertained his guest so well that the latter became intoxicated, the host owed a duty in law to see that the guest reached his home safely; if the guest should be allowed to go home unattended, and if he should die or suffer injury on the way through illness, exposure, snake-bite, attack by robbers or by wild beasts, the host was liable to pay full compensation. The principle of contributory negligence was also known to Burmese law, and the following rules of law regarding "travelling at night with due caution" will serve as an illustration:

If there be occasion for a person at night to go about the city or the town, or the village, he shall go only with a lantern, for if he goes about without a lantern and is stopped, or hindered, or attacked, he shall not be entitled to damages. If, however, he is going about in search of a doctor, and if he shouts out this fact in the darkness, he shall be entitled to full compensation from the offender who stops or strikes him, even though he carries no lantern. In the same way, if a young woman goes about at night beyond the usual hours when people go about, and if she wears no kerchief on her breast, and if her modesty is outraged, she shall not be entitled to any damages.

The unity of Burmese society has always been the family, but unlike the rigidly knit Roman family or the Hindu joint family, it easily disintegrates. A Burmese family is loosely knit by ties of blood, and sometimes of marriage, and thus it usually consists of the father, the mother, and their unmarried sons and daughters. The sons however can leave the family even before marriage on attaining the age of puberty (sixteen years of age), and the daughters on attaining the age of majority, but sons and daughters of course usually leave the family only on marriage. Sometimes sons and daughters decide to remain in the family even after marriage, at least for some time. The head of the family is the father, and on his death, the mother succeeds to the headship of the family, as in Burmese law the husband and wife are heirs to each other. The head of the Burmese family exercises general control over the family, but unlike the heads of the Roman and Hindu families, he performs no religious duties. He or she has the right to betroth his or her daughter under the age of majority to a male of his or her choice, but the right is subject to the daughter's right of repudiating the betrothal, either by refusing to marry the man chosen by her parent, or by compelling the parent to recognize her betrothal to the man of her own choice. The head of the Burmese family can also give away children under the age of puberty or majority to another family for adoption, but when the child attains the age of puberty or majority, he or she has the option to choose in which family (i.e. his original family or his adoptive family) he will remain. Acquisitions by members of the family accrue to the family, but as in Roman and Hindu laws, certain classes of acquisition by members of the family accrue to the acquirer and not to the family. Gifts from grandparents, from the king, and in certain cases, from strangers, and earnings through exercise of skill in the arts and in astrology, medicine, advocacy, and alchemy accrue to the acquirer. When a member of the family wishes to leave the family, there is no necessity to gain the assistance of a court of law. By mutual consent among the members, he is permitted to leave and he is given his share of the family estate. When the whole family decides to break up also, no formality is required, and by general consent, the family estate is divided between the members according to the rules of law pertaining to the partition of an estate into various shares.

One of the main features of Burmese society is the high status of its women. Unlike the situation in Hindu or Chinese society, the Burmese woman has never been a mere chattel at the disposal of the Burmese man. Since prehistoric times Burmese women have enjoyed an equality of status, rank, and opportunity with men. Under the Burmese kings, the women held high office, and served often as headman, chieftainess, and queen. In Burmese folktales dealing with strange disputes and wonderful decisions, which are known as Juristic Tales, the judge is a woman, namely Princess Learned-in-the-Law. At the present day, all the learned professions are open to women, and approximately 25 per cent of the students at the University of Rangoon are women.

The high status of women in Burmese society is reflected in the Burmese customary law relating to marriage, divorce, and inheritance. In Burmese law, marriage is purely a civil contract, founded on the consent of the man and woman to openly "eat and live together." Religion has nought to do with the marriage, and no special ceremony is necessary, and therefore in a court of law proof of marriage is not to be found in certificates of documents or evidence of a marriage ceremony, but in the testimony of witnesses that the man and woman lived together as man and wife. No Burmese man or woman can be forced into marriage without his or her consent. After a son has attained the age of puberty, or a daughter the age of majority, even the consent of the parents is no longer necessary. Divorce results without much formality when both the husband and the wife mutually agree to part. Burmese jurists in their writings often describe the husband as the lord of the wife, but that seems to be mere opinion, and they often advise the wife to obey her husband, but it does not mean that their advice is always followed. The wife has a right to divorce her husband without his consent, if he is guilty of cruelty or serious matrimonial misconduct. On divorce, the wife takes a substantial share of the joint estate, and if she should marry again, she remains absolute owner of her estate from her previous marriage, and does not share it with her second husband. But although divorce therefore is comparatively easy, and the wife enjoys an important position in the family, divorces have always been rare, and an atmosphere of cordiality and harmony prevails in the Burmese family.

Burmese women have always possessed full rights of inheritance. As the husband and wife are the heirs of each other, on the husband's death, the wife inherits a major share of the family estate, and full authority as head of the family if the family decides not to disintegrate and partition the estate. On the death of the surviving parent, the daughters have full rights of inheritance in competition with their brothers. As the Burmese customary law has never recognized a right to dispose of property by will, these rights of inheritance cannot be defeated in any way.

These, then, briefly are the main features of Burmese customary law. The loosely-knit family with an atmosphere of cordiality and harmony is still the unit of Burmese society at the present day, and the essence of Burmese customary law at the present day is the same as many centuries ago. My colleagues of this conference who spoke before me have emphasized the fact that Southeast Asia as a region has been the cross-road of many cultures. Burma has borrowed freely from the great cultures of her neighboring countries, but at the same time, she has been able to preserve her own national character and her own national institutions. I have emphasized the similarity in spirit of Burmese and English law, in an attempt to show that the Burmese people have evolved a system of law as fair and just as the common law of England, which lawyers and jurists all over the world have learned to admire and respect. I have also emphasized the Burmese love of freedom and personal liberty, in an endeavor to prove that the idea of democracy that prevails in the Union of Burma at the present day is not a mere borrowing from the West. And as long as the Burmese people retain this love of freedom, and as long as Burmese law retains its spirit of justice and fairness, the Burmese do not need to be anxious of their future in a changing and uncertain world.

R. Supomo

THE FUTURE OF ADAT LAW IN THE
RECONSTRUCTION OF INDONESIA

SINCE THE POLITICAL liberation of Indonesia has become a fact, there emerges another problem, equally urgent and difficult, viz. the problem of the reconstruction of Indonesian society, which, up to a few years ago, was largely controlled by foreign forces in its economic, social and political life.

Our revolution against the West has been more than a struggle for political independence. It is also a social and economic revolution, unchained by a people absolutely determined to take the destiny of Indonesia in its own hands.

Political freedom was nothing more than a bridge, on the far side of which we were to rebuild our society. From this time onwards, it is indeed a most important task for the leaders to make this freedom meaningful to the masses of the people. Colonial society has been left to us as a legacy of the former Dutch colonial power. That period being closed, we are confronted with the problem of reforming Indonesia, which means the breaking up of the colonial social order of the past and the creation of new standards based upon the national needs of the Indonesian people and adapted to the exigencies of modern life.

The creation of a new social order in Indonesia, as well as in all the young national states in Southeast Asia, should first of all satisfy the primary urge of nationalistic self-assertion. No longer should Asian social, political and economic development be a function of Western requirements which imposed such a terrible distortion on Asian life. Henceforward, since foreign political domination has been swept away, our national sovereignty will permit the expression of national purposes and characteristics.

On the other hand, we live in an age in which all countries are increasingly involved in all the economic, social and political processes of the world, so that the problem of the social reintegration of Indonesia, or of any other state of Southeast Asia, cannot be solved solely by reviving national cultures and national values. Indeed, creative nationalism has to go hand in hand with sound internationalism. The new social order should be formed by adjusting the cultural heritage to the process of modernization. All South Asiatic countries, which are only now emerging from what may be called a "colonial economy," are to be brought up to the level which Western nations have reached. Raising of standards seems, therefore, the very first thing on our national program. This is the sense of modernization, however, which is not identical with Westernization, although we must confess that it is the Western world-expansion which up to now dominates the international world-picture. Thus, modernization, in many cases, practically means adoption of Western institutions or Western ideas, and, in particular, the Western idea of progress.

Nevertheless, the fundamental fact remains that Asia has become more and more conscious of its own dignity and worth. The new nations of the East have determined to retain their historic cultures. At the same time, Asiatic peoples demand, no matter what their institutions might be, that the new national structures provide a means of realizing the fundamental goal of international equality in all fields of human endeavor. This makes the evolution of new solutions inevitable.

It is in this context that we may envisage the problem of the future of adat law in the reconstruction of Indonesia.

Adat law is a non-statutory law which is mainly customary law and, for a small part, Muslim law. It also includes case law, viz. decisions of the judge containing legal principles in the milieu in which he delivers judgment. Adat law is deeply rooted in traditional culture. It is a living law because it expresses the actual feeling for the law of the people. In accordance with its very nature, adat law is permanently growing and developing like life itself.[1]

Adat law, viz. adat civil law, is valid for Indonesians in so far as civil law is not replaced by statutory enactments. Europeans and Chinese, who have become Indonesian citizens since the transfer of sovereignty from the Netherlands to the Republic of Indonesia, are subject to European civil law. The dualism in this significant field of the Indonesian legal system is an inheritance of the Dutch colonial administration and is, up to now, still in force. Adat criminal law and adat procedural law apply in so far as they are not replaced by regulations in those regions of Indonesia where so-called "native justice" is still functioning.[2]

Adat constitutional law and adat administrative law apply in so far as they are not replaced by statutory enactments in the village communities and higher self-governing adat-territories.

Questions have been raised as to the extent to which the formation of national governments in Southeast Asia will affect the relative status of Eastern and Western law. As stated above, the determination of the Asiatic peoples to retain their historic cultures goes hand in hand with the desire to bring the internal economic and social development of their respective countries into harmony with the demands of modern statehood and to participate fully, on an equal basis, in the world structure of international intercourse.

What will be the future of adat law in the light of the need to modernize the whole Indonesian society? In order to ap-

---

[1] Das Recht Hamlich hat kein Dasein für sich, sein Wesen vielmehr is das Leben der Menchen selbst, von einer besondern Seite angesehen (Savigny, *Über den Beruf unserer Zeit zur Gezetzgebung und zur Rechtswissenschaft,* 1814).

[2] On Sumatra in Atjeh, Tapanuli, Benkulen, Palembang, Jambi and Riauw; on Borneo; on Celebes in Gorontalo; and in the Moluccas.

preciate the scope and sense of this problem, it seems useful first to look back at the past and to find out what role the adat law played in the former colonial structure. What was the policy of the former Dutch colonial government toward adat law and, in particular, on what motives had this policy been formed?

The adat law as a problem of law-policy came up for discussion for the first time in about 1848. Before that time, the Dutch East Indies Company formulated no conscious law policy, but left the Indonesians subject to their own laws without asking itself what the nature of that law could be. In 1848, codes such as the Civil Code, the Commercial Code, and the Code of Civil and Criminal Procedure, based upon the Dutch pattern, were provided for the European inhabitants of Indonesia.

As for adat law, the question arose for the colonial government to what extent this law could serve Dutch purposes and Dutch economic needs, and to what extent the adat law could be fitted into the framework of the Dutch colonial policy. The interest or the will of the Indonesian people was of no account. The first effort to supersede adat law, about 1848, resulted from the mentality of the generation which overestimated the bearing and importance of codification. Mr. Wichers, the then President of the Supreme Court in Indonesia, was commissioned to examine if adat private law could not be replaced by Western codification. In those days, people had not the faintest notion of adat law, but it was generally assumed that the Western law was not suitable for the so-called "simple" legal relations of the Indonesian people. It was due to this misconception that Mr. Wicher's codification drafts resulted in failure.

It was only for the sake of the European commercial interests that the Chinese and Arabs in Java became, in 1855, subject to the European law of property and to the European law of contracts, thus falling subject to the European civil and commercial laws, save in the field of family law and inheritance. This was gradually extended to other territories, so that, since 1925, this has been the law of non-Indonesian Asiatic inhabitants, other than Chinese, throughout the whole Archipelago. As for the Chinese inhabitants, they had been wholly subject to the European civil and commercial laws since statutory enactment of 1919 and 1925.

When, about 1870, Western private enterprise was introduced in Indonesia, replacing state-exploitation, the Dutch Minister of the Colonies, Van der Putte, proposed application of European land law to the rural population of Indonesia for the sake of the agrarian interests of the Dutch employers. But this effort failed because the Dutch Parliament insisted that first local inquiries should be made into the rights of the population to the soil.

In 1900, the Minister of the Colonies, Cremer, stood for local and partial codification of adat law, preferring to begin with regions where the population had embraced Christian religion, since, in the view of the new state of life of the population in those regions, the absence of legal security would in all probability be most perceptible. In this connection, codification was always understood as comprising the entire civil law of a region or population group. By 1904, it seemed as though the entire codification of adat law would become the cheered password of Indonesian civil law.

But things took a turn when the Cabinet Kuyper, which was in power in 1901, introduced a bill on November 15, 1904, aimed neither at maintenance of unwritten adat law nor at codification of adat law, but at the ousting of adat law by European law. In other words, for the security of the interests of approximately 300,000 Christian Indonesians, the Netherlands Government wanted to subject the entire population in the directly governed territory of the colonial government, which was then approximately thirty million inhabitants, to unification of the law along Western lines. This was a consequence of a policy of Christianization which asserted that adat law was wholly incapable of fulfilling the needs of the twentieth century.

This effort at unification came to nought owing to the fact that the Dutch Parliament adopted an amendment, Van Idsinga, which only tolerated replacing of adat law by Western law for reasons of social needs of the people. Adoption of this amendment can be credited to the publication of an article entitled "No Jurists' Law for the Indonesian," in the periodical *The XX Century* (1905) by Professor Van Vollenhoven, the founder of the science of adat law and the formulator of the system of adat law. It was recognized that interfering with the legal system in Indonesia was inevitably doomed to failure because there was a general lack of knowledge of the real relations in the Indonesian society.

In 1914, the Dutch Government published, in complete variance with the letter and the spirit of the amendment Van Idsinga, a draft civil code for all population groups, which was also challenged by Van Vollenhoven in his article, "Struggle for Adat Law" (De Gids, 1917). This draft civil code, based on unification, was not presented to the Dutch Parliament.

The third attempt at unification came off in 1923 when the Dutch Government published a new draft civil code of 1920, drawn up by Mr. Cowan, Director of Justice, in Jakarta. This draft failed of acceptance, again as a result of the criticism of Van Vollenhoven in his work: "Juridical Ready-made Work. Uniform Private Law for the Indies" (*Colonial Studies*, Vol. 9, 1925). It must be said, however, that Mr. Cowan was motivated by pure and high ideals. His attempt to introduce codification and unification for all sections of the population was not inspired by political or economic motives, but it was based on the following twofold consideration:

First, codification because the unwritten adat law gives rise to legal insecurity. One cannot guess in advance how a judicial decision will turn out, since the law is unwritten. Second, unification because the applicability of different legal systems for different sections of the population brings forth confusion of the law principles.

In this connection, one often cites the well-known words of Macaulay, who designed a codification for India in 1833:

> Uniformity when you can have it
> Diversity when you must have it
> But in all cases: *Certainty*.

Moreover, for Mr. Cowan it was a matter of course that unification must be based upon Western law, for, in his own words: "We have always seen the East adopting new social institutions from the West, never has the reverse happened, and private law must follow the social institutions."

Indeed, legal security is important, but the codifications designed up to that moment were not to provide legal security. The question of the diversity of law was still there, since the draft codifications, which were achieved, contained code-articles only applicable to a special population group or part of that group, as well as articles referring to the unwritten adat law. If codification of the law is wanted, it is according to Van Vollenhoven absolutely necessary for the draftsmen to restrain themselves to a complete, well-studied and synoptical whole, for which the intervention of the legislator is urgently needed. Van Vollenhoven was no opponent of unification of the law for all population groups of Indonesia, this being the final object to be realized. It is obvious, however, that the Indonesians, who form the vast majority of the population, could not be subject to the law which is most convenient for the Europeans, as the latter form by far the numerical minority. Neither could they be assimilated to the Europeans so far as private law is concerned. It should have been obvious to the former colonial authorities that the coming generation in Indonesia would need its own law in which neither the Europeans, nor the Chinese, nor the Arab residents would have the privilege of an exceptive private law, but, as anywhere else, would fall under the general law of the country.

The widely divergent state of the Indonesian population does create difficulties in the evolving of a uniform law. But, it is after all not necessary that uniformity of law be based upon the Western legal system. The dogma, at the end of the nineteenth century, which said that Asiatic peoples are not regarded as awakened until they have adopted the Western institutions and Western ideas, does not hold good any longer in the twentieth century, this being the period in which one has learned to appreciate the significance of Oriental cultures and civilizations.

Van Vollenhoven advocated systematic descriptions of the real law concepts of the population from law area to law area, subsequent to an investigation led by experts, and this for the promotion of the legal security and for the support of the judge who has to administer justice according to adat law. The strife and struggle of this authoritative professor was backed and justified, on the one side, by the bitter experience gained in scores of years which confirmed that imposing the Western law from above was always doomed to failure, and, on the other side, by the ever-growing realization of the significance of adat law in the environment of the Indonesian population.

At last, in 1927, his conceptions met with a response, and the Dutch colonial policy, from that date to the occupation of Indonesia by Japan in 1942, was marked by a purposeful return to dualism. But now it was "enlightened" dualism, as Adamson Hoebel and Arthur Schiller call it.[3] Accordingly, the maintenance of adat law is coupled with its official study and description, while this principle can only be abandoned in so far as this is required by the real exigencies of the modern world.

If it was Van Vollenhoven in the first decade of the twentieth century who made every endeavor to prevent adat law from being overcome by Western law in the guise of unification and codification, after him, it was his disciples, notably Ter Haar, who strove after the maintenance and realization

---

[3] In their introduction to *Adat Law in Indonesia,* translation of Ter Haar's *Beginselen en stelsel van het adatrecht.*

of adat law as most appropriate to the needs of the Indonesian society in its actual state. Here, it was particularly the rural population in the agrarian communities which Ter Haar had in mind, for in these parts legal intercourse is largely governed by adat law. By means of description on the results of investigations by experts, the law must be explained as distinctly as possible, in order to acquire greater legal security, and, not in the least, to support the judge who has to apply unwritten law. The new adat law policy, since 1927, required, in accordance with Ter Haar's views, also reorganization of the system of justice.[4] It was chiefly Ter Haar who reorganized in the ten years prior to the Second World War the courts to give village-justice, the so-called "native" courts at the higher levels, the administration of justice in the self-governing territories, the religious courts and, finally, government justice, so as to promote a good administration of justice by the law courts which apply adat law.

Investigations have been made into the adat law in West and Central Java, the results of which are recorded in my book on the adat private law of West Java (1933), and in the book on the adat private law of Central Java, written by Djojodigumo and Tirtawinata (1939).

In South Tapanuli, in South Celebes and in East Java investigations into adat law were conducted as well, but they were untimely interrupted by the outbreak of the Pacific War in 1942.

In summation then, subsequent to 1927, it appeared as though adat law should remain valid for the Indonesians and should be studied and described officially. Why this change of course? The answer seems to lie in the considerable increase of publications on adat law during this period, as well as the dedicated work of such men as Van Vollenhoven and Ter Haar.

When Van Vollenhoven began to write, in 1906, his basic work, *The Adat Law of the Dutch East Indies,* completed in

[4] Ter Haar, "Halfway the New Adat Policy," *Colonial Studies,* 1939, p. 1ff.

1931 and comprising three prodigious volumes, there emerged a tendency, among those who had been occupied with law policy, to acquire a better comprehension and appreciation of adat law. I also wish to mention by the same author a most important series of publications which are bound together in another three volumes, bearing the title of *Verspreide Geschriften van Van Vollenhoven* (*Spread Publications by Van Vollenhoven*). In addition, by means of the studies of reports and accounts of ethnologists, missionaries, and civilians, Van Vollenhoven was able to discover that the law of the Indonesian population has character of its own, and that it cannot be understood if approached in terms of a Western legal system or Western law doctrine.

In 1929, Ter Haar published his book, *Principles and System of Adat Law,* which, by virtue of its translation into English by Professor Arthur Schiller of Columbia University, is available to a wide reading public.[5]

Since the Second World War, the political structure of Indonesia has been altered principally in so far as Indonesia has emerged from a colony into an independent and sovereign state. The problem of adat law arises in connection with this whole new situation. A plural colonial society divided into different racial groups ruled by different law systems was left behind by the colonial government. It is not that an immediate dramatic change has been made from one kind of social order to another. The Indonesian society is still to be reshaped into a new social life which shall satisfy the national need for self-expression. The greater part of the Indonesian population is living, and will live in the near future, in village communities which will retain their basically agrarian character.

There is the need for raising the living standards of the masses and the broader problem of the evolution toward the self-reliance of communities which, at the same time, must try to adapt themselves, in some way or other, to the forces of

[5] See book review of this English translation, *Pacific Affairs*, June, 1949, p. 194.

the modern world. The reconstruction of Indonesia has, there-fore, to take place along national lines adapted to the exigen-cies of modern times. The question arises whether, and to what extent, adat law can be used for this purpose, and whether and to what extent adat law can rejuvenate itself. Van Vollen-hoven was right when he wrote that if it has been decided from above to maintain adat law, and it is dying out, the regu-lations are commanding in vain; with the corollary that, if it has been decided from above that adat law has to be replaced, but it remains vigorous and in force in the village and on the fields and on the markets, the judge will preside in vain.[6]

The place of adat law in the whole legal system which is in force in new Indonesia is still the same as at the end of the colonial period. According to article 142 of the Provisional Constitution of the Republic of Indonesia (1950), regulations by law and administrative provisions existing on August 17, 1945, remain in force unaltered, as regulations and provisions of the Republic of Indonesia, as long and in so far as they have not been withdrawn, supplemented, or altered by legislation and administrative provisions in virtue of this Constitution. Concrete directives as to the contents of the future law in Indo-nesia are not stated in the Provisional Constitution. Article 102 of this Constitution prescribes only that civil law, com-mercial law, penal law, and civil and criminal procedural law are to be regulated by law in legal codes, except when the legislator deems it necessary to regulate certain matters by spe-cial law.

Thus, *codification* is prescribed here, not *unification*.

In fact, it is clearly stated in article 25, paragraph 2, that differences in social and legal needs of the various groups of the population shall be taken into consideration. This seems to me a sound clause, for legal equality is only acceptable if it is based upon the real equality of conditions and needs; other-wise the legal uniformity works as a grievous injustice.

Only in the sense of prohibiting discrimination is unifica-

[6] Van Vollenhoven, *Adat Law*, Vol. 2, p. 878.

tion mentioned in the said Constitution. Article 7 states that all citizens are entitled to equal treatment and equal protection under the law, while article 25, paragraph 1, forbids the authorities to connect any advantage or disadvantage to the fact that citizens belong to a particular group of the population. Moreover, although the former short-sighted and indiscriminate colonial policy of unification has been rejected, the Indonesian Government supports wholeheartedly the trend toward a unified system of law if it is required by modern social realities. The Indonesian legislator shall, therefore, have to consider those spheres of the law where uniformity is expedient and should be realized. First of all, the sphere in which an intensive legal intercourse has been developed along uniform lines between Indonesian citizens of different races and between Indonesians and persons of another nationality, as in the sphere of contracts and other commercial topics, comes into consideration.

In the modern international commercial intercourse in Indonesia, Western concepts of civil and commercial law have long applied in practice as the law of the Indonesian commercial and industrial world.

According to the legal system of the former Indies, the Indonesian has considerable freedom in choosing the form of law under which he wishes to place himself. Since 1848, the Indonesian can voluntarily accept European law, and according to the regulation of 1917, he can do this in three ways: first, complete acceptance of European civil law; second, acceptance of the European property law; and third, acceptance of the European law in respect to a particular legal act.

In practice, however, little use is made of the first two possibilities. The possibility to accept the European law for a particular legal transaction is used to a greater but uncontrollable degree and is limited to contracts involving personal, or rather, movable property. It is usually in virtue of their relations with European or other non-Indonesians that the Indonesian uses the European law of contracts. The 1917 regulation stipulates further that he who performs a deed which is only known to European law is tacitly presumed to subject himself to that law. In practice, this amounts to the application of the commercial code regarding cheques and bills of exchange to Indonesians, since the legal transactions on these matters are not covered by the adat law. Entering into an insurance contract, or the creation of a partnership under a firm name are also instances of implied acceptance of European law.

It seems to me that uniformity of law can be established in the sphere of contracts and other commercial subjects enacted, in general, in the city and modern centers where Indonesians have long been accustomed to enter into business relations with their own people, as well as with non-Indonesians, inside and outside the country, under the vigor of Western legal rules. This uniform law would sanction the existing practice of using Western law concepts which have already been assimilated in the modern legal life and have, therefore, already become "modern" adat law. At the same time, the establishment of this new legislation would put an end to interracial law conflicts in this sphere.

Another field of the law which also demands the urgent attention of the national legislature is the domain of *labor*. The labor law in Indonesia is still dominated by various regulations of the colonial period which do not fit into the framework of the modern time. The European Contract Law, embodied as articles 1601 to 1603 of the Civil Code of 1848, only relates to labor contracts of "domestic servants and labourers." This applies, of course, solely to Indonesians, who were hired in the colonial days to do the most subservient work in domestic or other services. All other forms of labor relations were not governed by statutory law, and consequently any decisions on disputed contracts were left to the discretion of the courts.

The Europeans in Indonesia received a modern labor law in 1926, which applies both to Europeans among themselves and to European employees in the service of Indonesians. On the other hand, this law covers only those Indonesians, or other Asiatics, who are employed in a capacity usually performed by a European. In all other cases, Indonesian employers and employees remain subject to adat law or the Civil Code of 1848. This does not only entail unnecessary complication of law, but is, as well, an evident example of disparity of law based on racial discrimination to the disadvantage of the Indonesian population. Indonesian laborers in modern factories and trades, on European agricultural enterprises and in offices in the cities have made themselves conversant with the organizational forms of trade unionism originating from the West, and are already familiar with organized mass-actions for improvement of their existence and with organized strikes as an economic and political weapon. Therefore, conflicts of labor are presently in Indonesia the order of the day, and the need of a modern labor law is felt by all, irrespective of the race involved, in modern labor relations.

The *agrarian* problem in Indonesia is no less pressing. I do not intend to go into the social-economic aspects of this problem, since they do not fall within the scope of this investigation. As for the legal aspect of this question, the national government shall have to break away from the colonial agrarian legal order and make new agrarian laws in accordance with national and social standards. According to the still existing legal system, inherited from the Dutch, there are and have been for ages so-called "European lands"—lands governed by European law—and so-called "Indonesian lands" which are governed by adat law. The prime rule of interracial law of real property is that the law applicable to parcels thereof remains the same, regardless of the racial group to which the owner belongs. Thus, "European land" which comes into the hands of an Indonesian remains subject to European law, while "Indonesian land" remains governed by adat law even if held by a European. Furthermore, the colonial Government created the so-called "agrarian property" of land which is governed by Western rules. The Indonesian received the right by the colonial administration to replace his adat-right of property to agrarian property, registered in a European way. In the course of time, however, very little use has been made of this right of replacement.

Finally, the domain-theory of the colonial government prevailed, according to which all the land not held under a Western right of ownership or an agrarian right of ownership belongs to the domain of the State. Thus, land over which adat legal rights are exercised belongs automatically to the State's domain, although it is not free domain, while land over which no legal rights whatsoever existed was classified a free domain of the State. The entire domain-theory is in conflict with the adat law in so far as it does not recognize the right of the village community to dispose of woodland or other uncultivated land within its territory. The long chain of agrarian injustice towards the Indonesian population forged by the colonial agrarian legislation was pointed out by Van Vollenhoven in his booklet, "The Indonesian and His Land," reprinted in 1925.

The Indonesian Government shall have to do away with this plurality of legal status of land and the artificial domain-theory. In rising Indonesia, only one agrarian system must be valid. Subjective rights to ground by persons, irrespective of the race group or nationality, should be derived solely from a national uniform agrarian system of Indonesia. For this much-needed uniform law, adat rights to the land have to be considered in the first place, as, in this field, adat law has maintained its living power notwithstanding "a century of injustice." [7] Above all, the right of ownership must not be understood in a Western liberalistic sense, but the social function must be primarily emphasized in accordance with adat concepts. Article 26, paragraph 3, of the Indonesian Provisional Constitution already gives the directive that "the right of property" is a social function.

In the sphere of the law of the family and of inheritance,

[7] Van Vollenhoven, "The Indonesian and His Ground." reprinted 1925.

unification of law will be difficult to realize in the near future, since the power of tradition in each of the different race groups is, in this respect, still strong. The traditional ideas of family life, the ideas about relationship in the family of Indonesians on the one hand, and of Europeans and other non-Indonesians on the other hand, diverge so much that, according to the previously-mentioned rule of article 25, paragraph 2, of the Provisional Constitution, the diversity of law system will remain in existence for the time being. For the Indonesians, this implies the continuation of the prevalence of the adat law. It must be noted that adat law itself, in this regard, is not uniform in the different adat law circles of Indonesia. Kinship relations among the Batak, Nias, Gajo and Lampongs (all on Sumatra), in the Moluccas and the Timor Archipelago are organized along patrilineal lines; among the Minanakabau, Korinchi, Semendo (all on Sumatra) and among a few of the lesser ethnic groups in the eastern islands of Indonesia, matrilineal organizations prevail; while the family groupings on Java and in many regions of Bornea and Celebes are bilateral. Consequently, the legal relations in connection with the law of the family or succession between members of different adat groups must necessarily involve interlocal law conflict problems which must be solved by the courts of law. Therefore, the judge must be fully aware of his responsibility as a decisive factor in the growth of the law, and it is his duty to take the social reality, which is always changing and developing, as his starting point. The recent trend, because of modern influences —in particular for those who have come from the interior to live in the cities and other modern centers—shows a development toward the smaller immediate family relations, and, correlatively, a weakening or even actual disappearance of the traditional larger group-relations.

Adat *criminal* law in the sphere of government justice has been legally abandoned since the first of January, 1873, when a criminal code composed along Western lines for Easterners was introduced, as well as since the introduction of the Criminal Code of 1918, which was almost an exact copy of the Dutch Criminal Code of 1881.

In the sphere of so-called "native" justice, which, according to the Provisional Law of 1951, arranging the unification of the judiciary in Indonesia, is destined to be withdrawn gradually, the adat criminal law—in so far as it is not replaced by statutory enactments—is still in force. If, in the near future, all the adat courts of law have disappeared, there will thus be a uniform criminal code applicable to everybody in the whole of Indonesia under its jurisdiction. The question arises, however, in what respect the Code of 1918 is still usable for the new Indonesia and whether adat law can be used for the reform of the criminal law.

It can be stated at once that, although all rules in the criminal code incompatible with the sovereignty of Indonesia are withdrawn, a new national criminal code, adapted to the new national public policy, will still be necessary. Where the Indonesian population for decades has been used to penalties of loss of liberty on the ordinary delicts against life, body and goods, these penalties have become indispensable. But in imposing such a punishment, one must not lose the connection between the correction claimed by the adat law and that indispensable to the community. A criminal law code adapted to the modern needs of the new Indonesia will, of course, contain series of articles which, having nothing to do with the Eastern or Western way of thinking, are imperative for the maintenance of any modern government, including, for example, penalty provisions concerning security of the state, maintenance of public order, counterfeiting, perjury, etc.

The two other problems which must be considered as well are: one, the insertion of the typical Indonesian delicts from the sphere of the Indonesian world of thought; and two, the connection between sanctions of the modern criminal law and rules existing in the adat constitutional law, adat administrative law and adat private law.

The part which adat law will play in the drafting of a modern national Criminal Code will, therefore, not be a small one.

Finally, I want to say something about the part which adat law is playing in the constitutional rebuilding of Indonesia. The constitutional order during the former colonial period consisted of colonial constitutional law of Western origin, with a European and half-Indonesian organization of civil service in the upper regions, and adat constitutional law of the villages and other communities in the lower regions. However, government administration also penetrated into the said communities. But, despite Western-style ordinances on local government—"dress the Indonesian everywhere in a European dress"—with all its consequential confusion,[8] and notwithstanding all substitutions, lack of appreciation and deformation, the basic adat structure of the communities survived. Since the transfer of sovereignty, the colonial government was replaced by a national government based on a modern constitution which adopted Western principles of parliamentary democracy, and the Western principle of elections by universal and equal suffrage and by secret vote or by an equivalent free voting procedure (article 35).

The Constitution also secures fundamental human rights and freedom in accordance with the exigencies of modern times.

The need for rebuilding the constitutional structure of Indonesia based on the principles of nationalism, humanity, internationalism, democracy and social justice [9] obligates the national leaders of Indonesia to rediscover the cultural traditions and the pattern of values dominating the social organization of the masses of the population. It is significant that the Provisional Constitution itself includes the possibility of maintaining adat law by upholding the principle of decentralization and autonomy of the local communities (article 131). It is self-evident, however, that the adat communities have

[8] Van Vollenhoven, *Adatrecht,* Vol. 2, p. 846.

[9] President Sukarno, "Pantja Sila," the basic philosophy of the Indonesian State, *Indonesian Review,* January, 1951.

to provide for the general welfare prescribed by the Constitution (article 82). Modernization of these communities cannot be avoided, but this modernization shall have to be in correspondence with the institutions of the population.

Free Indonesia is, as we have seen above, facing unparalleled problems of reconstruction. The Western world-expansion, in general, and the colonial supremacy, in particular, have imposed on the Eastern peoples Western institutions of law and Western forms of government and society.

In Indonesia, in consequence thereof, adat law and Western law rule together—seldom regulated and corresponding, most of the time in a certain dissonance, occasionally in full conflict.

After the political liberation of Indonesia, Western influence and Western intercourse cannot be completely curtailed. This is also not the intention of the Indonesian Government. Since the end of the political supremacy of the West, the acceptance of the challenge of the West by the East takes place under fair circumstances. The East shall pose its own way of thinking against the Western way. Thus, the responsibility for the choice lies with the Asiatics themselves.

The gist of the problem is how to unite Eastern and Western concepts and needs into a harmony. The only effective answer seems to be: the assimilation of Western concepts in a form adapted to the national structure of the Indonesian society.

Traditional adat law expresses such universal values as the principle of mutual aid, the social function of man and property in the community, the principle of consent as a basis of public authority, and the principle of representation and consultation in the system of government. All these values should find new expression in modern institutions derived from the West. By rejuvenating the great forces of the Indonesian culture in this way, Indonesia will be able to consolidate its domestic position and to make a positive contribution to world peace, social justice and freedom in the international sphere.

Philip W. Thayer

THE IMPACT OF THE NEW STATES OF SOUTHEAST ASIA ON THE DEVELOPMENT OF INTERNATIONAL LAW

THE SUBJECT TO WHICH I rashly have committed myself is one which ought to be—and I hope at some later date may be—the theme of a book rather than of a paper. The impact of the new states of Southeast Asia on the development of international law is a matter of far-reaching consequence to the future of international relations generally. If I can give some brief indication today of the direction in which this impact may lead, I shall feel that I have laid at least a bit of a foundation for more complete consideration, discussion and study.

I am proposing to deal with the topic in this way: in the first place, I shall suggest what appear to be the principal imminent problems in the development of international law. In the second place, I shall look into the past in order to outline in a few words those factors in the legal, and particularly the international legal, heritage of these Southeast Asian states which might be pertinent to the problems previously enumerated. Finally, in the light of this background, I shall attempt to speculate on the trends most likely to be followed by the new States in their influence on international legal development.

Let us begin with the first point: what are the great pressing problems in the current state of international law? Those of you who do much reading in the field of international law are aware of an increasing tendency to dwell heavily on the interest of the international community in the substance and enforcement of international law. In his recent book, *A Modern Law of Nations*, Philip Jessup says:

Under the traditional international legal system, a breach of international law is considered to be a matter which concerns only the state whose rights are directly infringed; and no other state, nor the community of states, is entitled to remonstrate or object or take action.

The implication is that recognition of an international community interest represents a break with the past and introduces something completely novel into international legal thinking. So Dr. Jessup continues:

The discussion will proceed on the hypothesis that a new principle is accepted, in this instance the principle of community interest in the prevention of breaches of international law.

Without deprecating in any way the value of such a principle, I should like to point out that the idea is by no means a new one. One of the earliest and greatest writers of them all found in such a thought the real reason for the designation "international law." In his work, *De Jure Belli ac Pacis*, Grotius wrote:

Haec vero . . . societatis custodia, humano intellectui conveniens, fons est ejus juris, quod proprie tali nomine appellatur.

Following the same thought even further, Lauterpacht felt that the original hypothesis in international law should be that "the will of the international community must be obeyed." Certainly, the principle of international community interest is one of long standing. If it has failed to receive general acceptance and implementation in practice, it is perhaps due not so much to nonrecognition of its existence as to the coincident rise of another concept regarded as equally, if not even more basic, the concept of sovereignty.

The system of law described by Grotius and his contemporaries was devised for the European community of the sixteenth and seventeenth centuries and purported to lay down rules for the guidance of Christian princes and sovereigns in their relations with each other. Many of the early writers, notably de Vitoria and Suarez, were primarily theologians rather than publicists or lawyers. Grotius himself, in addition to his legal attainments, was also theologian, historian, diplomat, and intermittently turned his gifts to the composition of poetry. It was quite natural therefore that in these early writings and in the subsequent development of international law there should be a strong flavor, if not of divine revelation, at least of Churchly influence, with violation of the rules something in the nature of mortal sin. The law of nature was paramount. Not until the eighteenth century did the naturalists become outnumbered by the positivists, who found the basis of international law in the customs and practices of states instead of in a law of nature. Even so, the customs and practices in question were those of states in which the Christian faith was dominant, and with the colonial expansion of the European powers, these were the customs and practices which followed the standards of their royal masters. In the case of the Western Hemisphere there was no reason why these customs and practices should not persist. In the new republics which came into being there during the eighteenth and nineteenth centuries, the ruling classes and eventually the majority of the population were people who were proud of their European backgrounds and eager to perpetuate their traditions.

It must be noted further that the triumph of the positivists over the naturalists brought no change in the idea of international law as a system of law for the guidance of princes in their sovereign relations with each other. The doctrine of sovereignty continued unimpaired, a sovereignty both absolute and uncontrolled, in possession of which each individual prince (a term for which we now may substitute the term "sovereign state") was the unquestioned master of his own territories and his own people, and on terms of complete equality with all others of the same status.

In the final analysis, therefore, international law has emerged as a system which, on the one hand, owed its name to the interest of the international community and, yet on the other, has continued to accept the notion of an uncontestable sovereignty. No deep thought is required to see the fundamental inconsistency of these points of view. And that, in truth, is a major problem of international law today. How, if at all, can any doctrine of the supremacy of the will of the international community be reconciled with the doctrine of sovereignty?

From this problem flow two others which I also wish to mention. The first of these is concerned with the rights of individuals. International law, we have said, is a body of rules for the guidance of sovereign states in their relations with each other. As commonly stated, nations are the subject of international law; individuals are the objects. The individual person has been regarded as the lowly pawn on the international chessboard. If he has suffered a wrong or an injustice at the hands of a state other than his own, he has had no direct rights against that state by way of redress because his hands have been tied by the doctrine of sovereignty. His own country, to be sure, has owed him a duty of protection, but his helplessness as an individual has been merely underlined by the fact that his only recourse has been intercession at the diplomatic level. Even this, moreover, has been somewhat illusory, and might vanish altogether in the face of overriding national policy. The problem of the rights of individuals is one which is receiving increasing attention in the writings of the publicists and in the documentary output of international organizations. It is bound to be an issue in the future of international law.

The second additional problem, also stemming from the doctrine of sovereignty, is that of the justiciability of international disputes. If the doctrine of sovereignty be taken in its unrestricted sense, it means that every sovereign state is the ultimate judge of its own conduct. We already have noted that this is basically inconsistent with the idea that the international community has an effective interest in the enforcement of its law. It follows in a similar way that no sovereign state can be under any obligation, against its will, to submit its disputes with other sovereign states to adjudication and final settlement. This is a situation which may lead the man in the street to ask of the international lawyer, what kind of a system is this anyway, which has no sanction, which cannot be enforced, and which can be flouted with impunity by any sovereign state which has a mind to do so? Let us inquire, however, is it necessarily true that all international disputes must be legal in nature? As William W. Bishop has pointed out in his recent *Cases and Materials in International Law,*

Usually the international law aspects of international relations are commingled with political, strategic, economic, geographical, social, and other elements, and in consequence it may be difficult to determine the exact part played by international law. Account must be taken of these non-legal factors in analyzing international incidents which have taken place or in predicting what states will do in a given situation.

Is it possible, then, that there may be a distinction between disputes having a legal basis, which ought to be justiciable, and others involving purely political questions, which are not justiciable in the same sense? Conflicts of interest between individuals, we may remind ourselves, do not always get into the law courts. I raised a question the other day concerning a tendency on the part of most of us who have European backgrounds—a tendency to place great faith in a book of rules. We like to lay down principles, to put things into legal compartments, to set standards for all to follow. We even have invented a person known to the law as "the ordinary prudent man"—some might consider him a rather moronic individual —whose behavior is something for the rest of us to emulate.

It is a neat and tidy way of doing business, and it leads naturally to a feeling of discomfort and even of distress when circumstances arise in the international field which do not seem to fit the rules too easily.

Up to this point I have been concerned with a statement of the problems which seem to me of the greatest consequence to the future development of international law: in the first place, the basic problem involved in the inherent conflict between the idea of an effective international community interest on the one hand and the doctrine of sovereignty on the other; and, following from that, the two problems of the rights of individuals and the justiciability of international disputes. Let us digress now for a few moments to take a quick look at the international legal backgrounds of these new states of Southeast Asia.

We heard this morning two extremely illuminating talks on the customary law of Burma and on the adat law of Indonesia. Although neither of these papers was concerned particularly with the field of international relations, both mentioned the background influences in the development of these bodies of law of the Hindu and Muslim systems and of Buddhist beliefs and ideals. Both speakers also stressed the fact that in the directions where these influences were most effective, they resulted not so much in a mere borrowing from the older systems as in complete absorption and adoption. Parts of the Hindu law, for example, became for all intents and purposes part of the customary law of Burma and of the adat law in Indonesia. Let us explore briefly the corresponding possibilities of influence in the international field.

The ancient states of India exchanged ambassadors and diplomatic missions and recognized a well-developed body of international law in their dealings with each other. The principle of diplomatic immunity was thoroughly understood and for the same reasons which are used to support it today, but with one interesting variation on the modern doctrine. The person of the ambassador was inviolable in the sense that he

could not be killed or imprisoned; there was, however, no ob-
jection to mutilation. In the event that an ambassador incurred
the displeasure of the receiving country, his recall would be
requested in precise accord with modern practice, but he might
lose his ears into the bargain—a loss which would have a deplorable effect on his reporting abilities at his next post.

At the back of the ancient system of Hindu law, whether
regarded on a national or international basis, was an ethical
concept known as *Dharma*. This was a concept which was just
as binding upon states in their relations with each other as it
was on individuals, and it meant in the final analysis that one
must do the right thing simply because it was the right thing.
Sanction lay in the source of the concept, as being in the nature of a divine command which could not be ignored. This
concept of *Dharma*, deeply rooted in the very foundations
of the Hindu law, exerted a profound influence on all its
branches. In the transplanting and absorption of some phases
of the law in Burma and in Indonesia, *Dharma*, with its emphasis on ethical values, was bound to play an important part.

In Muslim law, as in Hindu, we find an historical background to which the subject of international relations was no
stranger. If the influence of the Muslim law has not been felt
to any appreciable degree in Burma, in Thailand, or in Indo-
China, it nevertheless has been a major factor in the legal
development of Indonesia and of Malaya, regions which now
embrace a population of more than eighty millions of people.
The Muslim law also resembled the Hindu in the spiritual
concept on which it was based. The two principal sources of
Muslim law were in the Koran and in the Sunnah—the word
of God on the one hand, the words of His Prophet on the
other. Both were of equal authority, the former because it
came direct from the original source and the latter on the
theory that the word of the messenger is an authentic echo
of that of the sender. Since the word of God naturally involved
an injunction to do right, the Muslim law, like the Hindu,
brought to the conduct of international relations a strong ethi-

cal motivation for fair dealing, based on a Divine command carrying its own sanction.

Buddhism is a system of thought rather than of law. Even so, it is a system of thought which has influenced profoundly the lives and social behavior of millions of people in Ceylon, in Burma, in Thailand, and to a lesser extent in India and in Indo-China. The teachings of Buddhism, so far as they might affect the course of jurisprudence, would lead in the same direction of right doing. In a recent article published by the Buddhist Association of Thailand, Dr. Luang Suriyabongs writes:

> The Universal Law of Karma, discovered by the Buddha, says that Kusol, i.e. the pursuit of good merit, is the only driving force that liberates the mind from the fetters which bind us to the Earth and finally leads to Nirvana. . . . Men are born and die according to their good and evil deeds, according to their Karma.

In glancing at three of the major forces which have combined to influence the international legal thinking of a large part of Southeast Asia, we thus find a common emphasis on spiritual values, on right doing, on fair dealing.

Before leaving this matter of historical backgrounds, two other factors should be mentioned which are the natural results of systems which emphasize righteousness and good living. The first of these is the deep regard felt by Hindu, Muslim and Buddhist alike for the welfare of the individual. In the ancient states of India, in the early kingdom of Burma, in the principalities of Indonesia, the chief of state, whether rajah, king, or sultan, had as his first and greatest obligation the well-being of his subjects. Muslim law and Buddhist thought in particular gave full recognition to the importance and dignity of the individual. Says the devout Buddhist: "We believe in accordance with the Buddha's world order that the State exists solely for the welfare of Man and society, and for no other purpose."

The second factor has been referred to by three other

speakers this week and concerns the tendency of the Southeast Asian peoples to use conciliation rather than concrete law as a basis for the settlement of disputes. In the customary law of Burma as well as in the adat law of Indonesia, the aim of the competent authorities in the handling of civil disputes has been not so much to enjoin conformity to inflexible rules as to bring the parties together in an effort to compose their differences through a better understanding of their conflicting points of view. To quote again from the same Buddhist writer:

> Our Buddhist or humanitarian State . . . is based on good human relationship; upon peaceful cooperation among our peoples; upon human persuasion and understanding, tolerance and mutual respect.

In the course of my remarks I have stated some problems, I have taken a quick look at history, and I have referred to the part played by custom and practice in the development of Western ideas of international law. In the light of these observations. I should like to hazard a few guesses as to what we may expect from these new states of Southeast Asia in their impact on international law. Let us consider first their probable attitude toward custom and practice. In the talk this morning by the Rector of the University of Rangoon, and in the paper which was read by the President of the University of Indonesia, we heard a great deal about the role of custom and practice in the growth of the indigenous law. If, then, we have noted the readiness with which Burma and Indonesia have been able to absorb and make their own the materials which they have taken over into local law from Hindu, Muslim and even Dutch and English sources, we may expect to find an equal facility in the field of international law. We must observe, however, that the picture in Asia is very different from that previously mentioned in the Western Hemisphere. Europeans rarely have gone to Asia with any expectation of making a permanent home there or of raising families which would become component parts of the population. Almost invariably they have had in mind an ultimate return to the countries of their origin. The recent achievement of independence by the new states of South and Southeast Asia therefore has not approximated in any way the birth of the American republics. On the contrary, it has resulted from an irresistible upsurge of nationalism on the part of native populations, and has been marked in consequence by a disposition to develop along strongly national lines. This is entirely natural and not peculiar to any one country.

I have no doubt whatever that the states of Southeast Asia will be able to accept without difficulty many of the customs and practices of international law as it exists today. We already have convincing examples in the field of international commercial law. Such usual instruments of the law merchant as bills of exchange and of lading, letters of credit, and marine insurance certificates are just as well understood and have the same effectiveness in Rangoon, Saigon, or Jakarta as would be the case in Valparaiso or New York.

I have no doubt either, however, that in the adoption of the customs and practices of international law, the states of Southeast Asia will proceed warily and with caution. They will wish to be sure, as has been the case before in the development of their local law, that the customs and practices in question are in harmony with their own needs and with their own heritage. The Burmese, you will recall, had no trouble in taking over the British Criminal Code substantially intact because British ideas of criminal justice were very much like their own.

Possibly there will be less difficulty in this respect with those customs and practices relating to procedural matters than with those of a substantive nature. As I have indicated, the diplomatic protocol of ancient India did not differ greatly in principle from that which we know today: and we may note in passing that the privileges of diplomatic immunity appear to be as thoroughly appreciated in the East as in the West, that the third person note and the *aide mémoire* are equally understood, and that the dubious specter of the diplomatic cocktail party is throwing its fitful shadow from Karachi to Manila. On the substantive side, the statesmen of Southeast Asia are in the unfortunate position of being confronted with a going system, the establishment of which they have had nothing to do. They have had little in the way of immediate background experience, and their countries have suffered from a lack of facilities for education and training in international law. This lack, I am happy to say, is by way of being remedied, but it cannot be a hasty process. For countries which have been obliged to send their students to the Netherlands, to England, and to France, it is no small task to build and to perfect the means of local instruction. Under these circumstances, I venture to believe that the statesmen and the jurists of Southeast Asia—and let us not forget that they are men of outstanding intelligence and ability—will approach the substantive problems of international law in a spirit of healthy skepticism, that they will look to the West for help and guidance, as indeed they must, but that they will not hesitate to select here and to discard there, and that in the final analysis they will contribute quite as much from the rich background of their own heritage as we give to them. In the result, the customs and practices which emerge will be just as truly the customs and practices of Southeast Asia as of the West; for they will have been made their own by the same process of adoption and absorption which has been so marked in the local law.

Let us turn next to the problems which I mentioned earlier as those most imminent in the development of international law, and consider the possible influence of the states of Southeast Asia in their solution. The first of these, you will recall, was concerned with the doctrine of sovereignty and its essential conflict with the will of the international community. If there are excepted the ancient kingdom of the Thais and the still undetermined peninsula of Malaya, these states of Southeast Asia have come by their independence only recently and under circumstances which would not tend to make them look with favor on any diminution of their sovereign rights. In the history of the last two-hundred years they have seen enough of outside influences, they are commendably anxious to run their own affairs in their own way, and it is to be expected that they should view with suspicion and distrust any overtures which might appear to encroach in any way, either directly or indirectly, on their newly-acquired status. Indications of this sensitivity are indeed not lacking in the events of recent months. In matters which pertain to their own area, the countries of Southeast Asia feel that they have a right to be consulted; in questions falling within the national jurisdiction, they are equally convinced that they should be free from any interference in arriving at their own decisions and in giving their own answers.

So far, therefore, as concerns any derogation of the attributes of sovereignty, I do not believe that we can look to the states of Southeast Asia for any positive action in the immediate future. This does not mean, however, that they do not believe in the idea of an international community interest. On the contrary, there is ample evidence of their complete awareness of the existence of such a community and of their increasing concern with their own place in it. A situation of this kind might seem merely to intensify in a new locale the ancient conflict between sovereignty on the one hand and an international community interest on the other. Before coming to this conclusion, however, it is desirable to turn to the two additional problems which were mentioned earlier as stemming from the question of sovereignty, those concerned with the rights of individuals and with the justiciability of international disputes. On both of these problems I believe that the influence of the states of Southeast Asia will be marked and vigorous.

It is impossible to come away from even a cursory examination of the Hindu, Muslim and Buddhist backgrounds of South and Southeast Asia without feeling that concern for the welfare of the individual will loom large in the future development of the countries in those regions. In the ultimate formulation of any international platform of human rights, in speeding the trend toward a better protection of the individual under international law, it is my conviction that the states of Southeast Asia will play an important and significant part. It is equally impossible to note the traditional legal procedures of the region without believing that these countries will bring to the settlement of international disputes a natural inclination toward the use of conciliation, as contrasted with strict law, which may have far-reaching consequences. Notwithstanding the sensitivity of the new states of Asia to any encroachment on their sovereign rights, it thus seems probable that in their concern for the rights of individuals, as well as in their attitude toward the justiciability of international disputes, the long-run effect is likely to be a weakening of the notion of an uncontrolled sovereignty and the consequent strengthening of the thesis of the will of the international community.

I do not wish to convey the impression that these developments will come overnight. The successful amalgamation of international legal ideas—based in one instance on the experience of the West and in the other on the traditions of the East—is something which calls not only for time and patience but also for good will and mutual understanding. I have no doubt about the good will, and with a continuing process of education on both sides I believe that we are daily on the road to a better understanding.

Carlos P. Romulo

THE POSITION OF SOUTHEAST ASIA IN

THE WORLD COMMUNITY

THE POSITION OF Southeast Asia in international society beggars definition, for it is part of a vast continent in ferment—of a mass of historical forces that may well recast the face of the earth. But as the dynamics of the East-West conflict, which is increasingly drawing attention in the Western countries to Southeast Asia, are largely ideological and economic in motivation and direction, it may be well to attempt to state the position of Southeast Asia in the world community in terms of political and economic geography.

Stated in those terms, the position of Southeast Asia in the international community, particularly in the struggle between freedom and communism, democracy and Soviet imperialism, becomes easier to comprehend. It is a position of vital strategic importance to the whole free world, dictated by the imperatives of the classic Lenin doctrine that "the road to Europe lies through Peiping and Calcutta" and the fact that Southeast Asia is the last remaining roadblock to Soviet hegemony in the whole of Asia.

In the intractable pattern of international Communism and Soviet imperialism, free Asia is the immediate and major theater of conflict between the free world and the Soviet world. The strategic position of Southeast Asia is in direct proportion to the fact that it is astride that theater.

None realizes the importance of Southeast Asia to the final outcome of the expanding conflict between the free world and the Soviet world more than the Communists. At the end of World War II, the democracies, including the United States, disbanded their armies in the mistaken notion that their mission to free the world from totalitarianism had been accomplished and that the world was again safe for democracy. The armies of Soviet Russia did not follow suit; their masters in the Kremlin had a new mission for them—the conquest and subjection of the non-Communist world. Within three years of V-E Day, ten countries of Europe were brought into the Soviet orbit by force from without or fraud from within. Since V-J Day, the Communists have resorted to open warfare in Southeast Asia, let alone other parts of Asia. In Burma, Indonesia, Malaya, and the Philippines, Communist-led bands continue to be a peace and order problem. In Indo-China, the battle is more formalized. In Korea, it is even more burdensome and more sanguinary. This series of Soviet aggression by proxy in Southeast Asia shows that the Kremlin regards the conquest and subjection of the Asian peoples as an objective condition for the final march on Europe of the vast Soviet armies, the prelude to which was enacted in Eastern Europe.

If the swelling tide of Soviet imperialism sweeps Southeast Asia—as it has swept the Chinese mainland—behind the iron curtain, South Asia, particularly India and Pakistan, and Japan would be menaced by Communist power, and the Soviet world would be in a position to muster most of the world's population and resources. More than that, she would be able to consolidate a new, incalculable force, both moral and physical, with which to launch a total war on freedom and everything that does not fit into her scheme of world empire and Communist society.

I have often said and will say now that with China lost to the free world, and Korea embattled and in a twilight zone, Southeast Asia represents in large measure the margin between victory and defeat for freedom as we know and cherish it. The struggle against Communism and Soviet imperialism may well be won or lost in Southeast Asia.

From this area comes two-thirds of the world's exportable rice, and were this rice to fall into Communist hands, the position of India and Japan would be in serious jeopardy. From Southeast Asia also come the raw materials, such as rubber, tin, rope, and oil, which provide the sinews of the economy and preparedness program of the West. If these raw materials were lost to the West, its whole economic and military position, already precarious, would be thoroughly undermined.

There are other reasons why Southeast Asia is vitally important to the United States and the rest of the free world. These are economic, strategic, moral, and psychological, and they bear examination in an objective assessment of the crucial position of Southeast Asia.

Southeast Asia dominates a vital corner of the globe and controls the communication lanes across two of the world's most strategic bodies of water, the Pacific and Indian Oceans.

Besides its normal contribution to Western industry and defense, it has substantial, albeit largely undeveloped, resources of nickel, bauxite, manganese, tungsten, and other critical minerals.

The only important producers of petroleum in more than half the world—from Iran eastward to California—are Sumatra, Borneo, and Burma.

With their surpluses of food, let alone rice, the peoples of Southeast Asia help feed free Asia.

By accepting payments for its exports in consumer goods, without requiring dollars, Southeast Asia has contributed immensely to the economic recovery of Western Europe. Without the trade of Southeast Asia, there could scarcely be a multilateral free world economy.

For numberless years, Southeast Asia has been bound to the West by strong economic and cultural ties, and most of its population, now free and independent, is psychologically conditioned to accept and live by the standards of free society.

Southeast Asia is potentially rich and strong. The American people can enable the peoples of Southeast Asia, with understanding and aid, to develop their potential and make their contribution to the stability and progress of the free world. Without such understanding and aid, they may fall prey to Communist propaganda or succumb to Communist aggression or subversion.

There, as in no other part of the world, there is need for the pragmatic approach to the problems that confront peoples and governments. Such an approach would call, above all, for a positive and well-rounded body of democratic doctrine, which points up the origins, historical development, ramifications, and adaptability to different cultures of democracy and the superiority of democratic processes over authoritarian methods as a solvent of the problems of mankind.

Reduced to their essentials, the problems of Southeast Asia are: self-protection, self-support, and self-government. They arise out of the strategic importance and untold wealth of the area, which the Communists covet, and the determination of the peoples of Southeast Asia who have recently achieved their independence to govern themselves and rise to a position of dignity, quality, and honor in the international community.

Through a painstaking survey, an obvious requirement of the application of experimental intelligence to the problems of Southeast Asia, experts of the United States, and also of England, have assessed the essential needs of the area. Specifically, these are:

1. Technical assistance and equipment to spark economies into action.

2. Trained specialists for the essential tasks of government: public health, agriculture, education, public works, etc.

3. Public service development: communications, transport, power, and agricultural extension services.

4. Engineering surveys to find out what the natural resources are and how they can best be used.

It cannot be overemphasized that these needs are the natural sediment of centuries of subjection to colonial powers. Peoples who have hitherto had little power, if any, over their own destinies are now suddenly faced with the problem of governing themselves and steering their countries through troublous times.

The application of experimental intelligence to the economic and social problems of Southeast Asia is already in progress. American aid, under the auspices of Point Four and the Mutual Security Agency, is gradually providing the basic mechanism for helping the free countries pull themselves up to a position of economic strength and health. It is progressively extending to them the resources and technology of the West, particularly of the United States, and by adapting these to local conditions, it bids fair to enable these young nations to prosper by their own efforts.

It is unfortunate that the sweep and movement of Asian nationalism have made many friends of Asia despair of the future of the Asian nations. They misinterpret the Asian urge toward mastery of Asian destiny as a drawing back from Western or American assistance. It is clear on the record, however, that Asian nationalism and the pressing need of the Asian peoples for economic and technical assistance from the more advanced countries of the free world can be, and have in actual instances been, brought into proper balance. Without doing violence to their independence and self-respect, the peoples of Southeast Asia, let alone the rest of Asia, must avail themselves of the demonstrable benefits of the Truman program of "cooperative effort to use science, technology, and natural resources for the benefit of all peoples, so that they may lead happier lives and create a better tomorrow for themselves and their children."

Free men everywhere must take heart from the contribution which free Asia is making to the development of democracy. Wherever the peoples of Asia achieve independence and are vouchsafed the opportunity to choose systems of government for themselves, as in the Philippines, India, Pakistan, Burma, Ceylon, and Indonesia, they have invariably taken a strong stand for democracy and chosen for themselves representative government. This unequivocal choice of democracy shows that there is a congenial climate in Asia for the development and growth of freedom.

The new world conceived in liberty that is steadily taking shape in the Far East, where, since 1946, Asians have been moving at the rate of a quarter of a million a day into the community for free states, is the most convincing proof of the validity of the thesis that freedom and more freedom is democracy's most effective weapon against Communism.

Those who doubt the efficacy of the American proposition transplanted to a foreign soil might look at its growth in the Philippines. Under the wise leadership of a proven statesman, a product of the school and political systems introduced in the Philippines by America, our young Republic, born in the devastation wrought by the last war, is addressing itself with vigor and vision to the maladies from which our country, like the rest of Southeast Asia, ails.

Our nation is embarked upon a program of economic development aimed at a wide and equable distribution of the fruits of free enterprise. By buying up landed estates and subdividing them into lots for resale to bona fide tenants on easy installments, our government is whittling down the vestiges of economic feudalism in our country. The Quirino resettlement program for Huks who have surrendered or have had a change of heart has proved an effective weapon—corollary to the magnificent effort of our armed forces—in our fight against Communism.

We have found no panaceas for poverty, misery, and the other ancient ills of man, as indeed no people on the face of the earth has found an easy cure for them, but, with American aid and by experimentation, we have succeeded in keeping them under such control as to preclude resort by any responsible segment of our society to any of the magic formulas with which the Communists seek to delude a weary and desperate world.

The Quirino administration has stamped out to a great

extent the favorite breeding places of subversive ideology, such as usury, absentee landlordism, and illiteracy.

On the whole, we have succeeded in the Philippines in proving that free institutions and the material progress that goes with them are not the exclusive patrimony of any race—that a people of whatever color, given the opportunity to develop self-government as the Philippine people had under America, can attain a position of honor and dignity in the international community.

With her experience in the Philippines to go by, America as the undisputed leader of the free world may well bear in mind that "money without love" is not the answer to the challenge of Asia. The voice of America to be heard in Asia must have the same rich spiritual content that it had when it rallied the free peoples of the world to a heroic defense of freedom in World War II. That voice must have the ring of humanity and universality of the Declaration of Independence and the Atlantic Charter.

It is of the utmost importance to the survival of freedom that the true and genuine voice of America be heard and understood in our part of the globe, for there is considerable skepticism in Asia today about the meaning and purpose of the spiritual and secular values of the West.

The free peoples of Asia must be made to feel that Soviet aggression has thrust upon them as well as the West a challenge which they can shirk only at the peril of their newly won freedom, a threat to the fundamental values, the faith and the hope, by which free men live. This feeling of solidarity can only be imparted through the moral force of precept and example.

To Communism's formula of "liberation" through world revolution, the United States as the leader of the free world can offer the alternative of America as a perpetual revolution. To the Soviet challenge of totalitarianism, the United States and the rest of the free world can give expanding freedom as an answer.

In the gathering storm of our age, in the struggle between the irreconcilable opposites of freedom and Communism which is upon us, these are the issues, the choices, upon which free Asia and the rest of the free world must make their stand. This, then, is the measure of free Asia's challenge to America.

Part 5: PROPOSALS FOR THE FUTURE

Clarence R. Decker

SOUTHEAST ASIA: PROPOSALS
FOR THE FUTURE

Proposing for the future is never quite so simple as disposing of the past, but, happily, Southeast Asia's phenomenal postwar recovery, her growing strength and stability, and her increasing influence in world affairs enable us to salute her future with considerable enthusiasm.

Some of the recent improvements, of course, are simply the surface result of the years of relative peace we have had, the gains are often more apparent than real, and many basic problems are still largely untouched. The Peace Treaty with Japan, for example, is a diplomatic triumph, but Japan has yet to find relief from the explosive population pressures inside her ocean-locked economy and this involves the restoration of hospitable relations with her none-too-friendly neighbors in Southeast Asia. The "neutralization" of Formosa is a military achievement, but what positive effect is it to have in building a free China's prestige in Southeast Asia, or on the mainland itself where—in terms of territory, numbers of people, and in immediate human appeal—Communism has achieved one of its greatest victories over the free world? The Philippines has pulled itself out of threatened bankruptcy and political collapse with courage and determination, but it has yet to solve the dilemma of a country politically independent but economically dependent on the United States. Indo-China's surface economy is improving, but the country is stalemated on the battlefield with the Communist-led Viet Minh and at the conference table with the French over the burning issue of independence. Thailand's long political freedom has yet to be implemented with genuine economic and social progress, and Indonesia and Burma, in addition to their problems of internal stability, have yet to spell out the full implications of their "neutralism" in a world more and more dependent on collective security.

Moreover Asia, unlike Europe, has developed little regional consciousness of her common problems and opportunities, and has found it almost impossible to bring an over-all political unity into her cultural diversity. The Western world has likewise seemed unable to construct a comprehensive and purposeful Asian policy. The United States, while waiting for the Orient's reluctant "dust to settle," has operated generally on a country-to-country or crisis-to-crisis basis. With Europe as our main line of defense, Asia often feels that she is a kind of after-thought in our global worries.

Communist successes in China and Korea jolted us into a late awareness that Asia, with over half the population of the world and with tremendous resources, physical and human, would play an increasingly vital role in world affairs generally and willy-nilly in the foreign policy of the United States specifically. Our Asia policy will undoubtedly continue to stress military and political security, as it should, but I suspect that its greatest and surest rewards will come in the field of economic, social, and cultural cooperation. It is this cooperation which I wish to stress this morning, and my observations are directed primarily to Americans.

The recognition of the importance of economic and cultural cooperation in international relations has already proved a major development—almost a revolution—in American foreign affairs in recent years. Before the thirties our foreign relations were left largely to the diplomat and, occasionally, to the soldier. Today a third person—whom we might describe loosely as the social economist—has been added to direct overseas undertakings such as the Marshall Plan, the Mutual Security Agency, the Technical Cooperation Administration, the Export-Import Bank and others. His is the task to help unleash the world's vast economic and human resources and to put them to work for a dynamic free society. Whether engineer, agriculturist, industrialist, businessman, health authority, administration expert, or teacher, this man embodies the ideal of attainment rather than of containment in international cooperation.

The United States is not alone in recognizing the historic necessity of this new international agent; indeed, we were not even the first. The Communists have long known that positive action on the social-economic front often produces results of more lasting significance than are achieved on the diplomatic or military front, and they have capitalized on this front deliberately and with undeniable success. The United Nations likewise has exerted effort along social-economic lines through organizations such as FAO, WHO, UNESCO, UNICEF, ILO, IRO and a host of others. The British have promoted their Colombo Plan.

All of these international undertakings proclaim lofty aims and many are achieving assuring results. Unhappily, there is far too little cooperation or coordination among them, especially in Southeast Asia. Like Stephen Leacock's knight we seem to have mounted our steed only to ride furiously in all directions. My own feeling is that more of our assistance programs should be channeled through the United Nations, but if this, for one reason or another, is not feasible or wise, we at least can reduce waste and confusion by insisting on greater cooperation both at top policy level and out in the field. Further, I think we have now reached the time when we might quite properly convene an international conference to review all international assistance undertakings of an economic or financial nature.

Such a conference, I believe, would approve my second proposal—namely, the development of a long-range program which would stress greater effort in fewer fields and focus our energies where they have the greatest leverage and the most lasting influence. The problems of the underdeveloped areas cannot be solved by opportunistic planning, nor can their vast resources be put to work with a handful of hoes, a Sunday contribution, and a few-score county agents.

The United States is not rich enough, strong enough, or, more important, wise enough to underwrite the globe—and the self-respect of foreign countries would not permit it if we could—but our unprecedented position of power and prestige requires continuity and boldness in our leadership. The long-range character of contemporary international politics obliges us to take the long view. Moreover, we owe it to ourselves as a country lest our efforts, as already charged with some truth, result in a multiplicity of crisis projects rather than in an over-all program geared to a major objective. We owe it to American business enterprise, which already has substantial interests in Asia, and we owe it to Asian enterprise, whose resources and products are flowing in steadily increasing amounts into our shops, stores and factories. We must face the clear fact that we shall be engaged, in one way or another, in an international economic program for many years to come, and we should put this fact plainly before the American people. We already have done ourselves and our friends abroad a disservice by giving the impression that our job was a stop-gap, relief, pump-priming undertaking which would solve all the world's ills quickly and cheaply. Further, it is becoming increasingly obvious that the American people neither understand nor wholeheartedly accept an appropriation-to-appropriation policy, presented one way one year and quite a different way another year. There is no evidence for the assumption that the American people and the Congress would not support a thoughtfully planned, long-range policy, especially if it were integrated with similar programs of the United Nations.

Third, the present bias in all Point Four programs toward food productivity, while vitally important, should be balanced

by development in industry, public works, and public administration. The riots in the Near East and the unrest in the
Far East come from city as much as rural people who demand
adequate housing, higher health standards, industrial employment, improved working conditions, and larger economic
and political freedom. Our "grass roots" fixation often leaves
the unhappy impression locally that our sole aim is to keep
our beneficiary countries as raw material hinterlands. They
are humiliated by our seeming contempt for their aspirations
to become, not necessarily self-sufficient, but more self-supporting. The "cheap" approach of the purely technical is lopsided
and dangerous. The problem is one of boosting and balanc-
ing the total economy.

Fourth, we must exert more influence on local vested interests. Without interfering in purely internal political affairs,
we can legitimately bring pressure on feudalistic forces that
frustrate necessary economic and social reform. I am thinking
particularly of problems such as land, tax, and labor reform.
At present we are frequently vulnerable on the charge that
we are helping the few rich to get richer and the many poor
to grow poorer. Certainly we are entitled to "moral collateral"
on our investment in underdeveloped countries.

Fifth, we need urgently to stimulate private and public
investment, which must eventually finance the continuation
and extension of our technical and economic pilot projects.

Sixth, we need to achieve a much closer coordination of
international banking facilities with grant undertakings in
order to insure an integrated and unified over-all policy.

Seventh, as previously recommended by three reports—
the Brookings Institution, the Gray, and the Rockefeller—
the Point Four programs of the Technical Cooperation Administration and the Mutual Security Agency should be
merged into one organization. Most Americans cannot understand the subtle distinction between TCA and MSA, and it is
doubtful that we do ourselves. With Iran and other TCA countries receiving military aid either from us or others, the dis-

tinction between military-nonmilitary countries can no longer be justified, nor can it be rationalized on realistic differences in methods and objectives with MSA as well as TCA deeply interested in agricultural productivity, and with TCA as well as MSA concerned with long-range industrial development.

Eighth, economic assistance programs should be clearly separated from both military and diplomatic agencies. Although the MSA economic program directly supports the military in several underdeveloped countries, it would undoubtedly be carried on even though there were no military threat. At present few Americans realize that we have a Point Four program in the Far East because it has been so completely overshadowed by the military. The confusion of economic assistance with military strategy, on the one hand, and diplomatic objectives, on the other, undermines our efforts to inspire confidence and good will on the only enduring basis— community of interest and mutual respect. A clear distinction would clarify our objectives and provide a strong psychological appeal to the highest idealism of our own people and of our friends abroad.

Ninth, the Far East, rightly or wrongly, feels that it is too often the orphan child in our foreign affairs. The recent criticism in the Asian press of the Australia–New Zealand–United States (ANZUS) meeting in Honolulu which was called the "Caucasian Conference on the Far East" is simply a case in point. This matter of morale, self-respect, or what Edgar Ansel Mowrer calls "equality of status" is one of the most delicate problems we face in our developing relations with Southeast Asia. Even the most casual traveler in the region quickly senses a strange mixture of admiration, anxiety, and disdain toward us. My own general impression, contrary to that of some others, is that the people of Asia genuinely like most Americans, but that they hold certain strongly-felt reservations, most of them psychological, about us.

(1) We are the rich uncle and they often betray an under-

standable envy of the vast power, wealth, and world prominence we have acquired in a relatively short period of time.

(2) They appreciate our economic help, but they know, as
some Americans occasionally forget, that our help is designed
to save us as well as them.

(3) They are inclined to feel that purely political considerations rather than need often determine the character
and amount of our aid.

(4) They sometimes suspect that we may try to force an
"imperialist capitalist democracy" on all the rest of the world,
or at least that we are so far to the "right" that we cannot
understand the peculiar nature of their social and political
problems. They may admit that our democracy works reasonably well in the United States, but they object to the notion
that it is invariably superior to their own or better adapted to
their needs.

(5) They think we are hypocritical on matters of social
justice. Our Negro problem, with the help of Communist
propaganda, is played up everywhere. Actually they may not
be deeply concerned about our Negroes—they have equally
onerous social injustices of their own—but they see the Negro
problem in terms of the Oriental problem.

(6) They are often offended by the naive insolence—the
exhibitionist and patronizing conduct—of some official personnel and tourists.

(7) They feel that while our culture produces high living
standards with a large amount of personal freedom, it also
produces high divorce rates, tawdry entertainment, and stom-
ach ulcers. Our movies abroad, for example, convey an impression of immaturity, crime, speed without direction, materialism, and plushness—and the villains frequently have Oriental features!

As Mayor Singh of Delhi said to some of us not long ago:

When the West is purely materialistic in conception as well as
in practice—and most of the ills of the modern world are due to

this materialism—we feel there is much that the West can learn from us, as there is so much that we in the East can learn from the West.

Unhappily, Asians are too often convinced that what they can learn from us is purely technological. They do not believe that we have much to offer about a way of life.

Most Americans believe that these criticisms are either untrue or grossly exaggerated, but at this crucial moment in history the important fact is that they are widely believed. Our task, therefore, is to demonstrate to our Southeast Asia neighbors in practical deeds that we are not a Frankenstein, not a technological monster and a crass materialist. Even as we send our bath tubs, tractors, turbines, and gadgets around the world, we must also share our nonmaterialistic culture—our education, our art, our philosophy of the good life. The most precious things we have to share are our Bill of Rights, our government of law rather than of men, our dynamic and creative culture. And as we export these spiritual values, we must indicate our eagerness to import the rich cultural resources of other peoples who can contribute to our strength and vitality. Who knows, perhaps the benefactor will benefit in the long run more fully than the beneficiary?

Americans are famous for their public relations. No important institution or organization would fail to provide generously for its "information services," yet, until recently, our country has not really tried to present its cultural way of life to its friends. Stalinism understands the power of ideas and the value of propaganda in disseminating ideas. In a statement not long ago, Andrei Vishinsky made it clear that the Communists consider ideological weapons superior to tanks and bombs: "We shall conquer the world," he said, "not with atom bombs, but with something the Americans cannot produce—with our ideas, our brains, our doctrines." In this connection, I recall, among the many slogans scribbled on the walls of buildings, on sidewalks, on vacant spaces everywhere in the Russian Sector of Berlin, this memorable bit: "Korea for the Koreans, Coca-Cola for the Americans."

In a very real sense that is the psychological problem in Southeast Asia: they want a Southeast Asia for Southeast Asians. I suspect that some kind of regional organization, perhaps Ambassador Romulo's Asiatic League—designed to satisfy this understandable desire for recognition and to relieve the "Europe First—Asia Second" frustration—is inevitable. Certainly Asia is the only major area of the world without a regional association of some type. I should like to suggest also that more personal attention from the highest officials of our Government, such as periodic visits to Southeast Asia by the Secretary of State and the Director of the Mutual Security Agency, would have a salutary psychological effect. The unofficial tour of Mrs. Roosevelt to parts of the Far East bolstered morale wherever she went. A visit to the Far East by the President-elect between the forthcoming election and the inauguration—a visit similar in its own way to that of President Roosevelt to Latin America in 1936—would help greatly to build good-neighbor relations between the United States and Southeast Asia.

In our stand against Stalinism, we are supporting the soldier munificently, as we should. We are supporting the statesman generously, as we should. But ultimately foreign policy is neither military nor political—like life itself, it is moral. There is no defense—not even an Atlantic Charter, a Pacific Pact, a hydrogen bomb, or an international army—against Soviet ideology except a superior moral understanding and courage. That is why we in the United States need so desperately to develop ambassadors of good will, whether they are high government officials or industrialists, businessmen, teachers, artists, students, or simply tourists. These need to be encouraged to go into all the world—especially into Asia—and share the gospel with every creature—the gospel of trade in goods, in services, in ideas, and, not the least, in ideals!

Melville H. Walker

VIEWS OF AMERICAN BUSINESS REGARDING
SOUTHEAST ASIA

ONE OF THE potentially most significant facts in the area with which we are concerned is the growing awareness of the extent to which the problems of individual countries in Southeast Asia are the common problems of all. While the urgency, respectively, of the military, political, and economic aspects may differ from country to country, there is a growing realization of the fact that a happening in any one of the Southeast Asian countries can be significant for all, and that what happens in Southeast Asia ramifies in its effects throughout the world.

We, in the United States, have had thrust upon us during and since World War II the responsibility of dealing with issues and learning much about areas and peoples in the world which were very remote from our direct contact or knowledge a few years ago. Ten years ago, for example, there were no universities in this country offering organized courses devoted especially to Southeast Asia. About ten years ago, to cite a personal experience, I received a call from a prominent person scheduled for a radio address. He asked to be told "about the Far East" in one phone call. In view of my own limited knowledge, that was not entirely feasible. Later he came to talk so that we might have benefit of maps, and one of his first remarks was "But Burma is an island, isn't it?"

We have come a very long way since then—a hard and far too costly a way—in learning about the Far East. We must go much further, and in government, business, and universities, through cooperative, broadly representative efforts, we must gain a better understanding of the realities of the situation with which each of us is called upon to deal.

Basic Problems

What are the basic problems on which attention has been focused at this conference? In a paramount sense, they relate to the protection of national freedom, and to the whole issues of security against Communist aggression and subversion, so manifest in the Associated States of Indo-China and in Malaya, which now together with Korea are active military fronts in the Far East. Secondly, every country in Southeast Asia shares in an urgent degree the problems of education and training of personnel for public and private administrative and technical responsibilities. Thirdly, the restoration or maintenance of productive economies and subsequent raising of living standards through economic development—these are the primary issues, in our judgment, on which the discussions of this week have centered. Most of our attention has been directed toward what is being done to meet these problems by the countries themselves, in cooperation with other nations, or through the United Nations or its specialized agencies. Particular attention has also been devoted to the policies and programs of the United States as they relate to Southeast Asian countries.

Here, in considering proposals for the future, my particular responsibility is the field of private business. Before proceeding to this discussion, however, and to suggestions relating immediately to trade and investment policies, I want to stress that any such proposals are largely pointless unless the military and subversive threats of Communist aggression are met and cast back. In addition to what has been done by United Nations forces in Korea, the people of Southeast Asia and the people of the free world now owe a debt far greater than most realize to the French, and to the struggle they are maintaining at great cost. That United States assistance to the French, and to the armies of Laos, Cambodia, and Viet-Nam has received the priority it has in the last year is a matter of foremost importance and satisfaction.

The Communist threat cannot be met by military means alone, but if the fight in all of its aspects including the military is not won in Indo-China and elsewhere, the shadow of a resurgent Russian imperialism will deepen throughout the whole area, with profound repercussions in Japan, in South Asia and the Middle East. Each of my business friends recently in the Far East has attested to this upon his return. I quote from one:

All of this is politics and not banking, but I would be leaving out the most important feature of the Far East if I did not cover this and try to impress upon you what I consider to be the Achilles heel of our age—the most dangerous threat to our future well being through the poisoned arrow of Communist victory in the East. I hope the French hang on, and thankfully our Government has finally recognized the need and urgency of assistance by sending military supplies.

What has happened in China provides irrefutable evidence in support of this view. In China the record was one in the first instance of inciting nationalism and of attaining political and military power by exploiting and fomenting agrarian discontent, by promising reforms and correcting some existing abuses. Once in power, the Communists imposed tyranny far worse than any previous colonialism. Their real record has revealed itself in wiping out whole sections of the population, in confiscation of property, in "brain-washing," in complete domination and control over every phase of every life.

With the forces of Communist tyranny seeking to advance throughout the world as they are in Southeast Asia, American business knows that the fate of the world hangs in the balance. We are not talking here about what financial statements will show, about dollars and cents. We are expressing our deeply held conviction that the political institutions, the economic liberties, the spiritual ideals of free men everywhere are under attack by a ruthless, authoritarian regime committed to the destruction of civilization as we know it.

Two global wars have laid upon the United States the burden of leadership in the struggle for survival which lies ahead. In the exercise of that leadership, the obligation rests upon us to make clear, to our own citizens and to the peoples of foreign lands, the course we intend to follow in our relations with other nations. The foreign policy under which our leadership is exercised must leave no doubt that the preservation of freedom, in its every aspect, is a goal we share with all mankind, and that we are seeking, in the attainment of that goal, a common effort and a common dedication.

Some Initial Observations Regarding Trade and Investment

Turning now to matters in the field of trade and investment, it is obvious that the United States is going to be deeply involved in problems of world-wide scope, for years to come. The more this is so, the more necessary it becomes to integrate foreign and domestic economic policies of the United States on a sensible basis, and the more necessary it is to follow consistently a policy of mutual benefit in our trade relations with others. With respect to Southeast Asia, we all saw how the prices of rubber, tin, and other products shot up after Korea. In some measure we pushed prices up against ourselves by so advertising our intention to stockpile. The sellers received dollars beyond their fondest expectations, and spent them on imports, with overtrading the order of the day. Then came world-wide complaints against high raw material costs, and demand fell off. With the slump, and inventories of imports high, in Southeast Asia banks were called on to carry merchants who couldn't sell goods fast enough to liquidate loans. Earnings from the shipment of raw products fell off in the exporting countries, with the inevitable effect on income levels.

In appraising the effects of this "feast or famine" approach, as in some measure it has characterized United States stockpiling, it is essential that we consider the repercussions abroad. Rubber is the largest single dollar earner for the whole sterling area—since 1946 it has earned $1,550 million or just over a quarter of the sterling area's total dollar earnings from commodities. Sharp fluctuations in the rubber market have pronounced economic and political repercussions, not only for the rubber producers, but for the tax revenues of the Malayan Government as well.

I am not saying that all private traders are whole-heartedly interested in developing orderly, steady business relationships that will endure and pay more over the long pull. To far too great an extent in the past, our foreign traders have not looked beyond the windfall profits to be gained in quick deals. The interest of too many American manufacturers in foreign trade has been sporadic, falling when demand in the domestic economy is high, and quickening when the domestic demand slackens. The export departments in responsible American companies engaging in trade need, and increasingly are gaining, the support of top management in adopting a consistent attitude of interest and participation in foreign markets. In this respect their attitude approaches that of American companies with direct investment abroad, who necessarily must take a long view, be equipped to withstand stormy weather, and contribute to the growth of the country in which they are operating. As this conception of steadiness spreads, it will be helpful not only in improving the position of the individual companies concerned, but also will aid in establishing and maintaining this country's foreign economic policies on a desirable basis.

Attesting the need of a steadier approach to trade relations from another direction, I am sure that many of us have observed the similar "feast or famine" attitude which exists in governmental administration in Southeast Asia, for example, in the administration of import controls. To cite the situation in the Philippines, the Import Control Commission now relaxes, and now tightens, the issuance of import licenses. The position of the importer is made even more unhappy by the fact that, when licenses are being issued, all importers, including many newcomers, are bringing in goods, so that prices are depressed.

On the other hand, when licenses are being held up and when goods might be moved profitably, he can't import them. Licensing by fits and starts in any country makes intelligent merchandising at fair prices on the part of the importer very difficult.

Education and Technical Training—A Major Contribution of American Business Abroad

Much needs to be said concerning the role that private business has played and continues to play in the economic growth of the nations in Southeast Asia. However, probably the least publicized contribution of American private enterprise, and certainly one of the most important from the standpoint of its long-run cumulative effects, has been that of developing and training personnel. I am not speaking here of educational grants, fellowships, contributions for schools, or formal training programs, in many of which phases American business abroad participates. I am speaking of "on-the-job" training.

Examples could be drawn from trade and from a number of industrial fields—sugar, automotive, public utilities, petroleum refining and distribution, and many others—and from different countries. Let me mention, however, the growing Philippine lumber industry. In 1951, three American companies accounted for better than 50 per cent of Philippine lumber exports, totalling 57 million board feet, worth $6.3 million. The importance of this industry to the internal economy of the Philippines is apparent, and its potential as an increasingly important Philippine export commodity is obvious from the rapid growth of export volume and the growing scarcity of world sources for first quality hardwood lumber.

The influence of American interests in Philippine sawmilling has always been far beyond their numerical propor-

tion. They have been almost entirely responsible for the introduction in the Philippines of modern production techniques,
of employment stability, of quality standards and of market
development. It has been these companies which have been
responsible for the opening up and development of almost
every foreign market for Philippine lumber, and it is again
their work and their attention to quality standards which has
kept these markets open. The influence of these measures on
the Philippine producers is slow, but over the years there has
been distinct and steady improvement in their operations
which is entirely due to their observation of the American
producers' methods. The American producers have also acted
as a trade school for the entire Philippine lumber industry.
American techniques have, over the years, trained literally
thousands of Filipinos in production skills previously unknown, and it is standard practice for the native mills to hire
their key men from these trained employees of the American
controlled companies. It is probably a safe statement that there
is no native sawmill of consequence which does not have at
least one key employee who received his training at an American mill.

The Responsibilities of Business

At this point, perhaps I should mention a second visit
with my "Burma is an island" friend. This occurred a couple
of years after the first, and not in Washington but in Chungking, China. Our respective circumstances had changed somewhat: my assignment was still to "seek, foster, and promote"
foreign commerce, but his had changed to another branch of
the United States Government, and he was making the Far
East tour with V.I.P. treatment the order of the day.

Almost his first request was to have some cards postmarked
"Chungking" to add to his collection. I sent the cards down
by messenger to have this done, and they were returned. My
friend quickly and unappreciatively informed me that the

Chungking postmark was illegible—it wasn't in English! The Chinese postal authorities were very obliging—they did fix up a rubber stamp that was "legible."

And then, my friend became impatient to call on Chiang Kai-shek. His question was, "What advice shall I give the Generalissimo?" At that point, a couple of us proved somewhat less obliging than the Chinese postal authorities. We said "none," and reminded him of the number of hours that he had been in China.

I mention these incidents as illustrative of a completely wrong approach that would be as rejected and ineffective in business, as it was in government.

In the productivity of this country we can be proud of our attainments, which fundamentally are based on private American enterprise. But we have no monopoly on the know-how in the world, and the world does not have to be "Americanized" to be free. We are good Americans only if, in our relations with other countries, we act with due respect for their traditions and institutions.

What I want to reaffirm concerning the responsibilities of American business was recently expressed by the Chairman of the Southeast Asia Committee of the National Foreign Trade Council in these words:

Narrowing private enterprise down still further for a moment to include only American private enterprise, it has an additional responsibility in the Philippines and in all of Asia—to be an apostle of good will between nations. In this direction the representatives of American companies, most of them with long experience and possessed of a genuine interest in the country to which they are assigned and therefore equipped with an intimate knowledge of its people, customs, and needs, can make an outstanding contribution. This can and should be done entirely outside the sphere of local or international politics. The representatives of American companies may be depended upon to take an interest in civic and community affairs, to understand and respect the people and the institutions, and generally to be good citizens of the country in which they live. To me, this is a vital function of American business in the entire area of Asia. Only by this means can the aims of private enterprise be reconciled with the honest nationalistic aspirations of young sovereign nations, and they should be reconciled because they can complement each other to their mutual advantage.

The Environment Necessary for Private Enterprise

In turning to the discussion of the environment necessary for private enterprise, it is to be observed that the situation differs markedly between countries as to the existence of a commercially or industrially inclined and trained population and the other requisites for industrial advance. It would not be very helpful to propose a prescription for industrial progress for Southeast Asia which merely reflected the situation which has been attained over many years in highly industrialized countries and presupposed that the basic requisites for such development already existed generally throughout Southeast Asia.

Sound industrial growth requires related developments in many fields. It requires a reasonable degree of law and order, access to a labor force which possesses or is able to acquire the necessary skills and has some sense of responsibility for its role in the productive process, access to an economic source of materials, purchasing power in the hands of the buyers of its products, transportation, power, and banking facilities, and access to capital markets—to name only some of the most important.

There is no greater fallacy than the idea that dollars can be magically transmuted into goods, or that industrial development is merely the obtaining of foreign government loans and the building of factories and buying of machines. To continue successfully in operation, such factories must not only be run by qualified personnel, but they must operate in an environment in which they can earn their way. They must be economically, and not only politically, justified. It is in these terms that United States private enterprise can make its greatest contribution toward accelerating industrialization in Southeast Asia.

The contributions and the responsibilities of private enterprise have been stressed. I have also spoken against the "fly by night" quick-profit artists, and have argued for a responsible long-view approach, in which private business can make a real contribution in raising technical knowledge, in improving living standards, and in helping other industries grow. But I must also emphasize that this whole proposition is not a one-way street: the advantages must be mutual advantages if they are to be long enjoyed by either party. The greatest need at the moment is for improved understanding of business principles on the part of the government officials concerned, and for effective action on their part in creating an environment in which such principles can operate.

Let us ask what opportunities and conditions must be clearly seen in Southeast Asia to induce a prospective investor —be he an individual capitalist or an executive in a large corporation—to decide that a given country will provide a favorable environment for his business. The opportunity must be for capital to be put to work there to earn a return commensurate with known risks.

Capital and managerial ability are scarce commodities in the United States and elsewhere in the world. Profits are the price which calls them forth in the United States and in any other market. This price varies from industry to industry within the United States, as it must vary from country to country. It tends to be whatever is required to keep an enterprise economically sound and, at the same time, attract the added capital required for its necessary expansion and growth.

The following are the important matters which the prospective investor will always take into account: Will he be free to operate his enterprise according to his best business judgment, without prejudice, discrimination or fear of seizure of his property by arbitrary government action? Has the country a strong socialistic bias with a trend toward nationalization of industry and intervention by the state in economic affairs? Are there deeply rooted inequalities in the social structure which may erupt into social conflict? What is the foreign exchange record, and the record in relation to administration of foreign trade restrictions and exchange controls? What is the level of taxation, and does tax or other legislation discriminate against foreign capital? If his enterprise is successful, will it be a matter of his choice whether his profits, the rewards for risk-taking, enterprise, and hard work, are to be remitted or reinvested? Are local men of wealth putting their funds into productive enterprises, or seeking speculative ventures or foreign refuge for their savings? Will nationalistic laws prevent the hiring of capable technicians? More than anything else, what has been the past record with respect to private investments? Nothing can be more impressive than a history of fair treatment over the years, a record of earnest effort by the country to meet its international obligations and to safeguard the capital already invested.

These are not academic questions. They are all questions which I have discussed on numerous occasions with businessmen contemplating investments in Far Eastern countries. They are questions on which businessmen, having responsibility for their own savings or those of their stockholders, must make their own decisions, on the basis of the totality of information and experience available to them. They are not questions for which answers may be found merely by filling out forms or paying insurance premiums.

This point must be kept foremost in mind. It isn't within the power of government in a free economy to turn on, as by a water tap, the flow to any foreign countries of the management and capital resources which are the property of its citizens. It is within the power of government, and its obligation, to work to create and maintain the conditions under which private enterprise can make the ever growing contributions of which it is capable, both in its own country and abroad.

Additional Views and Proposals

Some further observations, together with the more specific proposals which either have already been made or are implicit in the views which have been expressed, may be summarized as follows:

1. It has been noted that there is a growing tendency for the countries of Southeast Asia to take a common approach to their problems, to compare notes as it were, with countries having problems similar to their own, and to gain from the knowledge of what is working well, and what is not, in their neighboring countries. This desirable trend has been manifest in the work of the Economic Commission for Asia and the Far East and the other agencies of the United Nations, in the Trade Promotion Conference held in Singapore in October of 1951, in the efforts of the countries participating in the Colombo Plan. The countries of Southeast Asia are also in greater contact with Japan, and this too is a development of much promise.

2. It has been emphasized that a great need and prerequisite for economic advance in many areas is further progress toward establishment of conditions of internal security and law and order, as well as protection against external threats. The present situation demands, therefore, integrated United States policies—military, political and economic—with respect to Southeast Asia. Military supplies and assistance should be supplied, within our capacities, where they are needed and requested. In view of the urgency of the situation, governmental economic assistance programs on a grant basis may continue in some instances to be required. In view of the evidence thus far, however, it would appear that only relatively modest and restricted programs of this sort would be required or practicable.

In continuation of a program of economic assistance with respect to any one of these areas, it should be carried out in such a way as to enhance and not diminish the prospects for trade and investment through normal commercial channels. The general emphasis on larger agricultural production in the Mutual Security Agency's program in the Philippines is regarded as sound, as is the work in the improvement and extension of roads and public health and education. These are fields within the competence of government in which the MSA program is strengthening the stability and productivity of the Philippine economy as a whole. Combined with this, however, is the need for action by both the Philippine and United States governments to overcome existing obstacles to normal private trade and to encourage increased investment.

It is the view of American business that public funds for economic assistance should not be extended even in the fields indicated above—except where justified by the most urgent, strategic or humanitarian considerations—unless the recipient government by its policies and actions is creating the necessary environment for private trade and investment.

3. Returning to my earlier comments regarding stockpiling, I quote from page 20 of the Final Declaration of the Thirty-Seventh National Foreign Trade Convention held in New York in the fall of 1950:

Stockpiling. The Convention favors the stockpiling of materials needed for the production of essential civilian and military goods, and holds that the supplies of such materials should, at all times, be adequate to meet emergency requirements. In order that this may be accomplished effectively, and with the least disturbance to prices and established channels of distribution, it is imperative that the stockpiling program be administered judiciously by men of practical experience and thorough understanding of the problems involved, and that the facilities of private enterprise be used in carrying out the program.

This view is one consistently advocated in annual Conventions since 1946.

4. In considering the timeliness of attempting to clarify trade and investment relations through comprehensive treaties of friendship, commerce and navigation, it is proposed

that careful consideration be given lest this step be accorded undue immediacy or emphasis. Unless and until it is possible to have real agreement on the provisions of such a treaty based on mutuality of conviction, a treaty so concluded would in practice provide very little assurance of a constitutional and legislative framework conducive to private trade and investment. Even more important than a treaty is the need on the part of the governments concerned for a solid conviction that private foreign investment is desirable and worthy of encouragement.

5. Finally, it has long been urged as the single greatest incentive for an increase in our foreign investments, that the United States Government adopt the principle, recognized in the tax legislation of some seventeen foreign countries, that income on foreign investments should be taxed only in the country where it is earned; and that tax treaties be negotiated with other countries embodying this principle and containing ample provisions for the protection of American business from discriminatory and unduly burdensome taxes abroad.

Application of the high United States rates to income produced in foreign countries creates a competitive disadvantage for American enterprises as compared with local enterprises or those of other countries which exempt foreign-earned income. Although precise figures are lacking, it is certain that the income which the United States Government would lose if it ceased taxing foreign-earned income would be very small compared to the tremendous sums we are spending in an effort to increase foreign productivity through government-to-government loans and similar devices. Our Government, therefore, at the present time, is not utilizing one of the most practical inducements which it could offer in assisting the less developed countries to increase the level of their production.

6. The improvement in statistical sources, and dissemination of information concerning the economies of Southeast Asian countries, should be encouraged. Representatives of these countries in the United States should be enabled to provide more prompt information, particularly with respect to

laws and regulations. The Department of Commerce in our own Government is undertaking to prepare informational handbooks concerning trade and investment with respect to certain Far Eastern countries, and these can serve a most useful purpose.

I have tried this morning to present the thinking of American business on matters which are of foremost concern with respect to the countries of Southeast Asia. Our conviction is that private enterprise offers the best hope, not only for early results in achieving economic development, but for results that will endure. In our view, the foremost need now is for governments to take those further steps which will create and maintain conditions under which private enterprise can make the full contribution of which it is capable.

In conclusion, I repeat our major theme: civilization as we know it now faces one of its greatest challenges in two thousand years. There are no easy or quick ways to meet this challenge. The free world must be united for many years to come in a shared determination; its military strength and economic productivity must be maintained and strengthened; the conditions of life in its presently less developed areas must be improved; and its peoples everywhere must work steadfastly to bring these things about. It is only through such common dedication and continuing hard work that a free way of life will be preserved.

Rufus H. Smith

THE ROLE OF THE AMERICAN UNIVERSITIES
IN SOUTHEAST ASIA

ALTHOUGH IT IS a relatively simple matter to transfer from the United States to Thailand, Burma or the Philippines the idea of a new irrigation project or an electric light plant, infinitely more finesse and understanding is called for in the transfer of university history, concepts, curricula and organization from one land to another.

Universities do not break easily with tradition; time is the essence of university change; it is always advisable to keep constantly in mind that the academic world is eminently respectable, equally conservative, and at times, I am inclined to believe, thoroughly asleep to the changing world about.

Furthermore, the American university world is not one but many. Because of their great variety it is exceedingly difficult to formulate a role for American universities in the plural; they are so utterly unlike in structure, in numbers, in curricula, and in adaption to their environment. Princeton and New York Universities—native American institutions to the core—would find few common denominators upon which to unite in any role in Southeast Asia. But the formulation of such a role becomes infinitely more perplexing when the attempt is undertaken to combine Cornell, Chicago, Illinois, Johns Hopkins, Notre Dame, Fordham, Southern Methodist, Tulane, California, Stanford, and Harvard under one tent in Southeast Asia. Because of their variety and complexity, these institutions would encounter great trouble in working in unison in a common overseas relationship.

But of one fact we can be very certain. Whatever role American universities may have in Southeast Asia must emerge out of the educational needs of that region, as they present themselves now or in the future. No one who has been in this area of the world can fail to come away without the feeling that these countries are in a dynamic ferment, that they are on the threshold of a new day and age. Only one of these states, Thailand, has been free of the colonial yoke; this nation is a fascinating mosaic of the new and the old; wherever one goes in this smiling land, he is conscious of the myriads of school children. Manila, too, is a beehive of higher education, throbbing with the competition of a host of institutions which attempt by day and night shifts to carry the mounting student demand.

Burma and Indonesia have acquired independence only recently; their universities must meet the challenge of a new-found nationalism. Immediate warfare throttles educational developments in the three countries of Indo-China—Viet-Nam, Cambodia and Laos; while Malaya is stalled in a disrupting Communist rebellion. It is only a question of time, however, when the educational forces of these governments must expand their university services.

Higher education in Southeast Asia is on the march. There is no doubt in my mind that these universities must become truly national in character—their very names imply this role in their respective states.

One deep conviction gripped me as I came in contact with or studied the problems of these countries. If these states of Southeast Asia are to move forward into fuller and more stable futures of competent self-government, their universities must begin immediately to make provision for the training of leadership in every walk of life. Time is short and does not admit of delay, the challenge is immediate: these universities must gird themselves to train a more numerous, a more broadly prepared, a more competent leadership in a greater variety of occupations. Herein lies the challenge to the universities of Southeast Asia; herein, too, will be found the opportunities for service on the part of American universities.

To meet this challenge of a new order, Southeast Asian universities must become truly national in character: they must root themselves in their own cultural soil; their students must be trained in the basic problems of their own countries and in the spirit of dedicated service. These universities must take talent wherever it can be found and train it for those walks of life necessary to the advancement of the nation.

Such trained leadership, I have no doubt, will become Southeast Asia's greatest single asset. May I make my position more emphatic: the free states of this region—new and old in the making—cannot reach their full stature of nationhood without this leadership.

In brief, the universities of Southeast Asia must become an expression of the age in which they live as well as an influence upon both the present and the future. They must be responsive to the pressures and to the needs of the whole of their national life; they must accept the fundamental premise that higher education is a public responsibility and not the privilege of a particular class. Only by the acceptance of this premise will these countries be able to locate and to train in sufficient numbers the manpower necessary to self-government and nationhood.

This national task is an old story to the American university—an indigenous institution always aligned with future trends, always living among the swirling currents of American life, always courageous and free enough to remain flexible and experimental. The founders of Cornell University desired to "found an institution where any person can find instruction in any subject"; while New York University over one-hundred years ago broke with classical occupational tradition in order to train engineers, architects, teachers and business men.

It is my further belief that the fundamental educational

objectives of both Southeast Asian and American universities are very similar, although they differ greatly in detail and in timing. Much of our experience is behind us; our universities have been partners in the American task of nation-building for well over a century and a half. A similar challenge to the universities of Southeast Asia lies in the immediate future. In the past these nations have depended upon foreign-trained experts or a small group of their own nationals trained in foreign institutions, a situation still true in many professions and in advanced graduate work. Southeast Asian university training and services, in my judgment, have only begun to gather volume and momentum.

In what ways, then, can the American university—an indigenous product which has flowered out of the dynamic demands of our national life and which is geared to provide the trained leadership so necessary to our complex civilization—be of service to the universities of Southeast Asia as they prepare to meet a similar challenge to train the leadership equally vital to the success of their own countries? Is it possible for the Southeast Asian universities to profit from our longer and more varied experience?

At this point it might be well to bring together the sum total of American university contacts with Southeast Asia. On the whole, they are few and largely of recent years. In colonial dependencies, university lines of communication, training and organization naturally stem back to the imperial power. American universities, because of this fact and for all practical purposes, have had no long-standing educational relationship with Malaya, Indo-China, Burma and Indonesia. For the same reason, however, the United States has had several decades of intercommunication with the Philippines. Thailand, the only non-colonial power of the group, has maintained educational contacts with the world, a practice begun by Rama IV and Rama V. The present king received his higher education in Switzerland. Also many of Thailand's government officials and students have been sent to the

United States for technical and professional training. I found a contingent of some fifty Cornell University graduates in Bangkok. Apart from these students, however, American universities, until recent years, have had no particular role, part or function to play in Thailand.

It is true that in 1923 the Rockefeller Foundation gave its cooperation to the reform of the teaching of medicine in Siam in order to make it possible to give medical degrees. This cooperation was ended in 1934. Recent history reveals renewed American assistance to the profession of medicine. Through the Technical Assistance Program of the United States, a team of twelve staff members of Washington University, St. Louis, Missouri, are now at the Medical School at Siriraj to teach and to supervise medical and nursing education. Similar services are being rendered at the University of Agriculture, although the American staff members have been drawn from a number of institutions. In the Philippines, the University of Michigan, with Mutual Security Agency support, will carry on a pilot project in public administration training at the University of the Philippines. It is my understanding that several other projects embodying the idea of university team cooperation have been agreed upon during the past few months. These are the only developments which involve the direct participation of American universities in a form which might be described as a role or a function. These are all of recent origin but they are suggestive of specific and fruitful avenues of cooperation for the future. Nevertheless, American universities have no funds of their own for such purposes; what they do depends upon the working and limitations of the statutes which set up various forms of governmental assistance—the Technical Assistance Program (Point Four), the Mutual Security Act, the Fulbright and the Smith-Mundt Acts. The activities of American universities, unless foundation funds are available, are limited to the purposes as enacted in federal legislation.

The Fulbright Act, in so far as American universities are

involved, works on an individual and not on an institutional basis. Although American lecturers must be assigned to specific universities abroad, the universities from whence they originate play no direct part in the appointment or the service rendered. Nevertheless, the services requested are to meet specific problems in the home universities. The University of the Philippines, for example, calls for a lecturer in business administration to train junior members of the faculty; a request is also made for an expert in agricultural extension to prepare teachers in the field of community organization. Burma is interested in a professor of geology capable of setting up a museum, building a laboratory, and with the administrative ability to organize a department of geology at Mandalay. Thailand is interested in public administration, also in an expert in library science to assist in establishing standard library procedures.

American universities might well cooperate with the Conference Board of Associated Research Councils in making available their best talent in the requested fields of service. I am very much pleased to learn that the Board of Foreign Scholarships has authorized the Conference Board Committee to invite a limited number of American scholars of national and international reputation to participate in assisting lecturers on a noncompetitive basis. This is an extremely important step and one with which American universities should cooperate to the limit.

Governor Dewey, in his chapter on Indonesia in his book *Journey to the Far Pacific,* makes this pertinent comment: "Small amounts of American aid in the hands of first-class people are infinitely more helpful than large amounts in the hands of mediocre or bad people." He also quotes the comment of a Japanese scholar: "When you send technical assistants to Asia, I urge you to send one good man instead of a dozen poor ones."

The quality of our university representation in Asia is all-important. It is right here—making available its top-flight men—that the American universities can well render its permanent and most far-reaching service to Southeast Asia.

There are no general avenues of university service which lead to Southeast Asia as a whole. The social, economic and political problems of this region have few common denominators: educational developments are on different levels; the Southeast Asia universities stem from European backgrounds. Only in very recent years have the governments of this region met to consider mutual problems, as in the Economic Commission for Asia and the Far East. There have been few common approaches on the university plane; no wide interchange or intercommunication among students or faculties of the universities of this region. To a great extent, colonialism has kept them apart; only in recent years have they begun to think of the mutuality of their problems.

The situation changes rapidly. Burma, Indonesia and the Philippines have recently assumed the status of full-fledged states. The three countries of Viet-Nam, Cambodia and Laos have achieved a large measure of self-government.

When, for example, we consider the amphibian Republic of Indonesia with its 743,000 square miles of territory and its 80 millions of people which now make it the sixth largest state in the world; when we analyze its enormously complex task of economic and social reconstruction; when we study its monumental problem of uniting thousands of separate pieces of geography, stretching three thousand miles from East to West; we are staggered by the challenge of national leadership training which confronts the University of Indonesia. The weakest link in the whole governmental structure of this island land is to be found, probably, in the fact that it has no large body of trained administrative talent to carry through to successful completion the gigantic tasks with which this new state is confronted.

May I turn at this point to a consideration of a few of the

directions in which the universities of Southeast Asia are likely
to move if they are to provide the trained leadership so necessary to the dynamic era in which they exist.

We cannot here exhaustively analyze the trends which,
during the next few decades, will shape the policies, the organizations, the curricula and the services of the institutions
of this region. National educational surveys should be undertaken by the university administrations in each of these countries. All that can be done in this paper is to sketch very briefly
a few of these national pressures, and then to indicate wherein
the experiences and the accomplishments of American universities may be drawn upon for help. My purpose is simply
to open our minds to the magnitude of the task, to the variety
of the demands which may develop, and to the possible opportunities for service on the part of the American universities.
These random examples are only suggestive of the searching
and imaginative process which must go on in the minds of
Southeast Asian university administrators as they plan to
shape their institutions to meet the expanding national market
for the nurture of home-grown leaders:

1. Raising the standard of living of the people and the
betterment of human relations, both rural and urban, will
command in the years ahead the lion's share of governmental
action in Southeast Asia. High-level attention must be given
to the common man. Much of this pressure for a higher standard of living will be reflected in social science teaching and
research, in better provisions for health, in educational up-
grading, in technological projects and improvements. The
betterment of standards of living and human relationships
will result in the expansion of university training and research
on many fronts.

2. All Southeast Asian countries possess agricultural economies. In Thailand, some 83 per cent of the population is dependent on agricultural pursuits for its living. Betterment
of rural life will bulk large in the building of future university services. In this task our wide-spread state universities

have had long experience; in fact, the improvement of rural life to a very considerable extent is the central purpose of this particular type of American university.

3. In this connection, however, we should keep in mind that the Southeast Asian universities—in nearly every instance big-city institutions and geared primarily to the training for what might be called the "prestige" professions—are immersed, because of their location, in urban pressures and demands. Commercial, cultural and governmental activities in these countries focus almost entirely in one great urban center. Bangkok is now a throbbing city of one million people, while Jakarta has increased its three hundred thousand of a few years ago to some two million today. One of the striking social phenomena of the whole of Asia today is this trend to the dominance of the big city. This is unlike the United States where a considerable part of our institutional higher education still smacks of the rural in location, atmosphere and purpose. If the Southeast Asian universities are to remain truly national in character, they must ever strive to strike a balance between urban and rural.

Nevertheless, the astounding growth of the Asian city will bring many new urban problems to the universities of this region. Because of the heavy concentration of government administration in a few great capital cities, attention has been centered on training in public administration and for public office. This development has been accentuated by the fact that the nationals of these countries look upon government service as the major and preferred occupational outlet. They have also flocked into a few prestige professions, law and medicine. But few have gone into private business. Furthermore, these Southeast Asian governments are in business, much of it monopolistic—rice, tobacco, salt, utilities, railroads. Political economy is the order of the day in these countries, with the emphasis oftentimes on the political. Here arises another push to government occupations rather than to competitive free enterprise on the part of the native population.

4. This unbalanced situation is further aggravated by the fact that in these big cities a large share—almost a monopoly of certain types—of private commercial pursuits are in the hands of the Chinese. Throughout this conference, there has been a continuous reference to the strangle grip of the Chinese on the trade life of these lands—some of the comments have been outspoken. One can readily visualize the danger of having an extremely large share of the private business entrepreneur activities in the hands of an alien group which accepts no national responsibilities. It is easy to state the problems and to portray the dangers of this Chinese monopoly; it is much more difficult, however, to suggest constructive remedies which will correct this national weakness.

Have the universities of these Southeast Asian countries any obligation to assist in the correction of this situation? The problem comes down to this simple equation: what constructive steps can be taken to increase the number and percentage of native young men and women in the private commercial, industrial, and financial ranks of each of these nations? Should the government of Thailand, for example, turn to Chulalongkorn University's Faculty of Commerce for an answer? What measures would the Dean of Commerce and his faculty suggest to increase the number of Thai men and women in high-level executive posts? Should the curriculum of the School of Commerce be bent in the direction of applied business training and away from a stereotyped four-year day course in traditional economics? Would it be of help to develop in-service after-hour extension courses for young nationals now in business? Should the School of Commerce take upon itself the task of dignifying business as a calling for young Thai nationals? Should these schools of commerce extend that kind of training which would make it possible for them to compete on better-than-even terms with the Chinese? Our urban university schools of commerce should be models for such developments in Southeast Asia.

The implications of this sketchy glimpse into the pressures of national life in Southeast Asia are clear as to the direction their universities must take in organization, curricula and services. These pressures will emerge out of rural and urban demands for better living standards. These in turn will make necessary, if these countries are to march forward in self-government and national competence, a more numerous, a more broadly trained and a more competent personnel—public and private. Here is the role of the Southeast Asian universities. To assist them in the fulfillment of this task with educational services of every possible character should be the privilege of the American university.

The role of destiny of these Asian universities will be very similar, almost identical in fact, to that played by our state universities in the development of our forty-eight states of the American Union. No aspect of state betterment has been exempt from the ministrations of these state universities. Likewise, the huge metropolitan centers of population in America are served by great urban universities. This role is undertaken in some cases by privately supported institutions—New York and Boston Universities; sometimes by a municipal institution—Wayne of Detroit; sometimes by a state university—Minnesota in Minneapolis.

The universities of Southeast Asia should find much of value in the organization, the services and the curricula of these two major and indigenous varieties of American universities.

In closing, may I bring the problems of university cooperation down to earth, to the practical details of daily teaching, to the student. Again, it is only possible to suggest a few of the difficulties inherent in the task. Since I have had experience in public administration in Thailand, this subject is selected for discussion.

The betterment of public administration, broadly defined, in Southeast Asia is the imperative need of the present and of the future; the demand for more and better trained public personnel is stressed again and again in government publications.

A cooperative pilot experiment in public administration training has been established by the University of Michigan in the form of an Institute in Public Administration at the University of the Philippines. Training programs in administrative techniques and methods will be given to Philippine government workers and students, and eventually, it is planned, instruction will be provided for officials and students from Southeast Asia countries. The project is being financed by the Mutual Security Agency of the United States. With what practical problems will such a project be confronted?

Thailand, among these governments of Southeast Asia, has had the most varied and extensive experience and background in public administration. As a matter of fact, Chulalongkorn University in Bangkok stems back to the establishment by King Chulalongkorn in 1902 of a Royal Pages' School with its emphasis upon public service training. By royal decree, this school in 1910 became the Civil Service College. By 1917, the status of this Civil Service College was raised to that of a university; it was named Chulalongkorn. The Faculty of Political Science of Chulalongkorn University is the lineal descendent of this Royal Civil Service School. Re-established in 1948, this faculty under the able leadership of Dean Kasem Udyanin, inaugurated this year, 1952–53, a new public service curriculum which holds great promise for the future. It was my privilege to be associated with Dean Kasem and his faculty in the shaping of this curriculum.

But much more is required than the reorganization of a curriculum if public administration training is to attain its full stature in Thailand, the Philippines, Indonesia or Burma. A number of weaknesses developed in the preparation of the Chulalongkorn program which will take patience, money and experience to correct. May I note several.

One urgent need is that of social science texts in the Thai

language, so the students at Chulalongkorn can study these subjects in their own national frame of reference. Although Thai university students have a reasonable proficiency in English, it is asking altogether too much to expect of them that they should be dependent upon basic textbook material drawn from a foreign frame of reference with which they have had no first-hand experience and little historical knowledge. Their time should not be wasted in this manner; furthermore, although procedures and techniques may be taken from other countries, they should always be adjusted to, and illustrated by, the conditions which prevail in their own native land. The problem of national social science texts is a difficult one to solve. The purchase demand for any one text will not be large enough to cover the cost of separate printing; authors, capable of writing such texts or of rewriting American texts under contract, are rare. Nevertheless, the lack of texts which portray the conditions which prevail in the local country is a real handicap in the training of national students. Some American foundation might make a fruitful contribution at this point.

Other urgent teaching needs grew out of the fact that in Thailand most of the faculty render part-time services, are poorly paid, and are drawn largely from the ranks of government officials. There are few scholars who devote full time to teaching or research.

Another lack is to be found in the absence of teaching materials other than texts. For example, the new public administration program at Chulalongkorn University would be greatly strengthened if it had a first-class statistical laboratory. Thorough statistical grounding of all public administrators would do much to upgrade all the government services.

May I, at this point, make a suggestion to the American agencies who are furnishing funds or personnel to improve educational conditions in Southeast Asia. In some instances, their assistance and services might be pooled so as to effect worthwhile educational results extending over a long period of time rather than to distribute their funds among limited objectives and scattered, ephemeral contacts. Public administration in Thailand is an excellent example where cooperative efforts would yield big dividends in the future. American agencies in this particular instance have an opportunity to gear cooperatively to a long historical background of public administration which provides a new public service curriculum supported by the Government of Thailand and a new building which affords ample facilities for expansion—an excellent opportunity and a sound psychological entry for American aid to cooperate in a project which should leave its mark upon the competency of Thailand's government services for decades to come.

The Southeast Asian countries aspire to become strong, well-governed, democratic nations. But of all types of government, democracy stands in the greatest need of capable leaders and experts in all walks of life. The obvious training ground is the university. This is the national role which must be assumed by the universities of Southeast Asia. Because American universities have filled a similar role in the United States, they are in an enviable position to be of service to their sister universities of Southeast Asia. The success or failure of self-government and democracy in this region may well rest on the shoulders of these institutions of higher learning in Southeast Asia.

INDEX

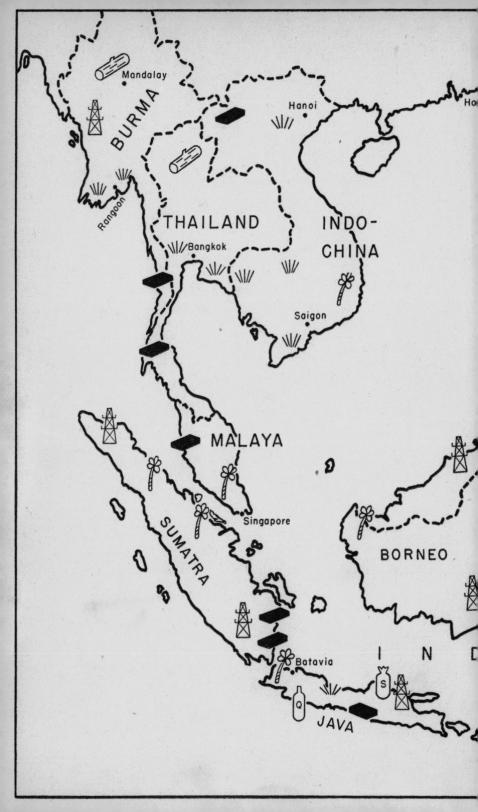